Praise for *The Devil's Half Acre*

"Harrowing and necessary. In bringing the story of Mary Lumpkin back into the light, Green has provided a powerful service for future generations."

—Anna Malaika Tubbs, author of *The Three Mothers*

"If we the people of the United States truly believe in forming a more perfect union, the unadulterated reality of systemic racism must be told. *The Devil's Half Acre* is an excellent book for readers looking to understand what life was like for enslaved African Americans like Mary Lumpkin, and to understand the impact that white supremacy has had on America as a whole."

—Dr. Johnnetta Betsch Cole, renowned educator, museum professional, and diversity and inclusion consultant

"Every Black woman must read the phenomenal book *The Devil's Half Acre*. It is our story—a true story, an erased story—of sisterhood and resistance. Mary Lumpkin, who rose from slavery, rape, and white supremacy–limited education to lay the foundation of one of America's first Historically Black Colleges, should be remembered alongside Harriet Tubman, Sojourner Truth, and Rosa Parks."

—Jodie Patterson, author of *The Bold World* and chair of the Human Rights Campaign Foundation Board

"Award-winning journalist Kristen Green's meticulously researched book *The Devil's Half Acre* is an extraordinary and unique portrait of the institution of slavery. Focused on the hidden, compelling life of enslaved Mary Lumpkin, this is a must-read for anyone committed to understanding the still-invisible aspects of slavery. It is also a story of resistance and the enduring legacies of survivors' contributions and even triumphs."

—Beverly Guy-Sheftall, director of the Women's Research & Resource Center at Spelman College and coauthor of *Gender Talk*

The Devil's Half Acre

Also by Kristen Green

Something Must Be Done About Prince Edward County

The Devil's Half Acre

THE UNTOLD STORY OF
HOW ONE WOMAN LIBERATED THE
SOUTH'S MOST NOTORIOUS SLAVE JAIL

KRISTEN GREEN

SEAL PRESS

New York

Seal Press
Hachette Book Group
1290 Avenue of the Americas, New York, NY 10104
www.sealpress.com
@sealpress

Printed in the United States of America

First Edition: April 2022

Published by Seal Press, an imprint of Perseus Books, LLC, a subsidiary of Hachette Book Group, Inc. The Seal Press name and logo is a trademark of the Hachette Book Group.

The Hachette Speakers Bureau provides a wide range of authors for speaking events. To find out more, go to www.hachettespeakersbureau.com or call (866) 376-6591.

The publisher is not responsible for websites (or their content) that are not owned by the publisher.

Print book interior design by Amy Quinn.

Library of Congress Cataloging-in-Publication Data
Names: Green, Kristen (Journalist), author.
Title: The devil's half acre : the untold story of how one woman liberated the South's most notorious slave jail / Kristen Green.
Description: First edition. | New York : Seal Press, 2022. | Includes bibliographical references and index.
Identifiers: LCCN 2021041088 | ISBN 9781541675636 (hardcover) | ISBN 9781541675629 (ebook)
Subjects: LCSH: Lumpkin, Mary F. | Virginia Union University (Richmond, Va.)—History—19th century. | African American women—Virginia—Richmond—Biography. | Women slaves—Virginia—Richmond—Biography. | Slave trade—Virginia—Richmond—History—19th century. | Jails—Virginia—Richmond—History—19th century.
Classification: LCC F234.R553 L864 2022 | DDC 306.3/62092 [B]—dc23
LC record available at https://lccn.loc.gov/2021041088

ISBNs: 9781541675636 (hardcover), 9781541675629 (ebook)

LSC-C

Printing 1, 2022

For my parents,
Faye Patteson Green and Charles Randall Green

When they told me my new-born babe was a girl,
my heart was heavier than it had ever been before.
Slavery is terrible for men; but it is far more terrible for women.

—Harriet Jacobs

Contents

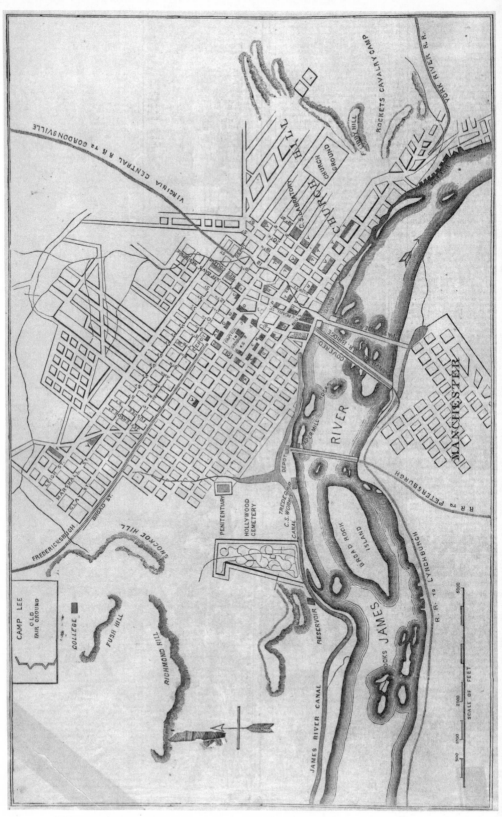

The city of Richmond, Virginia, 1862. (Library of Congress)

A Note from the Author

FROM THE MOMENT I first learned of Mary Lumpkin, I knew her story needed to be told. She had suffered unspeakable hardships as an enslaved woman, but had also accomplished incredible feats, helping to free her girls and playing a role in founding a school that improved the lives of generations of Black Americans.

But telling her story would be challenging. When I started looking in 2014 for clues about her life, I did not uncover much. Yet I was committed to finding a way to write about her. Niya Bates, who worked as a public historian at Thomas Jefferson's Monticello, was reassuring. She told me that even without a paper trail, "we can still learn quite a lot of information about enslaved people."

Bates had helped to bring into the light Sally Hemings, an enslaved woman who had at least six of Jefferson's children. "If we look harder at the evidence, we can put together a narrative of who she was as a person, as a mother, as a daughter," she told me.

I spent years collecting tiny tidbits of information about Mary Lumpkin's past—an entry in the US census, a listing in a city directory, a mention in a book. Over time I compiled more: her testimony in a court case, a will naming her and her children as beneficiaries, her burial record. I used genealogical research to trace her children and grandchildren, and I attempted to map her life from these scraps of knowledge.

I also spent years reading and thinking about the world that Mary Lumpkin inhabited. Eventually, I saw her on the pages I turned—in the stories of enslaved children sold away from their parents, of girls who learned to read and write, of girls who did not have enough to eat, of girls forced to have children with their enslavers. I could see her in women negotiating for freedom for their children and themselves. I envisioned her as I read about Black abolitionists, property and business owners, leaders of slave revolts. I pictured her laughing with friends, hugging her children, walking freely in a city of her choosing.

Over time Mary Lumpkin emerged from the shadows. As I wrote, I used the research I had conducted to imagine the spaces where she dwelled and fill the gaps in her story. Historians Daina Ramey Berry and Kali Nicole Gross suggest that such imagining is a way to "correct the erasure," and that is what I have tried to do.

In the time I have worked to excavate her history, the American conversation about slavery has begun to change, if ever so slightly. The *New York Times*'s 1619 Project has worked to reframe the history of slavery, emphasizing the contributions of enslaved people in forming the new country and building on the work scholars have done for years to educate Americans. In the aftermath of George Floyd's murder in Minneapolis, the Black Lives Matter movement has raised awareness of police brutality and racially motivated violence against Black Americans, revealing a past that had been rendered invisible, buried by white supremacists.

Perhaps the BLM movement also created more space for stories like Mary Lumpkin's to be heard. Black women have long been viewed as disposable in this country even though their wombs allowed America to expand and grow. Learning about our treatment of them could enable Americans to confront the complex question of what it means to be a Black woman in America.

I hope the story I wove about Mary Lumpkin's life inspires, opens minds, and motivates readers to work for racial justice. And I hope others will build upon what I have learned, expanding on Mary Lumpkin's story, just as I built upon other scholars' work.

I have taken care in how I present the history. I've chosen to use the term "Black" and to capitalize the word as a sign of my respect and recognition of the shared community and racial identity of Black Americans. I've chosen to keep "white" in lowercase because white people generally do not share a common culture or history or face discrimination because of their skin color. I also avoid capitalizing "white" because some hate groups have done so. I choose to capitalize "Indigenous" as well because I am using the term to identify people who belong to a group of political and historical communities with a shared experience.

I occasionally use the term "multiracial" to underscore, when important to the narrative, that a person is the child of a Black parent and a white parent or, in some cases, has Black and white grandparents or great-grandparents. I've also used the term in reference to laws that were meant to prevent the existence of mixed-race people and to control them. The multiracial people I refer to in this book—people like Mary Lumpkin and her children—are also Black, and when possible, I use that term instead.

I've chosen to use the term "enslaver" rather than "slave owner" or "slaveholder" in order to emphasize that white men and women made a choice to keep people enslaved and that there was a system in place to support them in doing so. I've chosen to use the phrase "enslaved person" rather than "slave" in order to recognize the humanity of these persons.

Some of the language I attribute to formerly enslaved people is imperfect. One of the best sources of interviews with formerly enslaved people is the Federal Writers' Project, conducted in the 1930s. The interviewers, many of whom were white, were instructed to transcribe the oral interviews phonetically, but they did not have the training to do this. Their own stereotypes about the speech patterns of the Black men and women they were interviewing are sometimes reflected in the text. Given these limitations, I chose to paraphrase and shorten quotes from many of the interviews. Still, I wanted to use enslaved men's and women's voices as often as possible, and in instances where it seemed appropriate to retain the enslaved person's words for their impact, I kept the imperfectly rendered language. I tried to do so sparingly and with care.

When writing about enslaved women who were forced to have the children of slave traders and later took their names, I also provide the names they were known by before they became mothers to their enslavers' children.

As I weighed how to present the information I uncovered, I found there was often no perfect solution to such issues as these. I have carefully considered the options and, in consultation with other texts and my editor, made the best decision I could in this moment. There were some paths I could not pursue and some stories I could not tell, and for these limitations I apologize. If I have caused offense or gotten things wrong, I take responsibility. I have tried to do right by Mary Lumpkin.

In this photo, Black laborers take a break from construction of Virginia Union University's new campus in 1899. The school, originally known as Richmond Theological School for Freedmen, first opened on the Lumpkin's Jail property. (Library of Congress)

Prologue

THE COBBLESTONE STREETS OF DOWNTOWN RICHMOND, VIRGINIA, gently slope to a low-lying area where a dark history is hidden.

One of the oldest neighborhoods in the city, Shockoe Bottom, is marked by throbbing nightclubs, an advertising agency, and a smattering of cafés, hotels, and restaurants. Tobacco warehouses perched on the James River are now stylish lofts, occupied by graduate students and young professionals. Interstate 95 roars over the neighborhood, and Amtrak rails run alongside the highway, picking up and dropping off passengers at the historic Main Street Station. The neighborhood retains remnants of a bygone era. Old advertisements painted on the sides of brick buildings give it a certain charm. Cluttered with parking lots and potholed streets, the neighborhood also feels abandoned and unloved, forgotten.

Tucked on the edge of Shockoe Bottom, a lush green field near a freeway ramp seems out of place in the urban landscape. It is not just a field, however, but a reclaimed African burial ground. Crossing under the freeway, a visitor finds more history, delivered up on a dull brown sign: LUMPKIN'S SLAVE JAIL ARCHAEOLOGICAL STUDY SITE. Three historic markers outline its significance.

This trio of metal signs next to a freeway, hemmed in by parking lots, is how the story of one of the most important chapters of the domestic slave trade in America is told. This is how the life of Mary Lumpkin, an enslaved woman who survived life inside the brutal jail, is shared.

This is exactly the way to tell a story so that no one will hear it.

In the mid-1800s, when Richmond was a hub of the domestic slave trade—the second-biggest in the South, after New Orleans—Shockoe Bottom was of ominous significance. Located down a hill from St. John's Church, where Patrick Henry uttered his famous words "Give me liberty or give me death," neighborhood businesses catered to the slave trade and to the people who relied on it. There were hotels where buyers could stay, taverns where they could have a drink and a meal, and stables where they could park their horses. Cobblers in the neighborhood fixed visiting enslavers' shoes, and tailors made clothing for enslaved people to wear when they were put up for sale. Blacksmiths fixed horseshoes for enslavers who had traveled long distances to buy enslaved people, and there were repair shops for their wagons. The neighborhood had auction houses for selling enslaved people and gallows for executing criminals. It was also home to a collection of slave jails that housed thousands of enslaved people, among them a girl named Mary Lumpkin.

One of two million girls and women enslaved in the American South in the decades before the Civil War, Mary Lumpkin's life was woven through with brutality and trauma, with family separation and abuse. But hers is also a story of resistance—and survival.

Described as "nearly white" and "fair faced," she may have been the multiracial child of an enslaved woman and her enslaver, one of his relatives, or a white overseer. Sold away as a young girl, probably from one or both of her parents, Mary Lumpkin was purchased by the slave trader Robert Lumpkin, a violent white man twenty-seven years her senior. When she was about thirteen, she was forced to have his children. She lived in his slave jail, where he imprisoned thousands of enslaved people over decades in the business. Some were held there before sale, and others were held after sale. Nearly all were to be shipped away to the Lower South.

In this wretched place, Mary Lumpkin managed to educate her children and find a path to freedom. After the Civil War, she inherited the jail when Robert Lumpkin died and bequeathed the property to her. Two years later, she helped a white Baptist missionary turn the "Devil's Half Acre"—a greatly feared place where countless enslaved people had long suffered—into "God's Half Acre," a school where dreams could be realized. The same grounds where enslaved people were imprisoned and beaten became the cornerstone for one of America's historically Black colleges and universities (HBCU). Virginia Union University is still in existence today.

"Virginia Union . . . was born in the bosom of Lumpkin's Jail," said W. Franklyn Richardson, chairman of the university's board and an alumnus. "The place we were sold into slavery becomes the place we are released into intellectual freedom."

In the aftermath of the Civil War, the school, founded as Richmond Theological School for Freedmen, provided Black students with an education. For more than 150 years, it has elevated and nurtured generations of Black men and women, helping them to realize their potential. It has shaped civic, education, and business leaders and developed activists who worked to desegregate whites-only lunch counters in Richmond department stores.

It is also one of the rare historically Black colleges and universities in America that can tie its origins to a Black woman.

"For Virginia Union to have a forming story rooted in Black womanness . . . it's a story of its own," said Virginia Union president Hakim J. Lucas.

Yet, for many years, Mary Lumpkin was invisible, even at the school she had played a role in forming. When Lumpkin's Jail was demolished and covered with fill dirt, her story went with it.

I FIRST LEARNED of Mary Lumpkin in 2011, soon after moving to Richmond. As a reporter at the local newspaper, the *Richmond Times-Dispatch*, I had been assigned to write about an African burial ground for free and enslaved Black people in Shockoe Bottom. A parking lot was believed to have been built over the bodies of hundreds of Black Americans buried between 1750 and 1816. Activists for years had called for the removal of a state-owned parking lot so that they could reclaim the burial ground.

Doing research for that story, I read about the nearby Lumpkin's Jail. In 2008, a team of archaeologists had gone looking for remnants of the slave jail compound, which was demolished in 1888. Overlaying old photos and maps, archaeologist Matthew Laird pinpointed the spot where he thought Robert Lumpkin's business had been located—now another parking lot in the shadow of Interstate 95. For eighteen weeks, his team searched for the jail's foundation by gently scraping away layers of earth in an excavation pit. In the course of its work, the team discovered hand-painted English china, an eyeglass lens, leather and fabric, and a piece of a child's doll. The archaeologists located the remains of a kitchen, a cobblestone courtyard, and a retaining wall that separated the upper part of the complex from the jail below. Then, during the last weeks of the dig, they uncovered the foundation of the jail down the hill eight feet from the rest of the Lumpkin compound and some fifteen feet below today's surface level. The history had been right there all along.

Years after the dig was completed and the burial ground had been reclaimed, I found myself thinking not just about Lumpkin's Jail and its role in American history but about the formidable woman who lived there with her enslaver, Robert Lumpkin. Mary Lumpkin had ministered to enslaved people imprisoned at the jail, and later she had made space for Black men and women to be educated. I wanted to learn more about her life and to understand why her story hadn't been told. I knew Mary Lumpkin did not simply find freedom but seized it—for her children and herself. It seemed to me to be an essential American story of a woman who had accomplished something incredible. With my experience working as a journalist and writing about Virginia history, I felt I would be able to research and write it.

A narrative about the erasure of women—and enslaved women in particular—unfolded before me. Mary Lumpkin's story had not been told for the same reason so many Black women's stories have not been told in this country. White men have historically told the stories. They were the ones who were educated, who managed the businesses, and who filed the court records. As the record keepers, they determined whose stories would endure the test of time and whose would vanish. By eliminating the stories of Black women—and those of Black men and children as well—white men preserved their positions of power, ensuring that a white supremacist society would continue.

Even the most detail-oriented plantation owners omitted enslaved people's names from plantation records or referred to them by only their first names, revealing the intentional nature of such omissions. Government records did not require full names, so when enslavers filled out shipping records for enslaved people they sent to the Lower South, they often provided only first names. The US census did not collect names of enslaved people for many years. Instead, census takers denoted them with a simple slash mark and recorded only their age and gender. This made it nearly impossible for enslaved people to find each other after separation by sale and, later, for descendants to trace their lineage. These gaps in the historical record also prevent historians and descendants from learning the details of enslaved people's lives, including Mary Lumpkin's.

Few enslaved people left the kinds of documents that historians use to trace and tell white people's stories. Though Mary Lumpkin was literate, she did not leave journals or personal papers—none, anyway, that I could locate. "People who are free have the ability to give their papers to someone specific. Enslaved people didn't have that privilege," said Niya Bates, the former public historian at Monticello.

Even wealthy white people had trouble preserving fragile papers. Important records put in a box and buried would quickly deteriorate. Enslaved people, many of whom could not read or write, did not typically have papers. If they did, their papers rarely survived. Only precious items like hair clips could be saved, passed down from one family member to the next. Moved around frequently as they were bought and sold, enslaved people's impermanent living conditions made it "very hard to keep track of personal belongings," Bates said.

Most enslaved people kept everything in their minds—"the only diary in which the records of their marriages, births and deaths were registered," wrote Henry Clay Bruce, who was born enslaved in Virginia. Oral histories were their primary means for preserving stories.

A handful of letters that Mary Lumpkin wrote to the administrators of the school now known as Virginia Union University were preserved. These letters and the court testimony she gave on behalf of a friend are the only records in her own voice. I couldn't find any documents that show where Mary Lumpkin was born or who her parents were.

Historians have had to rely on the records created by their oppressors in order to reconstruct the lives of Black men and women. But such records were unavailable for Mary Lumpkin, as only a few pages of a ledger book from Robert Lumpkin's renowned slave jail operation were preserved. While his will instructed that his assets be distributed to Mary Lumpkin, and then later to their children, other documents that might have revealed more about the relationship—and more about his role in the slave trade—were either lost or destroyed, perhaps intentionally.

To flesh out Mary Lumpkin's story, I went to a Richmond courthouse, where crinkling, 150-year-old court cases were still tied in "red tape"—the ribbon that has become synonymous with government bureaucracy. I went to Ipswich, Massachusetts, a tiny seaside town, and sat in the town museum and town library, flipping through records for the school her daughters attended. Poring over old property records in a Philadelphia basement, I discovered that Mary Lumpkin had purchased a home in her own name. I visited the hillside cemetery where she was buried in New Richmond, Ohio, and learned about the abolitionist roots of the community on the banks of the Ohio River. An outline of a life began to emerge that seemed to be defined as much by the freedom that Mary Lumpkin forged in her late twenties as by her enslavement.

As I traced her movements, I discovered that in her role as the mother of Robert Lumpkin's children she was part of a community of girls and women, hidden from view, who were chosen as sexual partners by slave traders and forced to bear their children. These women probably managed their enslaver's household and operated some part of the business of running a slave jail. As witnesses to the slave traders' violence and participants in the system of slavery, they were in some ways separated from other enslaved people. Yet choices were not theirs to make. They were unfree, and their lives were a paradox.

These enslaved women may have encouraged each other to seek more independence and assert themselves in the slave jails and in their relationships with the fathers of their children. Perhaps they supported each other in their quests to educate themselves and their children, and they may have bolstered each other's attempts to move their children out of slavery. Maybe they shared not only tactics for enduring their lives of enslavement but also methods for seeking better lives.

Mary Lumpkin forged such friendships and connections, first as an enslaved woman in the Richmond slave trade district where the slave jails and slave markets were located, and then as a free person in Philadelphia, New Orleans, and, later, New Richmond. Her relationships with other enslaved women, including Lucy Ann Cheatham Hagan, Corinna Hinton Omohundro, and Ann Banks Davis, may have helped protect her in her interactions with Robert Lumpkin and must have made her daily life easier to bear.

In her relationship with Robert Lumpkin, Mary Lumpkin exercised her agency and limited authority, finding a way out of enslavement. She told him he could do with her what he wanted but required that the children be freed. She demanded that he give her money so that she could free them. She showed empathy and concern for other enslaved people who were tortured and held captive in Lumpkin's Jail. She was highly mobile, seeking out opportunities in new places, and she would eventually make a home for herself in three American cities and a village. Not only did Mary Lumpkin ensure that her children were educated, but she helped make education available to newly free Black men in the aftermath of the Civil War and, subsequently, to generations of Black Americans.

Why, then, don't we know her story?

WHILE WOMEN'S STORIES have rarely been preserved throughout history, silence surrounds the lives of enslaved women because of what scholars call "triple constraints" or "triple invisibility." Being Black, female, and poor, enslaved women were devalued and forgotten, in spite of evidence of their leadership, resistance, and survival of monumental hardships. The institution of slavery relied on their bodies, yet their contributions were not recognized. They were exploited in every way.

Throughout American history, Black women have been marginalized or excluded from national narratives. They are rarely given credit for their role as abolitionists. Their attempts during the suffragist movement to improve their own lives were blocked, and their contributions to the civil rights movement were overlooked. Even today, after the deaths of Breonna Taylor, Rekia Boyd, and Atatiana Jefferson at the hands of police, they are left out of the prevailing narrative about state violence against Black people.

The stories of enslaved women have traditionally been lumped together and presented as one monolithic tale, rather than as distinct stories of hardships and triumphs. But "slavery was not just one enormous act of oppression against a nameless, interchangeable mass of people," writes the historian Annette Gordon-Reed. "It was millions of separate assassinations and attempted assassinations of individual spirits carried out over centuries." And yet, Gordon-Reed acknowledges, "We will always know little or nothing about the vast majority of enslaved women and the scores of them who suffered rape."

Traditionally, only the stories of the most exceptional women and their narratives of triumph have broken through. The only enslaved woman many Americans know about is Harriet Tubman, who not only fled her enslaver but returned to the South to help other enslaved people find freedom too. More recently, the story of Ona Judge, who fled her enslaver George Washington and was never caught, came to light. But her story is not yet widely known.

There are so many others whose stories need to be told. Female enslavement was more complex and varied than has been portrayed in the limited narratives to which Americans have been exposed. There are women like Harriet Jacobs, who hid in the attic of her grandmother's home for nearly seven years while her children played below in order to escape the threat of sexual abuse by her enslaver. Jacobs was the first woman to author a narrative of escaping enslavement in the United States. Louisa Picquet, sold away from her mother and brother at age thirteen, was forced to have the children of her enslaver. After she was freed at his death, she raised funds to purchase her mother's freedom. Reverend Hiram Mattison, an abolitionist pastor, helped her to tell her story in a question-and-answer format. Both books were published in 1861.

Telling only the stories of those who escaped slavery left out the stories of most enslaved women's lives. Many felt that they could not run away because they had family obligations and children they would not leave. "Apparently many women concluded that permanent escape was impossible or undesirable," writes the historian Stephanie M. H. Camp.

Instead, they fled temporarily when violence became too great to withstand. They fought back to avoid abuse, and they protested beatings. When they could not avoid rape, they attempted their own birth control and chewed cotton root to abort pregnancies. In despair and defiance, some took the lives of their own infants rather than see them grow up enslaved. A few killed their enslavers. Others slit their own throats, cut off their own hands, jumped from windows. They rescued other enslaved people, and they led slave revolts—stories that are only now coming to light.

They resisted in quiet ways too, using their agency to secure better jobs in enslavers' households, to get education for their children, to provide their families with some security and extra food. Because historians for generations have limited the scope of storytelling about Black women to those who are better documented and those deemed exceptional, the lives of women like Mary Lumpkin have not been explored, resulting in their omission from the history books.

Mary Lumpkin's story was even forgotten by her own family. Using public documents and newspaper stories, I built her family tree and traced the movement west of her children, followed by her grandchildren and great-grandchildren. During Reconstruction and Jim Crow, they headed farther and farther away from the land of her birth and enslavement, from her Blackness, from all that Mary Lumpkin endured and all she survived, until her descendants did not know she had existed at all.

Bringing Mary Lumpkin's story forward not only honors her contributions but deepens our knowledge of the enslaved experience. Revealing how her life unfolded expands our vision of women's lives and identities beyond the circumstances of their enslavement. It allows us to see their joy as wives and mothers, sisters and daughters, as living, breathing human beings. It allows us to explore the female friendships that enriched their existence.

Understanding their lives also enriches our collective humanity. With each story that is told, a more complete portrait of enslavement emerges, allowing Americans a deeper understanding of the lasting trauma of the nation's abuse of Black bodies—and Black women's bodies in particular. These abuses have continued throughout history. After emancipation, they took the form of lynchings and rape, which were common during Reconstruction and Jim Crow. Mass incarceration and police violence against Black Americans, which have continued for generations, are a direct outgrowth of the criminalization of their ancestors during slavery.

Sharing Black women's stories enables us to reclaim and recenter the contributions of all Black Americans. It allows us to honor Black women for making a way forward for themselves and their descendants through sheer determination and hard work. If we can acknowledge not only their history of trauma and survival but also that they are deserving of more care and respect in this country, we can begin to address the many ways in which the legacy of structural and systemic racism still disproportionately impacts Black women and girls today.

For instance, the health of Black women is at particular risk, and there is an urgent need to reform medical care to meet their needs. They face disproportionate rates of partner violence, are two and a half times more likely to die giving birth than white women, and have a lower life expectancy than white women. Black women routinely report that doctors ignore their pain and don't listen to them.

Nearly one in five Black women lives in poverty. They are paid 63 cents to every dollar a white man makes for full-time work, and they are less likely to get promoted. Black girls are given less support than their white peers in school and are punished more severely—they are five to six times more likely to be suspended than white girls. Black girls are sexualized at a younger age than white girls and subject to an "adultification" bias: authority figures perceive Black girls as older than they are and, rather than protect them as children, handle them violently.

As America considers its legacy of slavery in the aftermath of George Floyd's murder and nationwide protests, the country must recognize the contributions of Black women, who have been marginalized from feminist and civil rights campaigns for generations. By making systemic changes, from reforming predatory policing to providing equity in educational opportunity, we can improve the lives of Black girls and women. America must reform mass incarceration, which disproportionately affects Black families, and create a health care system that provides high-quality care for Black women and their families. By protecting Black women, we can change the culture of violence that has long been normalized in American policy.

We can draw attention to Black women's contributions, integral not just to their families and their communities but to the entire country. Women like Sojourner Truth, an abolitionist and author, and Rosa Parks, a civil rights activist, have given us all so much. Alicia Garza, Patrisse Cullors, and Opal Tometi, founders of the Black Lives Matter movement, and Tarana Burke, who launched the #metoo sexual abuse campaign pushing back against shame and patriarchy, are making America a better country. So, too, did Mary Lumpkin.

In tracing the contours of Mary Lumpkin's life, I am placing her inside America's story right where she lived—at its heart.

LUMPKIN'S JAIL.

This is an illustration of Lumpkin's Jail that appeared in *A History of the Richmond Theological Seminary* (1895), written by its longtime leader Charles Henry Corey. The jail, known by enslaved people as the "Devil's Half Acre," was built at the bottom of Robert Lumpkin's sloping Shockoe Bottom property. (Library of Virginia)

1

Chosen Ones

BEFORE SHE WAS ANYTHING ELSE, MARY LUMPKIN WAS SOMEONE'S daughter. Before she was the mother of a slave trader's children and a woman seeking freedom for herself and her descendants, she was an innocent baby girl.

Like her mother before her and most likely her grandmother and great-grandmother too, Mary Lumpkin was born enslaved. From the time she was in her mother's womb, her mother must have feared the day they would be separated. That would have been her persistent worry, layered on top of the devastating knowledge that her child likely would experience hunger, beatings, and sexual abuse in addition to exhausting forced labor.

One enslaved mother, trying to explain to her child that they would likely be separated, put him on her knee and pointed to the bare autumn trees. She held him close, tears slipping down her face.

"My son, as yonder leaves are stripped off the trees of the forest, so are the children of slaves swept away from them by the hands of cruel tyrants," Henry Box Brown recalled in his autobiography.

Mary Lumpkin, born around 1832, probably spent her early years with her mother on a Virginia plantation, perhaps in Hanover County north of Richmond. She may have also lived with siblings or her father. She was described as "mulatto," raising the question of whether her father was white. It's also possible that Mary's father was enslaved and that her mother or grandmother was fathered by a white man.

As a young child, Mary might not have realized that she was enslaved. White and Black children were often allowed to spend their days playing together. But as she grew to a young girl, she would have been given jobs to do. Enslaved girls were put to work earlier than boys, and by age five, some were taking care of infants or removing bugs from tobacco plants in the fields. At the age of six, they were taught to cook and clean, and by the time they were ten years old, they were doing the same work as grown women. Mary's mother knew that her daughter's carefree days were numbered, as was their time together. The odds of children being separated from their parents increased with age, and the fear that Mary's mother had harbored since before her daughter was born surely intensified.

As the slave trade changed from an international trade into a domestic one, the sale of children without their parents became increasingly common. By the 1820s, girls and boys were sold separately from their parents and siblings in order to feed the insatiable demand for enslaved people to work sugar and cotton fields in the Lower South and to maximize enslaver profits. From 1800 to 1860, prices for enslaved people more than tripled.

Peter Randolph, enslaved in Virginia, recalled the loss suffered by his mother when her oldest son was sold away from her and "carried where she never saw him again."

"She went mourning for him all her days, like a bird robbed of her young—like Rachel bereft of her children, who would not be comforted, because they were not," said Randolph, referring to the biblical story of Rachel weeping because her children were in exile.

Josephine Smith, born enslaved in Virginia, recalled being separated from her father as a toddler and "put on the block at Richmond," where she and her mother sold for $1,000. She compared their sale to a cow being sold away from the bull.

Perhaps Mary Lumpkin's mother had already had other children taken from her. In Richmond, an enslaved man named Pete told a visitor in 1860 that enslaved people could not tell "when our turn will come" to lose a family member to sale.

"I was sold away from my father when I was so young that I shouldn't know him now if I was to meet him," recalled Pete. Acknowledging the brutal realities of slavery, he added, "It may be [that] I'll lose my children as my father lost me."

An estimated one-third of enslaved children in Virginia were separated from their families. A child could be sold away from both her parents, sold with her mother away from her father, or left behind when her mother or father was sold away from her. "I never knew a whole family to live together, till all were grown up, in my life," recalled Lewis Clarke of his twenty-five years enslaved in Kentucky.

When an enslaver was ready to sell enslaved people, the ties of family were typically disregarded, except when it came to mothers of very young children. Yet even that small act of grace wasn't guaranteed, as infants were sometimes sold away from their parents. In 1854 a sleeping baby named Rachel was sold for $140 on the auction block—the platform from which enslaved people were sold—wrapped in a "coverlet," and cradled by an enslaved man who had been ordered to bring her. Cornelia Andrews, enslaved near Smithfield, North Carolina, watched hysterical mothers being separated from their newborns. If the master heard the desperate mothers sobbing, they would be "beat black an' blue," she recalled.

Mary Barbour, enslaved in North Carolina, recalled that a dozen of her siblings were sold away, each as soon as they turned three years old. Chancey Spell, also enslaved in North Carolina, was sold from her mother's arms. Harriett Hill, enslaved in Georgia, remembered being removed from her mother's care at three years old. Mingo White of Alabama was separated from his parents and put on an auction block at the age of four or five. He recalled potential buyers feeling his arms and legs and asking him "a lot of questions."

At the age of ten, Priscilla was taken from her enslaved parents in Virginia. Her mother, Di, wept silently as she and her husband Jim watched the girl sleep during their final night together. Was Mary Lumpkin's mother warned that her daughter would be sold? Did she mourn the loss before it happened?

Virginia—like North Carolina, South Carolina, Tennessee, Arkansas, and Texas—did not have laws in place to prevent enslaved children from being taken from their parents, and it happened frequently. Only Louisiana passed legislation to prevent the sale of children younger than ten years old without their mother.

It's possible that Mary was sold with her mother away from her father. If her father was also her enslaver, they may both have been sold to appease his white wife. At fifteen, Elizabeth Ramsay gave birth to a daughter by her South Carolina enslaver. When his white wife noticed that the enslaved child looked like her own baby, she became enraged.

"Mother had to be sold," recalled Ramsay's daughter, Louisa Picquet. The pair were sent to Georgia when Louisa was two months old.

Perhaps Robert Lumpkin purchased Mary alone, away from her family. At eight years old, children were worth more to enslavers without their mothers, though children of all ages were sold alone. She could have been sold to pay for a wedding in her enslaver's family or separated from her family when the estate of her enslaver was liquidated. One of Robert Lumpkin's relatives sold his farm and the people he enslaved when Mary was a girl—perhaps she had come from his property.

The sale of children to erase a debt was deemed "common and necessary" for enslavers who borrowed money using enslaved people as security. A small child could serve as a pledge on a deed of trust for a small loan. In April 1852, the sheriff in Eatonton, Georgia, sold a two-year-old girl and a pair of six-year-old girls in order to recoup borrowed money.

"For the payment of unsecured debts, it was an everyday occurrence to bring suit for the seizure and sale of slaves, including little children," the historian Frederic Bancroft writes.

Laura Clark's mom writhed on the ground, crying, when the girl, at the age of six or seven, was taken from her in North Carolina. She was sold with other children and put in a wagon with a pair of white men. Laura watched, unsure why her mother was upset, eating the candy she had been given to keep her quiet. Did something similar happen when Mary was taken?

Mary could have been removed from her enslaver's property while her mother was working in a field or cooking inside her enslaver's kitchen, a common tactic of enslavers hoping to avoid a scene of a mother and child's utter heartbreak. Sarah Gudger recalled watching the tragedy that unfolded when an enslaved mother returned to her North Carolina cabin after a day of work in the fields and realized that one of her children was missing. No one wanted to tell the panicked mother that a slave trader had taken her child, and tears rolled down her face when it dawned on her what had happened.

We don't know the exact details of Mary Lumpkin's beginning, but we know it must have involved separation from some or all of her family. What must it have been like for her to be led away from her home? How did she cope with leaving her family and possibly being taken from her parents and everyone she knew?

"I can't describe the heartbreak and horror of that separation," recalled John W. Fields, who was sold away from his mother and siblings in Kentucky at age six.

In 1840, an enslaved child was in Robert Lumpkin's possession, and it may have been Mary, then eight years old. If she was not yet enslaved by him, she soon would be.

By 1844, when Robert Lumpkin bought the jail that would make him famous, the center of the domestic slave trade in Virginia had shifted to Richmond from Alexandria, which lacked railroad access.

Richmond had been founded more than two hundred years earlier at the site of a Powhatan Confederacy town, which had been briefly settled by white colonists from Jamestown in 1607 and then again in 1644 as a trading post. Colonel William Byrd II named Richmond in 1737 for a town in southwest London, and the Virginia Assembly passed an act establishing the town in 1742. Shockoe Creek became its northern and eastern boundary, and the James River its southern and western boundary.

After the British surrendered at Yorktown, Richmond was officially named Virginia's new capital. By 1788, when construction of the gleaming State Capitol building designed by Thomas Jefferson was completed, Richmond had become a boomtown with a population of 3,800— 2,300 white and 1,500 Black. Shockoe Bottom was also developing as free Black masons, working under the direction of the Quaker George Winston, built more than one hundred brick buildings. The city market was located at Seventeenth Street. The slope down to Shockoe Creek, "a green pasture," was "considered a common, much used by laundresses whereon to dry the clothes which they washed in the stream."

As the slave trade took hold in Richmond, the growing industrial and manufacturing city was home to ironworks and flour mills, and with more than forty tobacco factories, it became the world's largest tobacco production center. Leasing out, or hiring out, enslaved people in urban areas was common by 1840, when there was not as much demand for their labor in the tobacco fields. Living away from their enslavers in rooms they rented, they had some freedom and were allowed to keep some of the money they made. Thus, leasing out led to communities of semi-free people.

The slave trade was the state's most profitable industry, and Richmond was alive with activity. In the 1840s, Virginia was responsible for shipping nearly half of all enslaved people who were taken across state lines in America. One slave trader sold about two thousand enslaved people each year of the decade. The big trading firms were selling one hundred to one hundred twenty-five a day by the 1850s. In 1857, the sale of enslaved people in Richmond totaled $4 million annually—about $440 million in today's dollars.

Clustered together east of the State Capitol at Eleventh and Franklin, slave jails were part of a thriving commercial district devoted primarily to businesses that served the slave trade. A visitor could walk one block south of the Capitol to Main Street, then head east, passing shops and stores, to go down the hill into Shockoe Bottom. In a three-block radius, there were churches, hotels, tobacco factories, and buildings associated with the slave trade. Many of the slave jails were clustered on or near Fifteenth Street, a narrow alley also known as Wall Street where Lumpkin's Jail was located.

In the 1850s, the Richmond trader Silas Omohundro owned a jail near Fifteenth and Main. An auctioneer, Hector Davis, lived next door and occupied buildings just off Fifteenth, north of Franklin. Robert Lumpkin's establishment was in a hollow to the north, between Broad and Franklin, and Shockoe Creek ran along the back of it.

Slave traders sold enslaved people to buyers directly from the slave jails, but there were also many other buildings in Shockoe Bottom that hosted sales, and Fifteenth was littered with auction houses. Odd Fellows Hall, located south of Lumpkin's Jail at Franklin and Fifteenth, held opera performances on its stage upstairs while slave sales went on in the basement. A red flag was hung outside the basement door to signal that enslaved people were for sale. Similar flags fluttered around the neighborhood, sometimes with slips of paper attached describing the enslaved people being sold.

Sales of enslaved people were held for years at the nearby Bell's Tavern, which was replaced in 1846 by the City Hotel, or the St. Charles. Hector Davis opened an office to conduct his slave trade business in the hotel, and livery stables and slave dealers were located behind it. The city's auction house, a three-story building with stone walls, was located near the Exchange Hotel on Franklin and Fourteenth and hosted slave sales in the hotel's post office.

Lumpkin's Jail was said to be one of the most characteristic and prominent features of the neighborhood. His compound included a forty-one-foot jail located in the center of the plot. In this "low, rough, brick building" surrounded by tall fences, Robert Lumpkin imprisoned and brutally punished enslaved people.

Farmers would come from miles away to sell enslaved people in the Richmond market. Cornelia Andrews, a formerly enslaved woman, recalled one enslaver buying enslaved people from the Smithfield, North Carolina, market and marching them on foot 160 miles to Richmond to resell. The enslaver had four horses that he hooked to a cart, and he chained enslaved people behind it, making them "trot" all the way to Richmond.

In 1851, the Swedish writer Fredrika Bremer visited several of Richmond's slave jails with a German resident of Richmond. In one jail courtyard, she encountered an enslaved man imprisoned there who had used an ax to cut off the fingers of his right hand after his enslaver separated him from his wife and children to sell him to the Lower South. In the same jail, an enslaved man greeted her in leg irons—a punishment meant to deeply shame him after he refused to work in the coal pits to which his enslaver had hired him out.

Bremer also pointed out that some of the enslaved people were light-skinned. In one jail, she noticed "a pretty little white boy of about seven years of age" waiting to be sold. "The child," she wrote, "had light hair, the most lovely light brown eyes, and cheeks as red as roses; he was, nevertheless, the child of a slave mother, and was to be sold as a slave. His price was three hundred and fifty dollars." Another jail Bremer visited kept "handsome fair" enslaved girls, "some of them almost white girls," who would be marketed for sex.

In yet another jail—perhaps Lumpkin's—she was taken to a room where enslaved men and women were flogged, a punishment known to last thirty minutes. "There were iron rings in the floor to which they are secured when they are laid down." She saw the cowhide used to whip them, which the overseer told her caused more harm to an enslaved person because the damage could not be seen.

This was the world where Mary Lumpkin lived, watching as enslaved men, women, and children came through the doors of the slave jail. She surely heard their moans, their wails, their screams of terror. Then she watched them leave again, shipped to new lives in the Lower South, separated from everyone they knew.

As a young enslaved girl, how did she make sense of life in the jail and her place in it? How did she cope with living in a place so terrible that it was known as the "Devil's Half Acre"?

SLAVE TRADING GOES back to the early days of recorded history, to a time when Nigerian Igbos traded their people as punishment for crimes. Europeans entered this established market in the sixteenth century, when the Portuguese purchased Africans who had been taken as slaves in tribal wars. Later, the Portuguese took their own captives from the west coast of Africa and, when they realized that was inefficient, relied on sales from Benin, where kings captured people from rival tribes. As other Europeans became involved in the slave trade, they purchased the captives who had been transported from the interior of Africa to the west coast.

In the seventeenth century, these people were shipped to the Americas as demand for slave labor rose on sugar plantations in the Caribbean and tobacco plantations in Virginia. The largest number of enslaved Africans were taken to the Americas during the eighteenth century. And once they arrived, they multiplied.

The historian Frederic Bancroft writes that the "cheapness and superabundance" of enslaved people in the colonies ensured that slavery would be used in the expansion of American lands south of Virginia.

Out of the slave trade was born the position of the slave trader—the person who profited from buying and selling enslaved people. The slave trader's role evolved in Virginia in the early 1800s, from selling enslaved people between Virginia farmers to then selling them to the Lower South. By 1820, landowners in Georgia, Tennessee, Kentucky, Alabama, Mississippi, Louisiana, and Missouri were all desperate to buy enslaved people, and demand remained high for years. By the 1840s, as the United States expanded, the price of enslaved people had risen dramatically.

The job requirements of a slave trader attracted a certain kind of person: a hardworking man—or occasionally a woman—willing to sacrifice for the job, a person who viewed enslaved people as less than human and had a particular flair for cruelty. The career was a good fit for calculating men, in that it required an ability to assess market demand, evaluate commodity type and quality, and forecast prices. One such man was the builder and carpenter John B. Prentis, the son of a Virginia politician, who abandoned his career—and his moral opposition to slavery—to pursue a life as a slave trader in Richmond. Prentis had been a landlord and a jailer, selling an enslaved person here and there in order to make quick money, before he committed full-time to the slave trade. As a trader, he would evaluate the cost of sending enslaved people south on foot or by boat and decide when and how to send them.

Slave traders plied their trade by making their way down dusty, rural roads, asking farmers in financial straits if they wanted to sell any of the people they enslaved. The trader could often convince a small farmer to unload a couple of enslaved people, as the sale could bring in as much money as the farmer would otherwise make in a year. Then the trader would turn around and sell the enslaved persons for a profit.

"My thighs is all blistered riding round or within twenty miles of Richmond," wrote the Louisiana enslaver Andrew Durnford, a rare free Black enslaver, who was looking for enslaved people to purchase during a June 1835 visit to Virginia.

A slave trader worked long hours for days on end, going to court sales, estate auctions, and slave markets. He had to be willing to separate enslaved families, to disregard family relationships between children and their parents, or between husbands and wives.

Robert Lumpkin's father died young and did not leave much for his family. Robert, the eldest of four brothers, may have tried other careers before settling on slave trader, just as John Prentis had. He worked as an itinerant salesman, for instance, traveling from town to town in the Virginia countryside selling household items like pots, pans, and pails from a platform on his wagon. He was most likely unmarried when he started out in the slave trade, probably by 1830. Trading in enslaved people could make a man a more lucrative living than selling household goods.

Robert Lumpkin would have known about Isaac Franklin and John Armfield's enormously successful slave trading firm. Established in Alexandria, Virginia, in 1828, the firm earned its outsized reputation by "vacuuming up people from the Virginia countryside," as the historian Edward Ball puts it. Robert Lumpkin must have noticed that other young, white men were roaming to far-flung Virginia and Maryland farms to buy enslaved people. Some of these "slave drivers" were rounding up men, women, and children, chaining them together in a line, or coffle, then putting them on southbound boats—or marching them hundreds of miles to New Orleans, Natchez, Mississippi, and other destinations in the Lower South. During the 1830s, more than 120,000 enslaved men, women, and children would be taken out of Virginia.

When he turned twenty-one in 1827, he was old enough to access his inheritance—what little of it existed. After the death of his father, Thomas Lumpkin, when Robert was a boy, his mother Elizabeth married George Lumpkin, presumably a relative of Thomas's. George Lumpkin became the legal guardian of Robert Lumpkin and his three brothers, Wilson, Thurston, and John. At least two of Robert's brothers would also enter the slave trade.

George Lumpkin had also gained custody of four enslaved people owned by Thomas Lumpkin. Robert Lumpkin told the Henrico County, Virginia, chancery court judge that he was "anxious and desirous to obtain a division of the said slaves, that he may obtain his portion thereof," and he asked the court to allow the sale of these four people, whom he had surely known since he was a boy. At the December sale, George Lumpkin bought Jordan and Peter for $854. The other two were sold—Reubin for $357 and Jenny for only $1, probably because, being either elderly or injured, she was unable to work. After the court expenses were settled, Thomas Lumpkin's debts were paid, his widow was given her portion of the proceeds, and their sons split the remainder. Robert Lumpkin's share amounted to $175.

Robert Lumpkin may have continued working as an itinerant salesman while also trying his hand at buying enslaved people, perhaps working as a headhunter on commission for Franklin and Armfield. At some point he began to focus exclusively on the traffic of enslaved people.

"Roaming over the country, and picking up a husband here, a wife there, a mother in one place, and an alluring maiden in another, he banded them with iron links into a coffle and sent them to the far southern market," wrote Charles Emery Stevens, the biographer of Anthony Burns, an enslaved man who would be imprisoned at Lumpkin's Jail.

The General Assembly of Virginia had passed an act in 1801 that enabled the governor to transport or sell out of state enslaved people condemned to die. The commonwealth then used the proceeds to reimburse enslavers for the loss of their property—a form of reparations for enslavers. Before long, Robert Lumpkin was winning bids to purchase enslaved convicts from the Commonwealth of Virginia. "Robert Lumpkin came out of nowhere," observed Philip Schwarz, the late professor emeritus of history at Virginia Commonwealth University, who spent much of his career studying slavery in Virginia.

The legislation had come in the wake of one of the most important insurrection plots in the history of US slavery, Gabriel's Conspiracy, which was planned for August 30, 1800. A blacksmith named Gabriel joined other enslaved men in planning to take the governor hostage with the hope of destroying slavery in Virginia. A rainstorm prevented the men from gathering as planned, and then a pair of enslaved men betrayed Gabriel and the other organizers. In the end, Gabriel was among twenty-six men who were believed to be responsible and were hung. Another eight were transported or sold out of state.

Slave traders purchased enslaved convicts and sold them for profit in the West Indies or Florida, which became a US colony in 1821, and likely did not reveal the enslaved convicts' backgrounds. In 1834, Robert Lumpkin and his brother Thurston Lumpkin won a contract from Governor Littleton Waller Tazewell to remove an enslaved man identified only as George. The governor paid them $1,000 and did not stipulate where George was to be taken.

Three years later, Robert Lumpkin, his brother Wilson Lumpkin, and a man from Baltimore named Thomas B. Small paid $17,000 to buy sixteen enslaved people, including three women. Enslaved in localities across Virginia, they had been convicted of crimes such as murder, assault upon a white person, burglary, arson, and attempted rape. Robert Lumpkin agreed to "truly and faithfully carry out of the said United States each and all of the said slaves," according to the purchase contract.

It's unclear where the trio took the enslaved people they had bought, but it seems likely that they transported the prisoners to the Lower South and hid their origins, echoing the tactic used by Britain to dump convicts in colonial America. Some states complained about this practice and made it illegal, and a few years later the Washington, DC, trader William H. Williams would be arrested and tried when he took enslaved convicts to New Orleans.

Robert Lumpkin probably also bought enslaved people at public auctions and courthouse "sheriff's sales," which were the sites of half of all sales of enslaved people. Established traders befriended tavern owners and other "middle men" in the countryside who alerted them when they knew of enslaved people for sale, but Robert Lumpkin may not have had those kinds of connections in his early years.

Enslaved people referred to slave traders as "soul-drivers" and feared them for their brutality and ability to change the course of enslaved people's lives by separating them from their family members and everyone they knew. W. L. Bost, enslaved in Newton, North Carolina, recalled slave traders bringing enslaved people through his town as they made their way to the Lower South. The traders stayed in the hotel his enslaver ran and put the enslaved people in slave quarters "like droves of hogs. All through the night I could hear them mourning and praying," he recalled.

Alex Woods, born enslaved in Orange County, North Carolina, in 1858, recalled that his enslaver's brother, John Woods, passed through with enslaved people chained together in coffles on the way to Richmond, perhaps headed to Lumpkin's Jail. They slept by the fire at night, their chains still attached.

A child at the time, Alex Woods later recalled that the sight of the enslaved men, women, and children, separated from their families, filled him with fear. He said, "I wus afraid my mother and father would be sold away from me."

With so many buyers and sellers of enslaved people making their way to Richmond, a young, ambitious man who had no ties and was free to travel the back roads of the state for weeks on end could earn good money in the trade. Robert Lumpkin came into the field just as it was shifting and growing in Virginia, and more widely in America, and he ran a business that was soon critical to the slave trade.

In the coming decades, he and his employees would hold thousands of enslaved people in his jail and torture and beat countless others on behalf of their enslavers. He would make a small fortune as a Virginia slave trader renowned for his brutality. And Mary Lumpkin would bear witness to the ruthless way he conducted his business.

To UNDERSTAND HOW the system of slavery forced Mary Lumpkin as a young, enslaved girl to live in the jail of a white slave trader, we need to return to the beginning of slavery in the New World.

The very nature of enslavement defined Black men and women as inferior, and this definition left enslaved girls and women vulnerable to abuse by white men. The rape of enslaved women by their enslavers resulted in children who, like Mary Lumpkin, would soon be subjected to the same kind of sexual abuse.

It is likely that the Black and white races in America mixed soon after the first recorded instance of Black men and women stepping foot on the shores of Jamestown in 1619. It may have even happened on the way to the Virginia colony. During the voyage from Africa to America, white overseers separated female captives from the kidnapped males. By the time a slave ship left on the journey from West Africa to the West Indies, known as the Middle Passage, it had become "half bedlam and half brothel," one slave ship captain recalled.

Thus, some of the Black women who survived the treacherous two- to three-month journey from Africa walked onto the shores of the New World with swollen bellies. Soon, they would deliver the country's first multiracial children of both Black and white heritage. At the time, the mixed children were referred to as "mulattoes," a term that came from the Spanish word *mulo*—a hybrid of two animals.

Once in America, the abuse of Black women continued. White planters and overseers raped the enslaved girls and women for whom they were responsible, creating an "endless trail of mulatto children sired by white men," writes the historian Joel Williamson. Enslavers and their sons sought sexual favors sometimes through gifts but more often by force.

If enslaved girls or women did not comply in exchange for a trinket, they would be "flogged" into submission. "Plenty of the colored women have children by the white men," recalled W. L. Bost. The women, he said, "know better than to not do what he say." Bost said the enslavers "take them very same children"—children they fathered —"and make slaves out of them."

Bost pointed out that, if the enslaver's wife found out, she raised "a revolution." But he said she rarely learned of the enslaver's abuse because he would never tell and the enslaved women were afraid to speak up. "They jes' go on hopin' that thing won't be that way always," Bost said.

John C. Bectom, born enslaved in 1862 in Cumberland County, North Carolina, recalled that "some of the slave holders would have some certain slave women reserved for their own use."

"Sometimes children almost white would be born to them. I have seen many of these children," Bectom recalled. "Sometimes the child would be said to belong to the overseer, and sometimes it would be said to belong to the master."

Enslaved women had few options. Martha Allen, born enslaved in Craven County, North Carolina, recalled the brutality her mother faced when she rejected the "young master"—probably her enslaver's son. When "she tells him no," Allen recounted later, he hurled a piece of wood at her head.

Minnie Fulkes, enslaved in Virginia, recalled that her mother was whipped naked by the overseer for spurning him. Fulkes recalled seeing "th' whelps an' scars," and asked her mother what she had done for him "to beat and do her so." "Nothin'," her mother said—except refuse to be with him.

Elisabeth Spark, enslaved in Virginia, said her enslaver, Shep Miller, whipped women the same way he did men. "Beat women naked an' wash 'em down in brine," she said. "Sometimes they beat 'em so bad, they jes' couldn't stand it an' they run away to the woods." The application of the salt solution was exacted as a second punishment.

William J. Anderson recalled his enslaver "divested a poor female slave of all wearing apparel, tied her down to stakes, and whipped her with a handsaw until he broke it over her naked body." The practice of stripping enslaved women either fully or to the waist for public beatings, exposing their breasts, reinforced the image of the uncivilized Black woman who was unworthy of respect and dignity and enabled enslavers to label them as "savages."

Even pregnant women were beaten. They were forced to dig a hole in the ground and then lie facedown with their belly in the hole, so that they could be whipped without harming the fetus, who would soon be born an enslaved person, if its mother survived the whipping.

Narratives of enslaved lives are filled with examples of sexual abuse and violence against enslaved women by enslavers. Squire Dowd, enslaved in Moore County, North Carolina, recalled that "Negro women having children by the masters was common."

No studies exist to tell us exactly how many enslaved women were forced to have the children of their enslavers. But analysis of DNA results by Katarzyna "Kasia" Bryc, a population geneticist and senior scientist at genealogy company 23andMe, found that the average self-identifying Black American has a genetic makeup that is about 24 percent European, or white—irrefutable evidence of a long-held truth about how common sexual abuse of enslaved people was.

Even enslaved women with live-in partners could not escape sexual predation by their enslavers, who were known to visit the cabins where enslaved couples lived and make husbands sit outside while raping their wives. One Mississippi court refused to offer clemency for an enslaved husband who murdered his enslaver after the enslaver raped his wife.

State laws didn't even allow for Black women to make a claim of rape against a white man. "No rape conviction against a white man, let alone a victim's owner, for raping an enslaved woman has been found between at least 1700 and the Civil War," writes the historian Sharon Block.

Enslavers had found that they could get the sexual fulfillment they desired while at the same time expanding the population of people they enslaved in the form of their own children.

SOME WHITE ENSLAVERS preferred light-skinned enslaved girls and women like Mary Lumpkin as their victims.

Colorism, the privileging of light skin over darker skin in people of the same race, stretched back to the earliest days of the colony. The most obvious way for a person to be evaluated under America's racist hierarchy was through skin color. Louisa Picquet wrote that her mother, Elizabeth Ramsay, who was forced to have children with at least two of her enslavers, was "pretty white" but "not white enough for white people."

Demand for light-skinned enslaved females in the slave market was high, and they sold for more money than darker-skinned enslaved girls and women. By the time Robert Lumpkin became a slave trader, girls and women like Mary were put in a separate category in the slave market: "fancy girls." By the 1830s, the term was used to refer to girls and women marketed for their sexuality. At the peak of the market, their bodies were sold for as much as $5,000, while a strong young man, or "field hand," would sell for $1,600.

"Traders gladly exhibited them and were proud of the high prices they commanded," Frederic Bancroft writes.

The term "fancy" reflected the buyer's ability to fulfill his sexual fantasies in encounters with these girls and women to which they need not consent. In this trade, slave traders were "selling buyers a fantasy" that others existed to satisfy them, writes historian Walter Johnson. "Fancy" was a double entendre, referencing the image of an educated, pretty, finely dressed, and well-mannered female. It also referred to what the enslaver desired or "fancied"—a sexual encounter with an enslaved girl or woman.

For enslavers, the price paid was "a measure not only of desire but of dominance," writes Johnson. In buying these women and girls, enslavers showed their power to purchase a female who was off-limits in contemporary society. The man took the sexual gratification he craved while also terrorizing and controlling enslaved women.

Slave traders were known to save some of the most beautiful enslaved women for themselves. Enslavers sometimes took the same approach. "Master would not have any white overseers," recalled Jacob Manson, enslaved in North Carolina. His enslaver, whom he referred to as Colonel Bun Eden, liked Black women too much "to have any other white man playing around them."

With "fancy girls," enslavers broke society's rules on their own terms. Coercing sex from girls and women over whom they had total power gave them a freedom they couldn't find in ordinary life. Because "fancy girls" were Black, they were off-limits to white men by law, making the taboo nature of these encounters more exciting for the men who raped them.

"Fancy girls" existed in a space of public erasure. The enslavers "sought victims, not companions," Johnson writes. "Enslavers mapped their own forbidden desires into enslaved women's bodies."

In the enslaver's estimation, women were registers for his power and for his secret desires. The abuse was hidden from anyone outside of his household—and sometimes from those within the household as well. Yet the evidence was there for anyone who wanted to see it. The children's faces mirrored those of their white fathers, proof of what was happening behind closed doors in the lives of those pushed into the shadows.

AFTER THE SHIP *White Lion* landed in Fort Comfort, Virginia, in 1619 with the first reported arrival of kidnapped Black men and women, a system of slavery developed that defined enslaved people by race. This is how Mary Lumpkin came to be enslaved.

White indentured servants from England worked the colony's tobacco fields alongside white convicts who had been sentenced to labor. Some Indigenous Virginians worked as servants, but most were enslaved. There were four enslaved Black people for every white servant in Virginia by the early 1690s. The passage of the Slave Code of 1705—an "act concerning Servants and Slaves"—limited the freedom of enslaved people and defined the rights of enslavers, allowing them to punish enslaved people without fear of legal repercussions.

When the United States banned the trade of enslaved people from Africa to the Americas in 1807, the decision was portrayed as a humanitarian achievement that would effectively end the slave trade. Instead, the transatlantic slave trade was quickly replaced with a larger domestic trade, which had been quietly developing for years. The domestic trade of enslaved people, termed a "second Middle Passage" by the historian Ira Berlin, would result in roughly a million enslaved people being moved from the Upper South (North Carolina, Tennessee, Virginia,

Kentucky, and Maryland) to the Lower South (South Carolina, Georgia, Florida, Alabama, Mississippi, Louisiana, and Texas) before the end of the Civil War. Enslaved people were literally "sold down the river."

Lobbied heavily by the Religious Society of Friends, commonly known as Quakers, some American leaders supported ending the transatlantic slave trade because they considered it immoral, but others did so to protect American investment in slavery. Farmers and plantation owners feared that an overabundance of enslaved people from Africa in the American slave market would reduce the value of the Black men, women, and children they owned. They realized that they stood to make a lot of money from selling the enslaved people already in America.

At first, the domestic slave trade was random and disorganized. By the 1820s, around the time Robert Lumpkin probably began working as a salesman, the trade had become more sophisticated, driven by surging demand for workers to pick cotton. The domestic trade of enslaved people was so widespread in Virginia that "the whole state was a slave market," says the historian Edward Baptist.

Virginia had been supplying enslaved people to the Lower South since the 1790s, when it had more enslaved people than work for them to do. Growing tobacco depleted the soil, and many Virginia planters went into debt after spending more money buying imported goods from England than the tobacco harvest would bring in. Tobacco production had slowed beginning in the 1750s, and with its decline, demand for the labor of enslaved people waned. Some Virginia property owners simply abandoned their lands when the soils became depleted and moved to the Lower South to start over on virgin territory.

Those who stayed in the Upper South were forced by 1800 to begin planting and harvesting grain, which earned a much lower profit than tobacco but did not require as much labor. For many enslavers, supporting the enslaved people on their properties became a financial burden. Feeding, clothing, and providing medical care for dozens of enslaved people was expensive, and if landowners were not making as much money off crops, the numbers simply did not work.

Meanwhile, Eli Whitney's invention and 1793 patent of the "saw-gin," or cotton gin, which separated the cotton seeds from the staple, had resulted in increased demand for enslaved labor in the Lower South because areas that could only grow the labor-intensive short-staple cotton suddenly had a way to harvest it. That demand increased with the 1803 Louisiana Purchase, which opened up a vast new area of land for cotton production and, later, sugar plantations. This convergence led to a vibrant downriver slave trade that enabled Virginia farmers to make up income lost from tobacco by selling enslaved people. Enslaved children and youth would become Virginia's most important export.

In this environment, Robert Lumpkin was positioned to make his mark as Virginia—and later Richmond in particular—became the center of the new domestic trade. Many enslavers in the Upper South traveled to this city on the fall line of the James River to buy and sell enslaved people, no questions asked. By the 1840s, Richmond held more enslaved people in jails, hosted more slave auctions, and shipped more enslaved people than any other American city, with the exception of New Orleans.

Over time, Virginia became "a nursery of slavery," according to a Confederate official. In the three decades before the Civil War, some 300,000 enslaved people were sold in Virginia, most of them through the market in Shockoe Bottom. They were delivered to new enslavers in a new land. Many were separated from everyone they knew and subjected to harsh working conditions, picking cotton in Alabama, Mississippi, Louisiana, and Texas. This displacement, and the trauma associated with it, would shape Black American life for centuries and is still vivid in the collective memory of Black Americans today.

The forced resettlement of enslaved people was "twenty times larger than Andrew Jackson's 'Indian removal' campaigns of the 1830s," writes Edward Ball. "It was bigger than the immigration of Jews into the United States during the 19th century, when some 500,000 arrived from Russia and Eastern Europe. It was bigger than the wagon-train migration to the West, beloved of American lore. This movement lasted longer and grabbed up more people than any other migration in North America before 1900."

Two-thirds of the people moved to the Lower South during this time would be sold by slave traders, including Robert Lumpkin.

THE MOST DANGEROUS time for enslaved girls like Mary Lumpkin was the onset of puberty. Adults dreaded its arrival for their enslaved children and grandchildren. Mothers tried to protect their daughters and paid attention to their development.

Enslaved women knew that their daughters' physical maturation would begin the cycle of abuse anew. Girls, too, learned to fear its onset, knowing it would soon lead to the separation they had feared all their lives. The value of their bodies rose when they were old enough to produce children and their sexuality could be commoditized. "A slave girl was expected to have children as soon as she became a woman. Some of them had children at the age of twelve and thirteen years old," said Hilliard Yellerday, who was enslaved in North Carolina.

At puberty, girls' chances of being sold away increased. Though prepubescent girls were also abused, puberty made them more vulnerable. "It marked the beginning of a period when all men could sexually assault them," writes the historian Daina Ramey Berry.

Enslaved boys and men were also terrorized by sexual abuse. Many enslaved boys were not provided adequate clothing by their enslavers and went naked on their plantations, and white enslavers subjected them to inspections of their bodies, including their genitals. Some enslavers were known to keep an enslaved boy or man for sexual abuse, and some brothels specialized in enslaved boys. Enslaved men were paraded around from plantation to plantation, forced by enslavers to have sex with women as part of breeding programs.

Harriet Jacobs wrote that puberty was "a sad epoch in the life of a slave girl." After a girl entered her teenage years, her mother "lives in daily expectation of troubles." Girls were taught by their elders to hide their physical development in order to protect themselves from abuse and perhaps delay being sold. Older women "understood the connection between their bodies and the institution of slavery," Berry wrote, and they passed down this information to their children and grandchildren.

Mary's mother—and other female family members such as a grandmother, aunt, or older sister—probably helped her hide her developing body. But ultimately, these precautions couldn't save enslaved girls from licentious enslavers. Nothing would save Mary from Robert Lumpkin.

THE FACT THAT Robert Lumpkin did not marry a white woman may indicate that he wasn't considered good marriage material.

He didn't come from a wealthy family. He spent lots of time on the road, putting in long hours but with little to show for it, as every dollar he earned was probably invested in buying more enslaved people. Certainly, any potential wives with whom he may have shared his vision of owning a slave jail would have been turned off by the idea of having to make their home in such a place. They also would have understood that slave traders had easy access to enslaved women. Besides, marriages were considered a financial arrangement between families: the parents of any white women Robert Lumpkin dated would have been looking to marry them to respected and admired men who had inherited money and owned land, homes, livestock, and enslaved people.

Perhaps Robert Lumpkin bought Mary with sexual abuse in mind as well as her future as a beautiful woman. One trader sold a "13 year old Girl, bright color, nearly a fancy," for $1,135 in Richmond, stating he believed the girl "had potential."

Theophilus Freeman, a New Orleans trader, refused to sell a seven- or eight-year-old girl named Emily to the enslaver who was buying her mother, Eliza, because he believed "there were heaps and piles of money to be made of her . . . when she was a few years older," recounted Solomon Northup in his *Twelve Years a Slave*. Freeman thought that men in New Orleans would pay $5,000 for "an extra, handsome, fancy piece as Emily would be . . . she was a beauty—a picture—a doll."

Robert Lumpkin may have bought Mary with the plan to market her as a "fancy girl" and then decided that he would rather keep her for himself. He needed someone to manage the household and help run the slave jail. Mary could do this, and he wouldn't have had to answer to her the way he would have to a white wife. The simplest explanation for why he chose Mary to have his children is that he could.

Robert Lumpkin had already been trading in enslaved people for years by the time he purchased Mary. Though he had not yet bought his namesake jail, he may have already been renting the property he would eventually buy, or perhaps another nearby jail. Robert Lumpkin may have purchased Mary with the intention of sexually abusing her. If she was sold alone, separated from everyone she knew, it would have only been a matter of time before Robert Lumpkin preyed on her.

"Soon she will learn to tremble when she hears her master's footfall. She will be compelled to realize that she is no longer a child. If God has bestowed beauty upon her, it will prove her greatest curse," Harriet Jacobs wrote in her autobiography, *Incidents in the Life of a Slave Girl*.

When Louisa Picquet was separated from her mother at thirteen and sold, her new enslaver "told me what he bought me for," she recalled. "He said if I behave myself he'd treat me well; but, if not, he'd whip me almost to death."

Louisa was forced to have children with her enslaver, likely the New Orleans hardware store owner John Williams. Two of the four children died in infancy. She was also required to care for him in his old age and to manage his household, which included children from his late wife.

To get Mary to comply, Robert Lumpkin may have bought her gifts, promised her a light workload, or agreed to assign enslaved people to help care for her children. He may have worked for years to encourage her to submit to sexual encounters with him, as Harriet Jacobs's enslaver attempted, or he may have beaten her, forcing her to give in immediately.

Mary may have rebuked Robert Lumpkin. She may have resisted. She probably considered her options, weighing what compliance would mean for her future, and what it might mean for the lives of the children she would be forced to have. Perhaps she came to the decision that giving Robert Lumpkin what he wanted was her best chance to get an education and attain freedom, both for herself and for her offspring. Maybe she saw being chosen by him as a way to build a better life.

Delores McQuinn, a Virginia legislator and Black woman who has worked for more than two decades to tell the stories of the enslaved in Richmond, said that she has thought a lot about Mary Lumpkin over the years. "I've tried to put myself in the position she found herself in," McQuinn said.

She believes that, as a young girl, Mary Lumpkin probably did whatever she was told to do. "But I also believe," McQuinn added, "that . . . by nature, we are inclined to look at our situation and figure out, 'how do I survive this?'"

An 1856 print of a Richmond slave auction depicts a Black woman, most likely alone and afraid, being sold in front of a group of white men. A Black man in the image, who was also likely enslaved, may have just been sold or perhaps was about to be sold. (Library of Congress)

2

"That Which Is Brought Forth Follows the Womb"

WHEN ROBERT LUMPKIN BOUGHT THE SHOCKOE BOTTOM SLAVE JAIL compound, it would catapult him into slave trader infamy and become Mary Lumpkin's home.

"Only the wealthiest or most powerful traders could afford to operate . . . jails," writes the historian Jeff Forret. Having one was "an important status symbol."

Lumpkin's new property was first developed as a slave jail by the slave trader Bacon Tait in 1830. Tait had built a two-story brick house that faced the street and a large boardinghouse, or hotel, for slave traders. In an advertisement in the *Richmond Whig*, Tait vowed to provide enslaved people with "general cleanliness, moderate exercise, and recreation within the yards during good weather, and good substantial food at all times." He had promised that their "confinement shall be rendered merely nominal, and the health of the Negroes so promoted, that they will be well prepared to encounter a change of climate when removed to the South"—sold to new enslavers to work on cotton or sugar plantations.

The *Liberator*, a weekly abolitionist newspaper published in Boston by the white abolitionist William Lloyd Garrison, mocked Tait's advertisement for his jail and its inherent inhumanity. "No danger of escape need be feared, as the windows are all grated with strong iron bars, a good watch is kept, and a large supply of chains, cart whips, thumbscrews, and other instruments of torture, are always on hand to restrain and punish refractory slaves," it read.

"P.S. Owners wishing to have slaves well flogged can have it done at Tait's Jail, at the lowest prices. He recommends his dungeons as very efficacious in breaking down the spirit of obstinate slaves," the *Liberator* continued. "He has some very secure interior rooms, in which negroes, claiming to be free, can be confined, so as to make it impossible for them to communicate with any one out of the jail by voice or letter."

When Tait built a larger jail at a higher elevation, he sold the property on Fifteenth to the trader Lewis A. Collier. In 1833, the new owner advertised his "Negro establishment, which consists of a spacious comfortable strong jail," and he "respectfully" suggested that "gentlemen wishing to deposit negroes in jail, for sale or otherwise . . . give me a call," promising that the enslaved people he housed were "carefully and well attended to."

Collier also offered, for sale or for lease, the enslaved people whom he personally owned. His claim that "I generally have on hand the use of one hundred" indicates that he was probably holding well over that number of enslaved people at the jail at a given time.

While he owned the jail, Collier continued developing the land, overseeing construction of three new buildings: an auction house with rooms to board visiting sellers and buyers overnight, a building that served as a bar and kitchen, and the jail. He pledged the lots as collateral for a loan from the Bank of Virginia. When he got into financial trouble, the bank seized the property and sold it to Robert Lumpkin, who took out a generous loan to buy it.

A ten- to twelve-foot-tall spiked fence, guarded by ferocious tracking dogs, protected the perimeter of Robert Lumpkin's property, and his brick home sat just inside the front gates. Fences were commonly used to hide what was happening inside slave jails. Bethany Veney, enslaved in Luray, Virginia, recalled one around the slave jail where she was kept for a night before she was to be sold at auction. "Arrived in Richmond, we were again shut up in jail, all around which was a very high fence, so high that no communication with the outside world was possible," Veney recalled.

Located at the center of his plot, Lumpkin's forty-one-foot-long, two-story jail was a "low, rough, brick building" across from an open courtyard with a large wash tank. Inside the jail, several people were crammed into each of the rooms, which had no access to the outdoors and contained only one small window, covered in bars. The smell of urine seeped into every crevice.

One enslaved man recalled being imprisoned among a thousand men in trader yards in Georgia and Virginia, waiting to be sold. When Henry Watson stayed in a Richmond jail for two days as an eight-year-old, "all sexes and ages are huddled together in a mass" until there were enough of them to chain together in a coffle, he wrote in his *Narrative of Henry Watson*. Some enslaved people were imprisoned for months. Over a ten-year period, the Richmond trader Silas Omohundro reported more than 1,800 enslaved people passing through his doors.

All of them needed to be fed and housed. At Lumpkin's Jail, a famous prisoner, Anthony Burns, who was being tortured, was fed corn-bread and rancid meat. Burns reported that he wasn't provided with a bed and that "a rude bench fastened against the wall and a single, coarse blanket were the only means of repose."

Solomon Northup slept on the "damp, hard floor" of William H. Williams's Yellow House in Washington, DC, where enslaved people were forced year-round to eat while squatting outdoors. Northup recalled being fed a meal of shriveled fried pork, a slice of bread, and a cup of water in his cell. Williams claimed that meals consisted of herring, cornbread, and sweetened coffee twice a day.

One enslaved man described an unnamed Richmond jail as "one of the most gloomy places I ever had been in before." The jail provided no beds, forcing him "to lie or sit by night on boards," and the cells were "full of vermin" and thick with lice.

Yet Robert Lumpkin was proud of the business he grew after he bought the jail. In the early 1850s, a visitor from Syracuse, New York, followed a potential buyer to Lumpkin's Jail. Otis Bigelow encountered Robert Lumpkin, whom he described as a fat man seated in a chair tipped back against a pole. The slave jail operator offered to give Bigelow a tour of the grounds.

"Mr. Lumpkin received me very courteously and showed me over his jail. The place, in fact, was a kind of hotel or boardinghouse for negro-traders and their slaves," Bigelow recalled. "I was invited to dine at a large table with perhaps twenty traders, who gave me almost no attention, and there was little conversation."

Bill Robinson, an enslaved man who had been imprisoned from boyhood by Lumpkin and served as an overseer, recalled the scene at the yard. "A number of the companions of these traders would be there of an afternoon, drinking and smoking and gambling . . .—gambling away men, women, and children," recalled Robinson.

When Robert Lumpkin hosted boarders, they sometimes asked to see the "bloodhounds" that Robinson trained in the jail yard to catch enslaved people who attempted to escape. He claimed to be a skilled dog handler who trained hounds for other slave traders too. "A negro boy was made to run all round the yard of the jail barefooted, and then hide himself in the large tree that grew in the yard," he recalled. "The hounds were kept out of sight, and then let loose and nosed the track of the boy round and round 'til he came to the tree. The discipline of the little dogs was to keep them to the scent and keep them under control."

When visiting enslavers urged Robinson to show off the dogs, he "would get them out and exhibit them on the trail of the boys," Robinson said.

Bloodhounds, of course, were "a terror to the slaves," recalled Harriet Jacobs. "They were let loose on a runaway, and, if they tracked him, they literally tore the flesh from his bones," Jacobs wrote in her autobiography. An overseer on Carter H. Edloe's Brandon Plantation in Prince George County, Virginia, where Peter Randolph was enslaved, "made his dogs tear and bite my mother very badly," Randolph recalled, and she died soon after.

Lumpkin's Jail also specialized in beatings, a service for which he charged extra. He had a special "back room" set aside to abuse enslaved people—a designated "whipping room" like the one Fredrika Bremer described where, for a fee, his employees beat enslaved people on behalf of their enslavers. A visitor described the setup: "In the rough floor, and at about the center of it, was the stout iron staple and whipping ring." The body of an enslaved person was outstretched so that his arms and legs could be attached to chains bolted to the floor, and then one of Robert Lumpkin's employees stood over the enslaved person and flogged him.

Robinson recalled that these floggings were rare, as "the chief object is to keep their slaves in good condition." Robert Lumpkin preferred to have an overseer force an enslaved person to "bend over a log, fasten their hands and feet and beat them." Robinson said the enslaved person was beaten with a board that had holes bored through it, which raised blisters but did not show marks on the skin, ensuring that the person could be sold without evidence of abuse. This was an important consideration because an enslaved person who appeared to have been badly beaten would be deemed unwilling to work and would sell for less.

Whipping enslaved people—even small children—on behalf of enslavers who considered themselves above such violence or who did not want to bloody their clothes was another way for Robert Lumpkin to diversify his income. He charged a fee on top of the 25 to 40 cents he collected per day to house each enslaved person. Robert Lumpkin also offered to board visiting enslavers' horses in his livery stable, and he probably rented out his bloodhounds.

In his compound, Robert Lumpkin provided access to this array of services for both enslavers looking to sell and those who wanted to buy. He may have generated significant income solely from his jail and boardinghouse, whereas other slave traders relied on income from buying and selling enslaved people. Under his watch, the property gained renown comparable to Joseph Bruin's slave jail in Alexandria, which Harriet Beecher Stowe used as the basis for *Uncle Tom's Cabin*. He was prosperous enough that the street where his jail was located was renamed Lumpkin's Alley. It would become the center of the Richmond trade.

Where did Mary Lumpkin fit in this world? How much freedom did she have, and how much responsibility? She is likely to have played some role in making the space comfortable and welcoming to other traders as well as enslavers looking to sell and buy enslaved people. Perhaps she offered to run errands for visiting enslavers or make special meals at a visitor's request.

Once Mary Lumpkin was chosen by Robert Lumpkin, she was likely separated from most other enslaved people in his compound. She likely received better treatment and lived in nicer quarters, but she remained enslaved nonetheless. She was witness to Robert Lumpkin's brutality and may have felt responsible for the abuse that other enslaved people were subject to, even though there was little she could do. She was probably just trying to stay alive.

It didn't take long for multiracial people—people like Mary Lumpkin—to become a noticeable segment of the Virginia population, and a growing one.

On land, the "first significant mixing," writes Joel Williamson, occurred between Black people and white indentured servants from Ireland, Scotland, and England. In the colonial period, enslaved Black people lived near European indentured servants, who outnumbered them. The rape of enslaved women by enslavers, their sons, and their overseers also continued unabated.

The Virginia colony first acted to prevent interracial relationships in 1630, eleven years after kidnapped Africans had landed in Fort Comfort. They publicly whipped a white man, Hugh Davis, for "abusing himself to the dishonor of God and the shame of Christians, by defiling his body in lying with a Negro." Ten years later, in 1640, the punishment was much lighter for another Virginia man, Robert Sweet, who was ordered to "do penance in church according to the law of England, for getting a negro woman with child." The Black woman was whipped.

The prevalence of multiracial people had raised a question for these British settlers: Should a child "got by an Englishman upon a negro" be free or enslaved?

White men realized that the answer to this question would impact their livelihoods, because they relied on enslaved people to do the difficult work of establishing farms in the Virginia colony. If children fathered by enslavers with enslaved women were white by law, the potential labor force would shrink. The answer also would determine the fate of enslaved people for generations, including Mary Lumpkin's children. White leaders concluded that they needed to control multiracial people in order to keep them enslaved. From the country's earliest days, white America legislated race to its own benefit.

In 1662, Virginia officials adopted a series of laws intended to discourage mixing between Black and white people and to classify multiracial people as inferior. One law in particular would change the face of slavery forever. Essentially, a child's race would follow its mother's. The principle of *partus sequitur ventrem*—Latin for "that which is brought forth follows the womb"—established that children born to enslaved mothers also would be enslaved. The decision was made specifically to protect white Americans' property rights, and it made the future of slavery directly dependent on enslaved women's ability to reproduce.

This law of the Virginia colony contradicted English tradition, which stipulated that a child's social status would match the father's. The new Virginia doctrine followed a Roman custom that had been applied to cattle since ancient times. When cows bred, the calves belonged to the owner of the female. If slavery relied on the status of women, then enslavers "needed not fear paternity liability if a pregnancy resulted from the rape."

The Virginia Assembly also outlawed marriages between whites and people of color as early as 1691. It was the first of the colonies to ban mixed marriages, and other colonies would soon follow suit. Of course, Virginia authorities often overlooked white men breaking the law. Even if they had wanted to enforce it, doing so would have been difficult, as Virginia law stipulated that enslaved people could not testify in court against a white person. White men had enacted the laws to punish white women for having sex with Black men—the law referred to the children born of these relationships as "that abominable mixture and spurious issue"—but continued to allow white men to rape Black women.

The Virginia government also moved in 1691 to prevent multiracial people from being freed, requiring enslavers to send formerly enslaved people out of Virginia once they were emancipated. Under these laws, the price for marrying someone of another race was banishment from Virginia forever.

Having children with someone of a different race also carried steep penalties. A white woman with a multiracial child could be subject to a fine or servitude for five years. An even harsher penalty was handed down to her child, who could be held in servitude for thirty-one years.

This law was renewed in 1696 and again in 1705, when the child's term of servitude was reduced to twenty-one years and the new punishment for marrying a multiracial or Black person was six months in prison and a fine. Even the minister who married an interracial couple was held accountable. At this time, the legislature defined a "mulatto" as any mixed-race Virginian with at least one-eighth African ancestry.

White Virginians began regulating multiracial people, in part, because they feared an insurrection by enslaved people. They pointed to Bacon's Rebellion in 1676 as evidence. Nathaniel Bacon, a relative of Virginia governor Sir William Berkeley, wanted Indigenous people removed so that whites could claim more property. To make his point, he organized a militia of indentured servants and enslaved Black men, who captured Jamestown and burned it down. The event stoked fear among colonial leaders that poor white and Black Virginians could unite against them and spurred the movement toward racialized slavery.

Colonial leaders continued to enact laws that limited the political power of brown and Black people. By 1705, Virginia prevented Black, Indigenous, and multiracial people from holding office even though they had never previously had any such opportunity. The colony also barred them from serving as witnesses in legal and court cases. By 1723, multiracial people were no longer allowed to vote and could own a gun only in rare circumstances. The laws shifted somewhat with each generation, but the rights of brown and Black people were always restricted.

In 1765, the Virginia legislature revised the amount of time that multiracial children served to twenty-one years of age for males and eighteen for females. In 1792, the state abandoned the term "abominable mixture" and passed a new act "preventing white men and women intermarrying with negroes or mulattoes." The codes of 1849 and 1860 legislated that "all marriages between a white person and a negro . . . shall be absolutely void, without any decree of divorce, or other legal process."

Yet, despite all the restrictions, multiracial children continued to be born.

In 1757, Rev. Peter Fontaine wrote in *Memoirs of a Huguenot Family*, "many base wretches among us take up with negro women, by which means the country swarms with mulatto bastards."

Nothing deterred white men from abusing the women they enslaved. Joel Williamson writes that white planters "surrendered sexually and fell over the race line," using the old tactic of blaming Black women for their seductiveness and promiscuity while casting white women as pure and self-respecting. "Whole clans of mulattoes were created," Williamson notes, ". . . to the almost inexpressible horror of their white neighbors."

They likely were more horrified by evidence that their world order was changing than by white men's abuse of Black women.

Ministers blamed the rise in the multiracial population on Black girls and women for "tempting" white men, a point of view that protected white supremacy. "Was the white man or the black woman the aggressor?" asks the Black historian James Hugo Johnston in his 1970 book *Race Relations in Virginia and Miscegenation in the South.* Johnston was one of the first Black men in America to earn a PhD in history and later became president of the Virginia Normal and Collegiate Institute, an HBCU later renamed Virginia State University.

White leaders found many ways to assign responsibility for the births of multiracial children. They labeled their fathers "fallen" men and "mavericks" and denounced the criminal character of a subset of white men who had been removed from their homes in England and relocated to the New World. They also blamed "immoral women" who had children with Black men. Yet they failed to acknowledge the most obvious cause: enslavers were sexually abusing the Black women they enslaved.

IN THE 1700S, some groups of Virginians began freeing the people they had enslaved.

When the first Quakers arrived in Virginia in 1655, they were not opposed to slavery, and many of them owned a few enslaved people to help with farming. Some Quakers soon claimed discomfort with the harsh treatment they witnessed enslaved people receiving, and at the London Yearly Meeting of Friends in 1714 and 1722, they raised the question of whether enslaved people should continue to be imported. At the request of the Friends, the Virginia General Assembly passed a law in 1771 that forbade the importation of enslaved people into the colony. The law was initially vetoed by the king, but it became law in 1778, during the Revolutionary War, when he no longer had a say. Friends also successfully lobbied the General Assembly in 1782 to pass a manumission act, which allowed enslavers to free the people they enslaved without government approval.

During the Revolution, enslaved people willing to fight for Great Britain were freed. In response, George Washington also allowed enslaved people to enlist, and some five thousand Black Americans who served in his Continental Army were also emancipated. After the war ended, evangelical preachers and some Virginia enslavers were inspired to set free some or all of the people they had enslaved.

In 1784, the Friends' Virginia Yearly Meeting decided to disown members who would not free the people they enslaved. Robert Pleasants, a Quaker who founded the Virginia Society for Promoting the Abolition of Slavery, had encouraged his father and half-brother to free in their wills the hundreds of people they enslaved. He believed that the laws would change to allow it, and after their deaths, when the manumission act was passed, Pleasants sued in chancery court to enforce his father's and brother's wills. He won, and some 400 Black men, women, and children were freed as a result. At his 1801 death, he left the people he had formerly enslaved a 350-acre estate and endowed a school for their descendants.

Free Black people owned land and socialized with white and Black people. They were expected to pay taxes. Yet Virginia leaders became alarmed as the free Black population grew from 1,800 in 1782 to 12,766 in 1790. By 1801, there would be more than 20,000 free Black residents and by 1810, just over 30,000. Legislators, fearful that the growing free Black population would lead to unrest among enslaved men and women, considered how to define a Black person by law. The sheer number of multiracial people—more than 60,000 in the colonies by 1776—made racial identity an important consideration. What would happen if multiracial Virginians started demanding freedom?

Two years after the American Revolution ended, in 1785, Virginia enacted a law stipulating that any person who was one-quarter or more Black—anyone with at least one Black grandparent—would be defined as "mulatto," a term also used to refer to people who were part Indigenous. The word "negro" in the statute would refer to both mulattoes and negroes.

Each state created its own definition of Blackness, determining the percentage of Black ancestry that would result in a person being stripped of his or her rights. Kentucky copied Virginia's definition, but other states came up with their own ways of defining "mulatto." In general, a person who was one-quarter Black was defined as a "quadroon," while someone who was one-eighth Black was an "octoroon." The people in these subcategories were deemed Black.

Whites knew that if they could control the definition of Blackness, they were more likely to be able to keep people enslaved. By legislating that children born to enslaved mothers would also be enslaved, white men and women not only protected their investment in human property but also ensured that Black people would be enslaved in perpetuity.

In 1801, Virginia legislators passed restrictive new laws intended to control the state's 346,000 Black residents. Lawmakers limited the movement of Black people and created a public guard to secure government buildings at night. Another law was passed in 1804 forbidding enslaved people from gathering to worship; it was amended the following year to allow enslavers to bring the people they enslaved to worship if the minister was white.

At the same time, legislators were considering a proposal to repeal the state's 1782 manumission act. Prior to the passage of the act, freeing the people one enslaved required the approval of the General Assembly. The act was amended in 1806 to ban the importation of enslaved people and to require formerly enslaved people to leave Virginia within a year of being freed unless they secured specific permission from the legislature to stay. The law was unevenly enforced in different localities and at different periods.

Black men and women found themselves forced to decide between going north, thus abandoning family members who were still enslaved, and staying in Virginia, where they risked being re-enslaved. Both choices involved great heartbreak.

YEARS BEFORE ROBERT Lumpkin bought the jail, forty-one of the people he enslaved managed to escape to freedom in the most successful slave rebellion in American history. The blow to his business—and perhaps to Mary Lumpkin's sense of security—was significant.

Slave revolts were inherently risky, and plans were often foiled before they could be executed. The free Black musician Solomon Northup was kidnapped in 1841 and shipped to New Orleans to be sold into slavery. He plotted a revolt during the trip south aboard the *Orleans*, but his plans were dashed when one of his co-conspirators caught smallpox and died.

Just a few months later, however, a group of enslaved people being shipped from Richmond to New Orleans accomplished a historic slave rebellion. The *Creole*, commanded by Captain Robert Ensor of Richmond, was carrying 135 enslaved people. In a dramatic turn, enslaved people overpowered the crew and took control of the ship.

Previously, Robert Lumpkin and other slave traders had sent enslaved people to the Lower South by land. When the number of domestic sales of enslaved people began to increase in the 1790s, most enslaved people sold out of Virginia were forced to walk in coffles to the Lower South. Either Robert Lumpkin or a slave trading partner whom Bill Robinson referred to as "Logan," an unmarried trader who lived near Lumpkin's Jail, took "gangs" of forty enslaved people south to Natchez, Mississippi, and New Orleans, covering twenty-five miles a day on foot. They were armed and accompanied by dogs, and they chained the enslaved men they considered dangerous.

By 1829, traders like Franklin and Armfield had adopted the strategy of using slave ships instead. This mode of transport reduced the total travel time from two months to about three weeks. But slave traders probably hadn't weighed the risks of slave revolts on ships, which Black rebels could take over and use to ferry themselves to freedom abroad.

When the *Creole* left Richmond on October 25, 1841, it was packed with enslaved people and boxes of tobacco. The captain, accompanied by his wife, his infant daughter, and his fifteen-year-old niece, was unprepared. "It is one thing to manage a company of slaves on a Virginia plantation," wrote Frederick Douglass, the Black intellectual and abolitionist, "and quite another to quell an insurrection on the lonely billows of the Atlantic, where every breeze speaks of courage and liberty."

The *Creole* left Richmond for Hampton Roads, Virginia, to pick up more enslaved people, including Madison Washington, who had successfully escaped enslavement to Canada, only to be captured when he returned to Virginia to rescue his wife Susan. He had been sold to a slave trader and was being shipped to New Orleans.

While at sea, Washington found allies among the other enslaved men who were willing to rebel after white overseers isolated enslaved females and sexually abused them. It was later reported that Washington's wife was on board, but that is unlikely.

Thirteen days after the ship left Richmond, Washington led the most successful slave rebellion in history, ultimately securing freedom for 128 people. He gained access to the deck by attacking an overseer who lifted the hatch on the forward hold. "I'm going up, I cannot stay here!" Washington reportedly exclaimed as he ascended the ladder to the deck and called on other male captors to join him.

Washington threatened to kill anyone who didn't comply, and a group of nineteen enslaved people participated in the rebellion, wounding Ensor and killing slave trader John R. Hewell. The enslaved men searched for and confiscated their enslavers' weapons and also seized documents related to their enslavement. They held the first mate at gunpoint and ordered him to steer the ship to Liberia, a colony established by Americans in 1822 as a place to send free Black people. Warned that there was not sufficient food and water aboard the ship to make it across the Atlantic, the enslaved people instead directed the first mate to head for the British colony of Nassau, Bahamas, where slavery had been abolished by 1834.

A year earlier, on October 9, 1840, the *Hermosa*, sailing from Richmond to New Orleans loaded with cotton, tobacco, and forty-eight enslaved people, had crashed on the shores of the Abaco Islands in the northern strip of the Bahamas. The local government had freed those aboard, including some enslaved people being shipped by Robert Lumpkin. Bill Robinson, Robert Lumpkin's overseer, who had been put in charge of shipments of enslaved people to New Orleans, was among the people enslaved by Lumpkin who were reportedly freed that day.

On the *Creole*, the mutineers "did not want to go anywhere else but where Mr. Lumpkin's negroes went last year," the *Richmond Enquirer* reported. According to the historian Anita Rupprecht, "They knew that having been rescued by Bahamian wreckers and taken into Nassau, 'Mr. Lumpkin's Negroes' had been freed by the British colonials."

Within a day, the *Creole* arrived at Nassau, and British officials sent a boat to meet it, while crowds of locals lined the beaches, watching the scene unfold. A crew of local Black Bahamian officers boarded the ship and "mingled with the slaves and told them they were free men, that they could go on shore and never be carried away from there," the *Richmond Enquirer* reported.

Washington and seventeen other people who were considered suspects in the death of the slave trader Hewell were detained and charged with mutiny at the request of the American consulate. US secretary of state Daniel Webster "demanded the insurrectionists' return for mutiny and murder."

Yet six months later, a court in Nassau freed the eighteen men, who became "free as air," Vermont's *Spirit of the Age* noted. What happened to Madison Washington and his wife Susan is unknown. Frederick Douglass, who wrote about Washington in both fiction and nonfiction accounts, praised Washington's heroism for striking down his oppressor on the deck of the *Creole* and referred to it as a historical precedent for slave rebellion.

"There are more Madison Washingtons in the South, and the time may not be distant when the whole south will present again a scene something similar to the deck of the Creole," Douglass said.

The incident raised questions for American leaders about whether England had the right to set free the enslaved people. The United States had not created a treaty with Britain establishing how the two countries would interact with each other's laws, and the incident renewed disputes over jurisdiction and interpretations of slavery in international law.

The Massachusetts abolitionist Charles Sumner argued that being at sea freed enslaved people from the jurisdiction of American laws. American supporters of slavery, including Senators Henry Clay and John C. Calhoun, reacted angrily to the British handling of the *Creole* mutiny. The *Richmond Enquirer* reported that New Orleans was "thrown . . . into a flame" over the decision to set free the enslaved people on Nassau.

Robert Lumpkin had insured some of the enslaved people on board, valued at $20,000, and was reimbursed for four of them. The trader James H. Birch of Alexandria, Virginia, had taken out $800 insurance policies on many of the thirty-nine enslaved people he shipped south on the *Creole*. When insurance companies denied some of the traders' claims, they filed lawsuits. Eight of the cases made their way through lower courts and to the Louisiana supreme court. Insurance companies prevailed in six of the cases, in which the court determined that the policies did not cover insurrection, and they were held liable in two policies that covered mutiny.

By the 1850s, shipping enslaved people by boat to New Orleans had proven to be a great risk. For the final decade of slave trading, nearly all of the enslaved people sold to the Lower South from Richmond would be sent out of the city on railroad train cars, not by ships or on foot.

For as long as there has been slavery, enslaved people have tried to find a way to freedom. The *Creole* passengers' path was more dramatic than most. The people enslaved by Robert Lumpkin who escaped on the *Creole* were an exception. It is unlikely that many others enslaved by him or held in his jail found liberation before the end of the Civil War.

If Mary Lumpkin learned of the *Creole* mutiny, she may have been happy for the enslaved people who escaped, but the event may have worried her too. Their escape—and the escape of people enslaved by Robert Lumpkin who were aboard the *Hermosa*—surely had a profound impact on his finances. Anytime an enslaver's bottom line fluctuated, enslaved people were at risk of being sold.

SLAVE JAILS WERE an outgrowth of the domestic slave trade, which required enslavers to move enslaved people between states. Sellers needed a place to house them before they were sold, and their new enslavers had to have somewhere to keep them until they could be delivered to new homes.

At first, traders relied on hotels and city jails that would agree to keep enslaved people temporarily. Early on, enslaved people were primarily sold in taverns, small hotels, and private jails, and they were kept in basements, rooms of houses, or outdoor pens. Over time a network of privately owned slave jails, also called "pens," developed to warehouse enslaved people before they were moved to the Lower South and would become integral to the domestic slave trade in America. In these places, Black men, women, and children, hidden away from the public, were tortured and abused.

A congressional investigation of the slave trade in Washington, DC, was called after an enslaved woman named Anna jumped out of a third-floor tavern window in 1815. She tried to end her life after learning that she had been sold away from her spouse and several of her children to Georgia traders. She survived, but because she suffered terrible injuries, the slave trader left her behind and took her two daughters. The investigation spurred by her jump found that enslaved people were "confined in their filth" in a "dungeon" in the average slave pen. Yet the slave trade in DC was not outlawed until 1850.

Richmond slave trader John B. Prentis made his way into the slave jail business by first imprisoning pirates on behalf of the federal government for a generous daily fee per prisoner. Prentis transitioned the business to a slave jail by 1822. The jail where Lumpkin would make his name had been constructed by 1830. By the 1840s, dozens of slave jails were located in Richmond, and the South was littered with them.

From the late 1700s until the start of the Civil War, Richmond was deemed "the slave trade control center." When enslavers arrived in the city with enslaved people to sell, slave jails promised to feed them and separate men from women. Auction houses needed jails not only for trading people they owned but to serve the enslavers and slave traders with whom they did business.

Charging a daily fee to board an enslaved person, slave jails became "booming businesses," Frederic Bancroft reported. In 1845, slave jail owner Silas Omohundro, who also owned a trading depot in Richmond with his brother R. F. Omohundro, asked 25 cents a day for boarding an enslaved person in his jail.

Some jails served as "fattening houses" that took steps to ensure that enslaved people would bring in more money at the slave market. They served high-quality food, such as butter and bacon, to add weight to enslaved people who would soon go on the market. Franklin and Armfield's jail in Alexandria had an outdoor courtyard where enslaved people were told to exercise and a medical center on-site to nurse them back to health or at least figure out how to make them appear healthy.

"I was ordered to have the old men's whiskers shaved off and the grey hairs plucked out," recalled William Wells Brown, an enslaved man who had been leased by a Kentucky slave trader. After his escape, he became an abolitionist and writer in England, authoring the first novel by a Black American. *Clotel; or, The President's Daughter* was published in 1853.

In Lumpkin's Jail, "each slave in the jail had a new suit of clothes, and when any purchasers came, they were dressed in the new clothes, the boys had their faces washed and greased, to make them shine," Bill Robinson later recalled. Franklin and Armfield had a tailor shop on site.

The experience of purchasing an enslaved person was also sexualized. Buyers were given the opportunity to inspect in private the women and men they were considering purchasing. In slave sales at Dickinson, Hill & Co. in Richmond, enslaved people were "stripped naked and carefully examined as horses are—every part of their body from their crown to their feet, was rigorously scrutinized," wrote James Redpath, an abolitionist and journalist.

Buyers watched enslaved people exercise in order to evaluate their bodies. Some buyers put their fingers inside enslaved men and women's mouths, "as they would to a horse," Robinson recalled. Enslavers were permitted to take off an enslaved woman's clothes and grope her, grabbing breasts or caressing calves, trying "all their feminine points," Robinson recalled. The enslavers claimed to be searching for histories of childbearing, but more likely they behaved this way because they could.

Enslaved women sometimes resisted this abusive treatment. "The greatest orator I ever heard was a woman. She was a slave. She was a mother, and her rostrum was the auction block," recalled John Randolph, a Charlotte County, Virginia, enslaver and longtime congressman.

Some women became so distraught on the auction block that their sales were postponed so that they could be "beaten into submission," writes the historian Stanley Feldstein. "Some refused to be sold," recalled Charles Crawley, a formerly enslaved Virginia man who described women fighting and kicking "like crazy folks." The enslavers responded by handcuffing the enslaved women and beating them, Crawley recalled.

Traders were also known for inflicting harm on enslaved people in order to ensure they would be easy to sell. Theophilus Freeman, the New Orleans trader, threatened the people he enslaved with torture instruments to induce them to follow scripts for how to behave during their own sales. He forced them to dance to violin music so they would appear content and happy when visitors toured the jail.

Precursors to today's private prisons, slave jails were spaces of extreme violence. What would it have meant to witness the trauma that unfolded there each day, to feel the weight of sadness and desperation caused by family separation? How could Mary Lumpkin, an enslaved girl, make a home in that heaviness?

THROUGHOUT HISTORY, SLAVE traders have been blamed for the slave trade. Pointing a finger at them was convenient for enslavers. As long as the public looked upon slave traders' operations as unsavory or immoral, enslavers could be relieved of the moral burden of selling people and separating children from their parents.

While some traders were certainly considered unethical, they were often respected. Traders were known to belong to Masonic lodges, boards of trade, and other business associations. Their financial success apparently erased the stigma of the slave trade. Many traders were proud of their business and even invited abolitionist visitors to tour the premises.

The Richmond auctioneer Hector Davis served on the Richmond City Council and became president of a bank he founded with Robert Lumpkin and others before the start of the Civil War. The slave trader Bacon Tait had a seat on the City Council for four terms and was a member of the Richmond Fire Association, an insurance company. John Prentis was a respected architect and builder before he became a Richmond trader.

Many slave traders realized the importance to their success of appearing to be honest. John Armfield welcomed visitors to his Alexandria jail and offered them a glass of wine while they waited for a tour. Dressed neatly, he patiently answered questions, attempting to persuade visitors that his firm treated enslaved people with decency and that the slave trade was humane. "Dealing in slaves was not worse than slaveholding," said the Baltimore trader Hope H. Slatter.

Richmond slave traders often banded together, living with each other during the trading season, selling enslaved people on each other's behalf, and executing wills for one another. "Despite all of their aggressive competition and cutthroat practices, the masculine lifestyle of the trade left many speculators to develop deep and sincere friendships with one another," writes the historian Steven Deyle.

At slave trader properties like Robert Lumpkin's, the men experienced "a certain camaraderie and male bonding as they boasted, cursed, drank, gambled, and shared women together," Deyle wrote. Some of the traders were not married, perhaps because they had difficulty finding suitable spouses, as Tait often complained.

Yet both married and single traders seemed to view sexual abuse as an entitlement of owning and, especially, dealing in enslaved people. Like other aspects of the slave trade, the jails were spaces of depravity. "The slave pen is only another name for a brothel," recalled John Brown, an enslaved man who penned *Slave Life in Georgia*. He noted that "the youngest and handsomest" of the slave women were chosen as a "mistress" of the enslaver and were swapped out weekly.

Isaac Franklin documented his abuse of enslaved women in letters he wrote to Rice Ballard, who worked as a buyer for him in Richmond. They both bragged about raping a light-skinned enslaved woman whom they sent back and forth between Richmond and Natchez, Mississippi. When Ballard freed two enslaved women and their children, who may have been his, Franklin mocked him, referring to the women and children as "your free family."

Franklin also impregnated an enslaved woman and then passed her on to a friend when he wed a white woman. His nephew, James Franklin, recalled his own rape and abuse of an eighteen-year-old enslaved woman. "To my certain knowledge she has been used and that smartly by a one eyed man about my size and age, excuse my foolishness," he wrote, referring to his penis. Armfield also fathered a child with an enslaved woman and married Isaac Franklin's niece.

Robert Lumpkin and a business partner sexually abused the enslaved women in their care. "They used to sleep with the girls, ordering me, at night, to bring such a girl or such a girl up to the house, just as they would order out such a horse to ride," Robinson recalled.

John B. Prentis, who was married to a white woman, may have fathered at least two children with enslaved women. At his 1848 death, he set free and provided money for "the mulatto girl Margaret Jackson" and her children. He also freed and left money for "my boy Edmond that was born at our house of a female servant named Mary."

Like many white women of her time, Prentis's wife, Catharine Dabney Prentis, "most likely turned a blind eye to John's fancies, refusing to know what she knew," writes the historian Kari J. Winter. John Prentis reminded his wife "that a dignified, virtuous, and affectionate wife tolerates and accommodates her husband's weaknesses, sexual and otherwise."

While many slave traders abused the women and girls in their care, some of the relationships extended beyond sex. Some slave traders even flouted them. Perhaps the most brazen was the trader Theophilus Freeman, who at one time partnered with Alexandria trader James H. Birch. Freeman was famously licentious—one historian went so far as to call him a "pimp." He was known in the 1840s to meet with visitors in the bedroom of his New Orleans home while lying in bed with Sarah Conner, a woman whom he had enslaved. Conner lived with Freeman "as his wife," and he took her on trips to New York and Philadelphia. It's unclear whether they had children.

When Freeman became insolvent in the mid-1840s, his creditors claimed that he had transferred to Conner some of his assets, including plantations in Louisiana and Georgia, in order to hide them. His creditors demanded that Conner's freedom be revoked and that Freeman forfeit her as an asset, along with her property, demonstrating just how vulnerable formerly enslaved women were, even when free. The bank was ultimately unsuccessful.

By the time Robert Lumpkin had opened his slave jail in Shockoe Bottom, several of his peers in the Richmond slave trade had not been able to achieve—or had chosen to forgo—marriage to white women and the white offspring that would follow. Slave traders he knew and associated with were having children with enslaved girls or women—relationships that went beyond sexual abuse. Several of these men were creating something that, to outsiders, may have resembled a family. Looking around Richmond's slave district, Robert Lumpkin saw multiple examples of slave traders living with Black women, most of whom were enslaved and unable to consent. Traders fathered multiracial children whom they educated, protected, and provided for.

Bacon Tait, who expressed frustration about being unable to marry, started a relationship with a free Black woman, Courtney Fountain, who worked as a housekeeper. The first of four children with Fountain was born around 1843. The Norfolk trader George W. Apperson, who frequently stayed with Lumpkin and by 1852 had his own jail nearby, fathered the first of two children with Louisa Girard, a Black woman whom he may have enslaved, in 1841. The Richmond trader

Silas Omohundro had five children with Louisa, who was approximately eighteen years old when she gave birth to his son, Littleton, around 1838.

Having children with enslaved girls and women allowed these men to create a family life—or something resembling a family life—that had otherwise eluded them. In this intimate Richmond slave trading community, the practice of fathering children with enslaved girls or women was normalized for slave traders, as was keeping these women and the children in their home or close at hand in the slave jail compound.

Looking around, Robert Lumpkin may have seen a clear path for his future in young Mary.

UNITED STATES SLAVE TRADE.
1830.

This abolitionist print, dated 1830, depicts a group of enslaved men in chains, as well as a woman and children. Two white men, one on horseback and one holding a whip, appear to be acting as overseers and preparing to load the enslaved people on a ship to be taken south for sale. (Library of Congress)

3

The Thing We Can't Name

WHEN SHE WAS ABOUT THIRTEEN YEARS OLD, MARY LUMPKIN GAVE birth to a baby girl, the daughter of Robert Lumpkin. Martha Dabney Lumpkin was born enslaved, just like her mother.

Like Elizabeth Hobbs Keckley, a Virginia-born enslaved woman forced to have a child with her enslaver even though "she did not wish to give him life," Mary Lumpkin may not have wanted a child. And yet, like Keckley, who later became a seamstress for Mary Todd Lincoln, and like many other enslaved women before her, Mary probably had little to no say in the matter.

On plantations, enslaved women built networks among themselves to support each other in birthing and raising children, but Mary Lumpkin, isolated from other enslaved people in the jail, likely did not have any such support. At most, she might have had one family member by her side if she had been sold with her mother or a sister. How frightening it must have been to bring a child into the world without older females who knew and loved her to guide her through pregnancy and childbirth, and then through caring for a baby. She must have felt incredibly alone.

If Mary Lumpkin gave birth in the slave jail, Robert Lumpkin may have called in a midwife to help her. The health risks for Mary Lumpkin and her daughter were great—about half of children born enslaved were stillborn or died in the first years of life. What must it have been like to deliver a child in a place that devalued enslaved people and stripped them of their humanity? As she labored, Mary Lumpkin knew that her child would be enslaved from birth.

On plantations, women who had given birth days earlier were forced to leave their infants, often without food or a caring provider, and return to the fields. As the mother of Robert Lumpkin's children, and because she lived and worked in the jail, Mary may have been allowed to stay with her baby. She would have been valued in ways that the other people enslaved and housed by Robert Lumpkin were not. If her place in the jail was not already secure, it became so once she gave birth to his child in 1845. Her new status within the jail would have given her some freedom of movement on the property and around Richmond. But her worries about her children were only beginning.

For nearly two decades, she watched as enslaved men, women, and children came through the doors of the slave jail, taken away from everyone they loved to be shipped to new lives of physically demanding work that could kill them. Not much separated her from them, or her child from their children.

As a new mother, Mary Lumpkin now worried not only about her own fate but also about the fate of her daughter.

THROUGHOUT HISTORY, ENSLAVED women were forced to have the children of their enslavers more commonly than has been acknowledged. Many people are only aware of one—Sally Hemings, an enslaved woman who had children with Thomas Jefferson, thirty years her senior.

Jefferson attempted to keep the relationship hidden, and for more than two hundred years, it mostly remained a secret. Like Mary Lumpkin, Sally Hemings had no way to tell her story. While many people in Jefferson's day knew about her, and even though their many descendants carried the story, a particular narrative was crafted about Jefferson that erased the Hemings family story. He would be remembered as the brilliant architect of ornate buildings and the author of the Declaration of Independence—a story that did not include Hemings. The legacy of America's beloved third president did not include his enslaved children and their enslaved mother, an omission that suspended Americans in a false understanding of their nation's history.

Yet the labor of enslaved people built this country, and it built the White House. Eight of America's presidents owned enslaved people while they were in office. At least one other president and one vice president fathered children with enslaved girls and women. James Madison's father, James Madison Sr., had a daughter, Coreen, with an enslaved girl. As a young man, James Madison, the future president, fathered a son, Jim, with this enslaved half-sister. Martin Van Buren's vice president, Richard Johnson of Kentucky, had two daughters with Julia Chinn, an enslaved woman. She managed his property while he was in Washington and ran a school on the grounds. How many more women like them existed?

Sexual abuse was woven through generations of Sally Hemings's family. She was the daughter of an enslaved woman, Elizabeth Hemings, and her white enslaver, John Wayles, a British immigrant who worked as a slave trader. Elizabeth Hemings was the daughter of an enslaved woman and an English sea captain named Hemings. When Wayles died, he left his enslaved children with Elizabeth Hemings to their white half-sister, Martha Wayles Jefferson, and her husband Thomas Jefferson. Sally Hemings was moved to Monticello as a child, and later she served as a "nursemaid" for the Jeffersons' young daughter, Polly. After Martha Jefferson died in 1782, Thomas Jefferson went to Paris to serve as minister to France, and fourteen-year-old Hemings was chosen to accompany Polly. While in France, Hemings "became Mr. Jefferson's concubine" at the age of sixteen, their son Madison Hemings later recounted.

The historian Edward Baptist notes that when powerful men like Jefferson chased "the Sable Venus," they always captured their prey. Robert Lumpkin took no risk in pursuing Mary Lumpkin. An enslaved girl or woman had no power to thwart the advances of powerful men. "She couldn't reject them," Baptist wrote. "Most enslaved women found it vital to go along."

Sally Hemings and her children with Jefferson were known at Monticello and in wider Charlottesville in the 1790s. Yet the relationship was not public during his tenure as US secretary of state and then as vice president, or during his bid for the US presidency in 1801. News that Jefferson had fathered children with Hemings didn't break until the following year, when he was serving as president.

"It is well known that the man, whom it delighteth the people to honor, keeps, and for many years has kept, as his concubine, one of his slaves. Her name is SALLY," wrote the journalist James Callender in the *Richmond Recorder*, noting that Hemings had a young son. "His features are said to bear a striking although sable resemblance to those of the president himself."

The scandal was quickly forgotten, and Jefferson never acknowledged his children with Hemings. After he died in 1826 and she in 1835, the truth was buried with them. Madison Hemings claimed Jefferson as his father in an 1873 article in an obscure newspaper, stating that he was born in 1805 when Jefferson was president. But his account either faded from history or was not believed.

Sally Hemings and her children with Jefferson were systematically erased, just as Mary Lumpkin and her children would be. More than a century later, when Black men and women began publicly claiming to be descendants of Jefferson, scholars initially denied that it was possible. This denial went on for decades, until a series of books made a persuasive case that Jefferson had fathered Hemings's children. Finally, in 2000, Monticello published a report that a direct genetic connection between descendants of Hemings and Jefferson had been established through DNA testing.

For decades, Jefferson's plantation had tried to ignore or downplay his relationship with Hemings, and she was not discussed on official tours of Monticello. And yet, as the *Washington Post* writer Philip Kennicott has pointed out, Hemings "might be considered the first lady to the third president of the United States if that didn't presume her relationship to Jefferson was voluntary."

Nearly two decades after releasing the report, Monticello shifted its position and began publicly acknowledging Hemings's role in Jefferson's life. The museum website was updated to share the story of Hemings, "one of the most famous—and least known—African American women in US history."

Yet it was the presidential estate's failure to acknowledge her role in Jefferson's life for so many years that kept Hemings's story from being known. In recent years, Monticello has been renovated, in part to showcase the room where Hemings may have slept—a room that had previously been utilized as a public restroom—and created a "Hemings Family Tour" that shares her history.

"For more than 200 years, her name has been linked to Thomas Jefferson as his 'concubine,' obscuring the facts of her life and her identity," the museum's website read in 2021. Until Monticello became intentional about telling her story, Sally Hemings was portrayed as a victim rather than as someone who had agency, someone who had an identity of her own.

"Though enslaved, Sally Hemings helped shape her life and the lives of her children, who got an almost 50-year head start on emancipation, escaping the system that had engulfed their ancestors and millions of others," notes the historian Annette Gordon-Reed.

We know that throughout history women who submitted to their enslavers often benefited in small, but tangible, ways. They may have been given better work assignments and nicer living quarters. Silas Omohundro, a Richmond slave trader, provided gold jewelry and diamonds to Corinna Hinton Omohundro, another enslaved woman with whom he had children, and he gave her some freedom of movement around Richmond.

Robert Lumpkin likely either taught Mary Lumpkin to read and write or hired someone else to teach her. While an 1830s law prohibited schools for enslaved people, some enslavers educated the people they enslaved but may have kept it secret. Harriet Jacobs was taught to read and write by her enslaver, Margaret Horniblow. "For this privilege, which so rarely falls to the lot of a slave, I bless [Margaret's] memory," Jacobs wrote.

While living in France, where she was free, Sally Hemings had laid out terms for going back to Virginia with Jefferson. "She refused to return with him," Madison Hemings recalled. "To induce her to do so he promised her extraordinary privileges, and made a solemn pledge that her children should be freed at the age of twenty-one years."

Over an eighteen-year period, Sally Hemings had at least six children with Jefferson, four of whom survived to adulthood—sons Beverly, Madison, and Eston and a daughter, Harriet. All four took Hemings as their last name, though later in life Madison and his children used the last name Jefferson. On the estate, Sally Hemings's workload was light compared to the work of other enslaved people; she was assigned to sew and take care of Jefferson's "chamber" and wardrobe.

Decades after their Paris negotiation, Jefferson freed Beverly and Harriet Hemings when they turned twenty-one years old. When Jefferson allowed them to leave Monticello in the early 1820s, they were apparently lost to him. He did not free his younger children, Eston and Madison Hemings, until his death, and he never freed their mother. Instead, after Jefferson's death, his white daughter Patsy permitted Sally Hemings to leave Monticello to live with her youngest sons, who had built a house in Charlottesville.

When Sally Hemings died in 1835, the location of her grave was either not recorded or lost, another erasure.

Though Mary Lumpkin lived in the slave jail with Robert Lumpkin, ultimately raising five of his children to adulthood, the nature of their connection is unclear.

The relationships between enslaver and enslaved are difficult to parse. Even with all that has been revealed in recent years about Sally Hemings's life, little is known about her feelings for Jefferson.

"How is it possible to get at the nature of a relationship between a man and a woman like Jefferson and Hemings when neither party specifically wrote or speaks to others about the relationship or their feelings?" asks Gordon-Reed, who wrote two books on the subject.

Mary Lumpkin may have detested Robert Lumpkin for separating her from some or all of her family. Perhaps she warmed to him over time, or maybe she saw their relationship as transactional and felt she had some control. Mary Collins, an enslaved Virginia woman who had two children with her Orange County enslaver Hilton Waddell, used her daughter to get items she wanted or needed. "She said it was no harm for me to ask him for things for her which she could not get," Collins's daughter, Harriet Ann Daves, recalled.

Perhaps Mary Lumpkin employed similar practices. She and the children probably lived in the main house on the jail property with Robert Lumpkin. She may have had the freedom to move about the grounds as she wished—or at least within Robert Lumpkin's house. He may have set aside a space in the main house to give her and the children some privacy, and he may have furnished it with ornate furniture and pretty linens. He likely bought instruments and provided musical instruction, along with tutoring and French lessons. He probably ensured that Mary and her children had better food to eat than he served in the jail. Perhaps he bought her dresses and silk stockings, as Silas Omohundro did for Corinna Hinton Omohundro. Maybe he bought household items she wanted and gifts for her friends.

After the birth of Martha, Mary Lumpkin had at least four other children by Robert Lumpkin. Another daughter, Annie, born in about 1847, was followed by three boys who lived to adulthood. The first was born around 1848 and named Robert for his father. Richard and John would follow around 1853 and 1857. While Mary Lumpkin's role as the mother of his children is likely to have improved her status in Robert Lumpkin's jail complex, her fears that she would be sold away may not have been alleviated. That was the ultimate fate of Cynthia, an enslaved woman who had been forced to have the children of the Louisville slave trader "Mr. Walker." When he married a white woman, he sold Cynthia and his four children with her, heartlessly removing them from his life.

Perhaps Mary Lumpkin had reached some kind of agreement with Robert Lumpkin, as Sally Hemings did with Thomas Jefferson. Did he promise to educate the children they would have and to free them? Did he promise to provide for them in death?

Mary Lumpkin told him "she would do anything he wanted, as long as he would let the children go free." "You can do anything you want to me, you can't hurt these children," she told him. "These children have to be free." Mary Lumpkin's great-great-granddaughter, Carolivia Herron, a writer, scholar, and English professor at the HBCU Howard University, recalled being told that Mary Lumpkin demanded money in order to free the children and was provided it.

We don't know what her feelings for Robert Lumpkin were, but their relationship should not be viewed as a love affair. The 1995 movie *Jefferson in Paris* imagined that Sally Hemings and Jefferson were in love, making the case that, if she didn't love him, Hemings would have left Jefferson in Paris. Yet her decision to return to Monticello does not prove that she had romantic feelings for him. More likely it shows that she missed her family and worried about never seeing them again. As a young girl without resources, she surely felt obliged to do as her much older enslaver asked. Finding herself in a similar situation, Mary Lumpkin must have felt forced to comply with Robert Lumpkin's requests.

"The man who is victimizing her is one of the most powerful slave traders in the country," said Niya Bates, the former public historian at Monticello.

Oral accounts of Hemings and Jefferson's relationship passed down to Madison Hemings's descendants indicated that Jefferson "dearly loved" Hemings. But if Jefferson had viewed her as a true partner, perhaps he would have freed her. Perhaps he would have publicly acknowledged the children he fathered with her, freed his children before they turned twenty-one, and stayed in contact with them when they left his estate.

Americans' desire to turn the relationship between Jefferson and Hemings into a love story speaks to the country's collective failure to process the trauma of slavery. It preserves Jefferson's standing as an American icon, despite his moral failings, and essentially forgives all American presidents who were enslavers, starting with George Washington. It extends grace to Robert Lumpkin, who possessed none of Thomas Jefferson's positive attributes of leadership and vision and was instead known for his brutality.

The desire to take something deeply despicable and make it palatable is an American pathology. At every step, white America wants to sanitize the trauma and abuse of slavery—trauma and abuse that Mary Lumpkin surely suffered. Yet, in the few existing references to her life, those experiences are erased and she is converted into Robert Lumpkin's "wife."

During this time, most relationships between white men and enslaved women involved violence and rape. But there was also space for other interactions, particularly when an enslaved woman had some agency. Mary Lumpkin was "first and foremost looking to stay alive and to not be separated from her children," says the historian Sharony Andrews Green. And like any white woman of that era, she would have been looking for security.

Robert Lumpkin clearly took advantage of Mary as a child and used his position of authority over her when she was powerless. That's not a love story. Mary Lumpkin didn't have the opportunity to choose whether to be with him—not until she already had birthed his children.

Once Mary Lumpkin had children, her focus must have been on how to keep them.

Children were an important part of the slave trade, and in Lumpkin's Jail, Mary Lumpkin surely saw families being separated and children arriving without parents. Their desperate, miserable cries must have echoed through the property, and this surely tugged at her heartstrings.

She surely knew that she was at risk of being separated from her own children—or they from her.

Half of the 666,000 interstate sales made by slave traders before the Civil War included forced separations of family members. One-quarter ended a first marriage and half tore apart a nuclear family, often separating children under the age of thirteen from their parents. Enslavers' intentional dissolution of all family bonds was yet another form of control over the lives of those they enslaved.

Across Virginia, children were picked up on back roads, bought from farms, kidnapped, and otherwise removed from their parents' care en route to the Richmond slave market. In 1835, ten Black boys ages six to twelve who had been taken from their families days earlier were marched two-by-two down a rural Virginia road. They were tied at the wrists and fastened together with a rope. When they arrived at a country tavern, a white overseer holding a whip led the children to a horse trough to drink and then pointed them to a shed to sleep. They were likely headed to a slave market to be sold.

In Ohio, a free Black girl named Jane was kidnapped when "a bad man got out of a covered wagon and took her into it with one hand about her body and the other upon her mouth to prevent her screams," wrote her son, Jermain Wesley Loguen. Other young Black children in the wagon were also taken over the river on a boat, most likely into Kentucky, where "the kidnappers sold them, one after another." When Jane was sold to three brothers in Tennessee, she was renamed Cherry, perhaps so that her origins could not be traced.

Viney Baker, born enslaved in Virginia, recalled how she learned that her mother, Hannah Murry, had been sold away from her. Viney "lay down on the straw mattress" with her mother one night, and the next morning, when she woke up, her mother was gone. Her enslaver had taken her mother without waking her. Acknowledging the trauma of being separated, Baker added that she was always glad that she was asleep when it happened.

Enslaved children were also separated from their parents when en-slavers gave them to their own offspring as wedding gifts. Frank Free-man, enslaved in North Carolina, was removed from his mother's care when his enslaver's daughter married and left home. "She took me with her, when I was two years old," he said.

Enslavers were despised both for threatening enslaved people with sale—its own form of control—and then later for following through on their threats. "I hope you will try to meet me in heaven," one man told his sobbing wife after being sold away from her in St. Louis. "I shall try to meet you there, too."

Harriet Jacobs's enslaver warned that he would sell her son away from her if she didn't submit to his sexual advances. "His threat lacerated my heart," Jacobs recalled, and she was consumed with worry.

Enslavers blamed slave traders for the evils of slavery, yet most of them separated families. "Virtually all enslavers were engaged in slave trading, and all slave traders were enslavers," observes Kari J. Winter.

Harriet Beecher Stowe asked in *Uncle Tom's Cabin*, "Who, sir, makes the trader? Who is most to blame?"

Even before the international slave trade was banned, family ties were disregarded by most enslavers, except when it came to mothers of very young children. Throughout the South, most traders marketed children ten to twelve years old, and many also sold those between the ages of six and nine. Girls ten and under, for example, sold for $800 in 1857.

J. T. Underwood advertised in the *Louisville Weekly Journal* in May 1849 that he was willing to sell an enslaved woman and her four chil-dren, ages eighteen months to six years, "separately to suit purchasers." The Savannah trader A. Bryan advertised in December 1859 that he was selling a five-year-old "likely intelligent yellow girl child" as well as eight-year-old and eleven-year-old "likely girls"—referring to their like-liness to produce offspring and their vulnerability to rape.

George Apperson, the trader who had a private jail in Richmond and an office at the United States Hotel, formerly known as Union Hotel, offered "cash for negroes" in 1848. "I will pay the highest cash for likely young negroes of both sexes, from 10 to 30 years of age," the advertisement read. He also offered to "attend to shipping of negroes to any of the Southern ports, free of charge, when left with me."

Even in Louisiana, traders worked around the rules meant to prevent the sale of children. Because orphaned children of any age could be sold, traders were more likely to label children as "orphans." The slave trader David Wise wrote that "witness has often sold little children . . . who had lost their mother."

Outside of Louisiana, some traders worried about the public perception of selling children and didn't want people to know that they were dividing families to pad their bottom line. But plenty did it anyway. Slave sale announcements rarely referred to single children as orphans, an indication that they had in fact been separated from their parents. A slave trader could profit most by buying a family of enslaved people and then selling the family members individually.

The slave trader Hope H. Slatter, who worked with trader John Hagan in New Orleans, claimed that he couldn't help what happened to families of enslaved people before he purchased them or after he sold them. Yet Slatter, who opened a Baltimore slave jail in 1838, sold children as young as seven, advertising the sale of "a sprightly, bright mulatto girl only seven years old, as fine a servant as he ever saw." The girl was offered for sale, alone, for $250.

In another instance, Slatter, whose brother Shadrach was a trader in New Orleans, advertised that he wanted to buy between seventy-five and one hundred enslaved people from eight to twenty-five years old and that he was looking for seamstresses and "small fancy girls for nurses." Yet there was evidence that he sold four-year-old and six-year-old girls away from their mothers.

For many families, the separation was permanent. Lizzie Baker, enslaved in Duplin County, North Carolina, recalled her mother, Teeny McIntire, crying as she told the girl that her siblings, Lucy and Fred, had been taken before Lizzie was born. They were "carried to Richmond" and sold as children. Her mother inquired about them "as long as she lived," but never saw them again.

"We tried to get some news of brother and sister," Baker said, but no information materialized. Even in old age, she hoped they would show up, but "ain't no use ever expectin' to see 'em," she said.

Henry Box Brown, born enslaved in Louisa County, Virginia, was separated from his parents when, at age fifteen, he was sent to work in a tobacco factory in Richmond. Most of his siblings had already been taken from their parents when they were left to their enslavers' family members at his death. Brown joined the First African Baptist Church, founded in 1841 as the first large all-Black church in Richmond, and he sang in the choir. He married Nancy, a woman owned by a different enslaver, and they had three children.

He would lose his family again when Samuel Cottrell, a Richmond saddler and the enslaver of his pregnant wife, told Brown that "he wanted some money today, as he had a demand for a large amount." When Brown informed him that he could not pay, Cottrell responded, "I want money, and money I will have."

After Brown went to work that morning, he learned that "my wife and children were taken from their home, sent to the auction mart and sold, and then lay in prison" in Richmond, he wrote in his autobiography, *Narrative of the Life of Henry Box Brown*. Perhaps Nancy and the couple's three children spent the night in Lumpkin's Jail.

The next morning Brown joined other desperate enslaved people standing on the side of the road, hoping for a final glimpse of family members as a slave coffle of 350 men, women, and children were marched out of Richmond by the North Carolina Methodist minister who had bought them. Brown spotted his eldest child on a wagon and spoke to him. When Nancy passed him, "I seized hold of her hand . . . and my tongue was only able to say, we shall meet in heaven!" He then walked four miles with her out of town, hand-in-hand, until they were forced to part. He did not see his family again. The next year he secured his freedom by shipping himself to Philadelphia in a three-foot-long box.

Harriet Jacobs recalled the horrific experience of watching a mother lead her seven children to an auction block. "She knew that *some* of them would be taken from her; but they took *all*," Jacobs recounted. "The children were sold to a slave-trader, and their mother was bought by a man in her own town. Before night her children were all far away."

The woman had begged the trader to tell her where he would take them, and he had refused. "How *could* he," Jacobs wrote, "when he knew he would sell them, one by one, wherever he could command the highest price?"

Jacobs described the "wild, haggard face" of the mother when Jacobs encountered her on the street. "She wrung her hands in anguish, and exclaimed, 'Gone! All gone! Why *don't* God kill me?'"

The breaking of familial ties—particularly the bond between parent and child—was among the most damaging and dehumanizing impacts of slavery. Even though the act of mothering was essential to slavery, the primal connections that are so important to the mother's health and the child's development were severed without regard. White mothers were put on a pedestal, but Black mothers, whose reproductive freedom was taken from them, were written off as irresponsible and sexually promiscuous, portrayals that have continued today.

An enslaved mother toiled in two shifts. "She had to work all the day for her owner, and at night for those who were dearer to her than life," Peter Randolph recalled of his mother. She would boil corn to feed her five children, and she would ask neighbors for cast-off clothing in order to dress them. "When they had none to give, she would sit and cry over us."

Frederick Douglass's mother would walk through the night as far as twelve miles to see her children, scattered to different enslavers' homes, and then, in the morning, walk back to the farm where she had been hired out to report for work. "My poor mother, like many other slave women, had *many children*, but NO FAMILY!" he wrote.

Sojourner Truth, an enslaved woman who escaped slavery with her infant daughter, Sophia, also successfully sued a white man to retrieve her son who had been taken from her. Speaking to a women's rights convention in 1851, she told the crowd that most of her children had been sold away from her. She addressed the hypocrisy of white men and women who disregarded Black women's humanity by taking their children and then by ignoring the pain it caused them.

"When I cried out with my mother's grief, none but Jesus heard me! And ain't I a woman?" she asked.

When an infant belonging to a woman the trader "Walker" had purchased cried as he led a coffle of enslaved people south, he removed the baby from its trembling mother's arms, ignoring her pleading and crying. "He took the child by one arm, as you would a cat by the leg," recalled William Wells Brown, and gave it away. Mary Armstrong's St. Louis enslaver beat her nine-month-old sister to death for crying. "She come and took the diaper offen my little sister and whipped till the blood jes' ran," Armstrong recalled.

Across the South, mothers were seen in cotton fields talking to children who had been taken years earlier as if they were there. The trauma of being separated from parents, siblings, spouses, and children would leave permanent imprints on the bodies and minds of those enslaved in America for generations to come.

Because of the way the heartless separations were conducted—slave traders rarely kept records of who went where—most children were unable to be reunited with their parents, even after emancipation. The separation of migrant children from their parents at the US border with Mexico during the Trump administration echoed slavery in this way. Some of the migrant children were sent to foster homes without a record of where they went and with no way to reach their parents. As in the slavery era, the fundamental need of children for their parents, and parents for their children, was intentionally disregarded.

Perhaps Mary Lumpkin experienced this kind of separation and was left without a way to find or reconnect with her family. The trauma of being taken from one or both parents surely stayed with her all of her days and shaped the way she mothered her children and, later, her grandchildren. The experience also may have played a role in her negotiations with Robert Lumpkin, making her more determined not to be separated from her own sons and daughters.

Mary Lumpkin would do what it took to ensure that her children's fate was different from her own. They were not going to be sold away from the person who brought them into the world. They were not going to lose their siblings. They were not going to toil anonymously in someone's field. She would see to that.

WHILE ROBERT LUMPKIN provided for his children and Mary Lumpkin, he also continued to sexually abuse at least one other enslaved woman in his care at the jail.

Mary may have worried that if he had children with another woman, he would reject her. She must have been concerned that if she fell out of favor with him, she and her children could be sold, as happened to a kidnapped enslaved girl. Cherry's enslaver, David Logue, fathered children with her and then, after several years, moved on to a white woman, with whom he also had children. When he got into financial trouble, he sold Cherry and her children to his brother and sister-in-law. Later, two of her children were sold away from her.

"A young negress is often her master's mistress, until childbearing and years render it tasteful or convenient to sell the offspring from his sight, and exchange her for another victim," wrote Cherry's son Jermain Wesley Loguen, who was known as Jarm Logue while enslaved. He escaped slavery on his aunt and uncle's horse after he, his siblings, and his mother were sold away from his father.

Most enslavers did not care about the happiness of the Black women they abused or that of the children these unions created. Some enslavers even sold their own children for profit. "White people were enslaving themselves," Joel Williamson points out, "in the form of their children and their children's children."

For some white men, the sexual abuse of enslaved females was "both a passion and a [business] pursuit," notes the historian Michael Tadman.

The enslaver Ephraim Christopher, who lived in Greenville, South Carolina, with an enslaved woman named Maria, reportedly sold as many as thirteen of their children. He put each child up for sale for $225 when he or she reached about nine year sold, a decision that certainly devastated not only the child but its mother and siblings as well.

A judge in an 1854 court case noted that, by selling a child a year, Christopher had "gained great profit from his dazzling abuse of parenthood." The practice of enslavers selling the children they fathered was concerning even to slavery advocates.

"We fear that fathers have made a traffic in their own children, as slaves," wrote the editor of the *Niles Register* in 1834. Chris Franklin, enslaved in Louisiana, confirmed that this happened routinely. "Dey sell dem jes' like other slaves," he said.

While serving as secretary of war under President James Monroe in 1817, John C. Calhoun, a staunch defender of slavery, raised concerns about white men trafficking their own children. He suggested that laws needed to be enacted to free multiracial people. Abolitionists started circulating photos of light-skinned enslaved children, making the case that if people who appeared white could be enslaved, then anyone could be. This was a popular tactic through the war's end.

Some white men—many of them married with white wives and white children—did not acknowledge the children they fathered with enslaved girls and women. White women were also skilled at denial, even when the multiracial children under their roofs resembled their own. "Every lady tells you who is the father of all the Mulatto children in everybody's household," wrote Mary Boykin Miller Chesnut in her *Diary from Dixie*, "but those in her own, she seems to think drop from the clouds or pretends so to think." Some white women appeared not to mind because their husband's sexual abuse of enslaved women meant they owned more enslaved people.

Just as Robert Lumpkin apparently sexually abused other enslaved women on his property, married enslavers were known to do the same in plain sight of their wives, some of whom were unwilling to tolerate the behavior. Lucy W. Norman of Henry County, Virginia, petitioned for divorce in 1848. She claimed that her husband, James B. Norman, brought a "negro servant girl" into their bedroom and slept with her on a pallet, kissing the enslaved girl in front of his wife. After keeping the girl in the home for two years, he moved out of his wife's home and took the girl with him, living openly in town with her.

Another Virginia woman told of her husband spending months traveling in South Carolina and Georgia selling enslaved people and then bringing home an enslaved woman, who served as a source of "great unhappiness to his wife." The enslaved woman surely was unhappy with her position too.

Some white women did not keep silent about white men's misdeeds. One Virginia woman called white men's sexual relationships with enslaved women "the one great evil hanging over the Southern states, destroying the domestic peace and happiness of thousands," though she failed to reflect on their impact on enslaved women. The practice, she said, was more common than Southerners would admit and "pervades the entire society."

"The white mothers and daughters of the South have suffered under it for years—have seen their dearest affections trampled on—their hopes of domestic happiness destroyed," the woman said.

White women tended to blame, not their husbands, but the Black women in their home, and they could be ruthless about removing enslaved women they viewed as a threat. White women would sell an enslaved woman and her children in an instant to keep their family intact or to seek revenge against their husband or the woman. The lives of enslaved women and their chances of staying with their children were often as threatened by white women as by white men.

Yet some enslavers made it clear that they did not want their own children sold into slavery. In his will, James H. Hammond, the depraved South Carolina governor, directed his white son, Harry, not to sell the children he had fathered with both an enslaved woman, Sally Johnson, and her daughter Louisa when she was twelve.

"I cannot free these people and send them North. It would be cruelty to them," he wrote, failing to grasp that sexual abuse and incest were also a form of cruelty.

Instead, his racist views dictated that the multiracial children remain enslaved by their white half-siblings and other family members. "Do not let Louisa or any of my children or possible children be slaves of Strangers," Hammond wrote. "Slavery in the family will be their happiest earthly condition."

Louisa Picquet, whose father was her first enslaver, noted that the faces of the South's multiracial children "stood out as a testimony to the deep moral pollution of the slave states." She suggested that multiracial people in the slave states were "to a great extent the contribution of enslavers and their sons to the common stock of southern chattels.

"Our chivalrous 'southern gentlemen' beget thousands of slaves; and hundreds of the children of our free white citizens are sold in the southern slave markets every year," Picquet wrote. She considered the root of these men's longing, asking, "What must the hidden life be?"

Henry Clay Bruce, the brother of the first Black US senator, Blanche K. Bruce, noted, "We would have been pure black, were it not that immoral men have, by force, injected their blood into our veins, to such an extent, that we now represent all colors, from pure black to pure white, and almost entirely as the result of the licentiousness of white men," Bruce wrote. "We are what they made us."

Enslavers failed to immediately recognize that multiracial people were more likely to become free because having light skin was "a presumption in favor of freedom," observes the historian James Hugo Johnston. They not only had an easier time escaping slavery than darker-skinned people but were also better able to stay free. Over time multiracial people became leaders of the abolitionist movement. Two of the first great Black leaders, Frederick Douglass and Booker T. Washington, could not identify their fathers, who were almost certainly white.

While some white enslavers violated multiple enslaved women, others had a long-term relationship with one Black woman. These enslavers at times attempted to do right by the enslaved woman and the children they fathered, but states worked to make it more difficult to set free women like Mary Lumpkin and her children.

Johnston argues that it "frequently appears that the deceased master is the father of certain slaves and seeks to make provision for his children." He cites John Stewart of Petersburg, Virginia, who, in his will, left "my natural colored daughter" Mary Vizzaneau a house, property, and "all I have at the bank." In Prince George County, Carter Edloe had also freed and provided for his enslaved children when he died. In Louisa County, Ralph Quarles, a wealthy white planter, had four children with Lucy Jane Langston, a Black woman. Quarles freed her and their daughter Maria, who was born enslaved. Quarles's three other children with Langston, all sons, including John Mercer Langston, were born free after their mother was emancipated. The future Virginia congressman established the law school at Howard University and was appointed president of the HBCU now known as Virginia State University. When Maria married an enslaved man, Quarles purchased and set free his daughter's husband. He then gave the couple a plantation and, in a cruel paradox, several enslaved people.

In New Orleans, white masters were known to leave large and valuable estates to their multiracial children. In Louisiana, whose legal system derived from French law, the condition of the child followed that of the father, unlike Virginia and the other states. Louisianans were generally more accepting of multiracial people because of the region's connection to Spanish and French colonists, who intermarried more freely than the English. But after the Louisiana Purchase in 1803, more Americans settled there, and Louisiana became less accepting of free Black people. Louisiana courts began shutting down enslavers who attempted to provide for their multiracial children. After 1808, the courts also made it more difficult to emancipate them. In 1832, Louisiana passed acts to protect white heirs from the "too great fondness of the natural parents of such children." An 1833 Louisiana court decision said that "an acknowledgement by the father of natural children, by his own slave, besides being an offense to morals, is a mere nullity"—an act that is legally void. Later, with the Act of 1857, Louisiana prohibited the emancipation of multiracial children.

Other states had for years been less accepting of free Black people. White leaders expressed worries that Black freedom could destroy Southern white society—or perhaps just end white supremacy. In Virginia, fear of uprisings like Gabriel's Conspiracy had led to the passage of more restrictive slave codes.

"The argument of the Quakers and of democrats like Thomas Jefferson that blacks are humans, too, lost much of its force," notes the historian Jay Worrall Jr.

"There can be no compromise between liberty and slavery," wrote the *Virginia Herald* in September 1800. "If we keep a ferocious monster in our country, we must keep him in chains."

By 1804, abolition seemed hopeless in Virginia as residents became increasingly hostile to the idea. The Virginia Abolition Society, which had been founded by the Quaker Robert Pleasants and joined by Methodists, quietly ceased to exist. The commonwealth also stopped sending representatives to the annual meeting of the American Convention of Abolitionist Societies in Philadelphia.

A slave rebellion by the preacher Nat Turner in Southampton, Virginia, on August 21, 1831, was the deadliest in history. It resulted in the deaths of at least fifty-five white men, women, and children. In response, white people reportedly killed some three dozen enslaved people without trials—although one historian has argued that far fewer were put to death. The trials of other enslaved people believed to have been involved started within ten days, and Turner, who eluded capture for months, was hanged.

The rebellion convinced some Virginians to end slavery and remove free Black people from the state to end the threat of violence. Some two thousand Virginians signed petitions asking the state legislature to act. Thomas Jefferson Randolph, the grandson of Thomas Jefferson, proposed a law that would have allowed for gradual emancipation. It was voted down and was the last time the Virginia Assembly seriously considered ending slavery.

In 1831 and 1832, the Virginia legislature passed a series of laws reducing free Black people to the same legal status as enslaved people. Black men and women were barred from assembling without a white person present. The legislation also restricted Black preachers. In 1849, Virginia gave local police the authority to "force open the doors of free Negroes and of slaves in the absence of their masters, when access is denied, when in search of firearms or other weapons, by authority of a warrant," and in 1860 the state permitted local courts to enslave free Black people convicted of felonies.

This is the world into which Mary Lumpkin and her children were born—a Virginia where even free Black men and women were not welcome and had few rights. She must have dreamed about escaping the restrictions that had limited her life and would limit her children's too. Perhaps she started planting seeds in Robert Lumpkin's mind that she wanted more for their children. Perhaps she was trying to persuade him to join her in protecting them.

This 1866 print was created from a sketch by J. J. Nevins, who captioned the work, based on an earlier sketch, "Richmond Virginia. Where Men and Women Are Sold like Cattle." (Provided by The Valentine's Archives)

4

So Well Acquainted

In the jail compound, Mary Lumpkin was most likely alone in her unique role—separated from other enslaved people and given some freedoms. Once she had a child, she was further isolated by the responsibilities of motherhood. She needed a friend, someone she could confide in. Someone to bring joy and hope to her life.

Her days may have been shaped by caring for her children and running Robert Lumpkin's household. She would have spent her time cleaning up after the children, feeding them, helping them learn their numbers. She would have also shopped for food, prepared the meals, clothed the family, and cleaned the home.

If she also managed Robert Lumpkin's boardinghouse, as Corinna Hinton Omohundro did for Silas Omohundro, she served meals and drinks, washed laundry, made beds, and kept the rooms tidy. She probably had help from other enslaved people with all these jobs, and she would have been charged with managing them.

It was through her work at the jail that Mary Lumpkin made a connection who would become a lifelong friend. Soon after giving birth to Annie, her second child, in 1847, Mary Lumpkin met Lucy Ann

Cheatham, also an enslaved girl. Mary Lumpkin had hired her from her enslaver, the Richmond trader William H. Betts, who may have been sexually abusing her.

"She used to do my sewing for me," Mary later recalled. "That is how I became so well acquainted with her."

Unlike the relationship she had with Robert Lumpkin and her role as a mother, her friendship with Lucy Ann was something she chose, something she could keep for herself. Although Mary Lumpkin had a higher status inside the jail than Lucy Ann, she allowed herself to relate to another enslaved girl who was about her age, to the benefit of both.

The young women—still girls by today's standards—may have sat together, talking about their shared experiences, while they sewed clothes for other enslaved people to wear at sale or perhaps clothes for Mary Lumpkin's children. They were both about sixteen, and a natural affinity developed between them. It may have been difficult for Mary Lumpkin to make friends, in part because of her status as the mother of Robert Lumpkin's children.

Yet Lucy Ann Cheatham and Mary Lumpkin struck up an immediate friendship, and they maintained it all their lives, despite the slavery that imprisoned them. "We . . . were very intimate since I first became acquainted with her," Mary Lumpkin said later. "She always confided in me."

The two women probably had much to talk about. Perhaps they discussed the slave traders who enslaved them, or the enslaved people they saw come and go. Perhaps they shared stories about their families—the families they had been separated from as well as the families still in their lives. They may have talked about their frustrations with enslaved life, but perhaps they also talked about what brought them happiness.

What did this friendship forged between two enslaved women in a slave jail mean for them? What did it mean for their ability to not just survive in their complex living situations, but also thrive?

When Mary Lumpkin hired Lucy Ann Cheatham, the girl regularly went to Lumpkin's Jail to work with Mary. Perhaps it was there, sewing with Mary, that she caught a slave trader's eye. John Hagan, a New Orleans slave dealer who owned slave pens in Charleston and New Orleans, may have been lodging on the Lumpkin property during his regular trips to Richmond when he encountered Lucy Ann.

Not long after the two young women met, Hagan purchased Lucy Ann from William H. Betts. Did Mary and Lucy Ann have any warning that it would happen? Did Mary overhear the traders talking, and if so, did she understand that Hagan was buying her friend? She would not have tried to interfere, but she would have been devastated by the news.

In December 1848, Hagan shipped Lucy Ann Cheatham out of Richmond, taking her from her mother, her two half-sisters, and Mary Lumpkin. They had been friends for about a year when Lucy Ann was forced to board the slave ship *Cyane*, bound for New Orleans, most likely in chains. She joined sixty-five other young enslaved people who had been separated from their parents, including twelve others purchased by Hagan. On the way to a slave market and, eventually, new enslavers in the Lower South, they huddled in fear, sobbing and shivering. Lucy Ann was surely terrified of the fate that awaited her in Louisiana.

When she arrived in New Orleans in January 1849, John Hagan did not sell Lucy Ann Cheatham. Instead, he made her his sexual partner. Her life would soon mirror Mary Lumpkin's in some ways.

If Hagan had chosen her for this purpose in Richmond, he could have spared her the twenty-eight-day journey on a slave ship, which put her in danger of getting sick and dying and of being sexually abused. Hagan could have protected her by having her accompany him on the boat he took home via Charleston, where his mother lived. Instead, he let her suffer.

Within five months of Lucy Ann Cheatham's departure from Richmond, Mary Lumpkin received a letter from her, brimming with news. "She wrote to me telling me about her marriage" to Hagan, Mary Lumpkin recalled later.

The marriage, as described, resembled what we know of the relationship Mary Lumpkin had with Robert Lumpkin. Lucy Ann probably lived with Hagan in his Esplanade Avenue slave jail property. She would soon give birth to his children, but Hagan did not legally marry her.

It's more likely that Hagan and Lucy Ann reached an agreement about their relationship that included a promise that Hagan would free her and any children they had—a vow that Mary also sought from Robert Lumpkin.

FREEDOM WAS SURELY already on the minds of Lucy Ann Hagan and Mary Lumpkin. Perhaps they found it encouraging that, in 1840, Richmond trader Silas Omohundro moved his two enslaved children and the enslaved mother of one of the children to freedom in Ohio.

Louisa Tandy was a young enslaved girl, like Mary Lumpkin and Lucy Ann Cheatham, when Silas Omohundro purchased her and made her the mother of his child. In the 1830s, before seeking more profitable work in the slave trade, he had owned a ferry across the James River in Fluvanna County, Virginia. He went to work for Franklin and Armfield's Richmond employee Rice Ballard and later started a business with his brother, R. F. Omohundro. The origins of his unique family surname are unknown, but it gained notoriety thanks to his nephew, John Burwell Omohundro, the frontier cowboy "Texas Jack."

During Silas Omohundro's tenure with Franklin and Armfield, he encountered Louisa Tandy. She gave birth to his son, Littleton, in 1838, when she was about sixteen. Soon after, he must have begun to think about how to get her to freedom.

As the first laws restricting free Black people were passed in Virginia, more Black men and women had moved out of the commonwealth and landed in Ohio. Quakers who had freed those they formerly enslaved helped them relocate. John Randolph's will called for the purchase of land in Ohio on which the people he enslaved could start new lives. Other white men who had fathered children with enslaved women realized that there was no future for their children in Virginia and also made plans to move them to Ohio. They were joined by enslavers from Louisiana, Alabama, and Mississippi who drove their children and the children's enslaved mothers to free states to emancipate them. Before long, free Black communities had sprung up in Ohio.

"The human attachment of fathers to their children could not be destroyed, and white fathers sought means to evade the law as it affected their own children," writes James Hugo Johnston.

Silas Omohundro may have chosen Ohio for Louisa Tandy because it was the free state closest to Virginia. Quakers from Virginia had been moving to Ohio for decades, along with the enslaved people they had set free. Some of Ohio's new residents devoted themselves to helping enslaved people escape slavery, and their state would become one of the most important in the network of helpers and hiding spots known as the Underground Railroad.

The state's location along the Ohio River across from Kentucky, a slave state, and the 375-mile border between them also made it popular for those escaping slavery. Black residents of Cincinnati lived in homes clustered around the riverfront, where it was easier to hide those attempting to escape. Home to free Black people who were prospering economically and providing educational opportunities for Black children, Ohio was a center of abolitionism in America.

Two years after Louisa Tandy gave birth to Silas Omohundro's child, the mother and son were in Cincinnati, along with six-year-old Julia A. Hopkins, who was probably the child of Silas Omohundro and another woman. Census enumerators labeled them as free people of color, but Silas Omohundro told neighbors that Louisa Tandy was his wife.

He purchased a house in Cincinnati where she and the children lived. In 1840, she gave birth to Martha, her second child with Silas Omohundro—and the first one born free. For the next two decades, Silas Omohundro continued to visit Louisa Tandy and their children in Cincinnati. The visits did not stop until the start of the Civil War, by which time she had given birth to three more children with Silas Omohundro—a son Sidney and daughters Cinderella and Florence, all born free.

Sidney and Cinderella would attend the Hughes School, founded in Cincinnati in 1853 to offer free education for poor white children. They were questioned about their race after other students reported to the teacher that their mother was a "colored woman," but the teacher ignored the reports.

Silas Omohundro provided money for their school expenses, but it's unclear how often he saw his children and what they knew about him. Perhaps Louisa Tandy Omohundro told them little of her childhood. She may have hoped they never knew what she had experienced as an enslaved girl.

Ohio's "Black Laws" were in place until 1849, nearly a decade after Louisa Tandy Omohundro moved to Cincinnati. The state stopped requiring Black men and women to post bond when they arrived in Ohio, and it lifted a ban on Black residents testifying in court cases against white people.

While life was difficult for Black residents of Ohio, Louisa Tandy Omohundro was essentially free. Four of her five children would be born free in Ohio, and she became legally free there too. Enslavers who wanted to free the people they enslaved either drafted manumission papers and told the formerly enslaved people to register the papers in the county probate courts where they moved or retained an attorney in Ohio to complete the paperwork, the route Silas Omohundro took.

Louisa Tandy Omohundro's life in Ohio was quite different from her life in Virginia. For much of the year, she was far out of Silas Omohundro's reach and would have been difficult, if not impossible, to control. She lived in her own home. She decided what she ate, when she left the house, where she went, and the shape of her children's lives. She did not answer to an enslaver or a slave trader. All the little decisions that make up a day were now hers to make. Silas Omohundro had hired a white man to check in on her, but other than him, she most likely answered to no one.

Yet neither slavery nor freedom was an absolute condition—not in Ohio, not anywhere. Louisa Tandy Omohundro experienced racism and remained at risk of being kidnapped and sold back into slavery. Luckily, in 1841, a year or so after she arrived in Ohio, the state enacted a law mandating that any enslaved person brought into the state be automatically emancipated. Before then, Southern enslavers regularly visited Ohio accompanied by people they enslaved. White enslavers from around the South took women they enslaved on vacation at Tawawa Springs near Xenia, and some of them probably tried to escape. State laws had allowed the enslavers to stay in the state for unspecified periods of time before the people they enslaved were considered free. Some continued to work as indentured servants once in Ohio, and others may have remained under the control of enslavers via threats that they would be returned to a slave state if they didn't behave.

Living five hundred miles away in Richmond, Silas Omohundro's primary form of control over Louisa Tandy Omohundro would have been financial. He sent her $12,000 a year for the children's education—a vast sum of money in those days, equivalent to more than $400,000 today—and he owned the home where she lived. She may have felt indebted to him and believed it necessary to submit to his sexual advances when he traveled annually to Ohio. Her last child was born in 1852, a dozen years after Silas Omohundro took her to Ohio.

Certainly Louisa Tandy Omohundro, a seamstress, benefited financially from her connection to a wealthy, white slave trader. Some, if not all, of her children passed for white, though neighbors gossiped about Louisa's race. She took Omohundro's distinctive surname for herself and for her children in an attempt to claim whiteness.

Some slave traders in Robert Lumpkin's circle worried about the welfare of the children they fathered with enslaved women. They realized that, as the value of enslaved people rose, their own children, born enslaved, were at risk. While many enslavers refused to acknowledge their children, and some even sold them away, there were men in Lumpkin's circle who cared for their offspring with enslaved women. Silas Omohundro's decision to relocate Louisa and his children surely encouraged other Richmond slave traders, including Robert Lumpkin, to consider freeing their enslaved children and moving them out of state.

These men knew that other enslavers would view their children as property, not as cherished offspring. Moving them to a free state could prevent them from being seized or stolen and keep them safe. When Silas Omohundro sent Louisa to Ohio, he not only protected her and his children but also provided Robert Lumpkin and other local slave traders with a road map for freeing their children and the children's enslaved mothers.

Perhaps more importantly, enslaved women like Mary Lumpkin and Lucy Ann Hagan could do more than dream about becoming free—they could see it as real possibility. They could lobby on their own behalf to be freed, just as Louisa Tandy Omohundro had been.

Isolated in their distinct line of work, slave traders made their own communities out of the men with whom they worked and lived in Shockoe Bottom. The enslaved women who gave birth to their children surely struck up friendships too.

Robert Lumpkin, Silas Omohundro, and Hector Davis lived in close proximity in the 1850s. By then, all three men had children with much younger enslaved women. After Louisa Tandy Omohundro was relocated to Cincinnati, Silas Omohundro had his first child with Corinna Hinton Omohundro by 1849, when she was sixteen. The auctioneer Hector Davis by 1852 had a child with Ann Banks Davis, a twenty-two-year-old enslaved woman. At that time, Robert Lumpkin already had three children with Mary Lumpkin.

These three men shared their homes with visiting slave traders. They executed wills for each other and may have loaned each other money. They also socialized together and may have occasionally chosen to do so with the Black women with whom they had children. Perhaps Silas Omohundro hosted dinner parties, using the collection of fine silverware and china he had amassed. Bacon Tait, who began having children with a free Black woman by 1843, once noted that he "had not sit at a table in a private house with [white] Ladies for more than twenty years," indicating that Black women—either free or enslaved—were a regular presence at their gatherings.

Outside of socializing, these Black women were likely to have already encountered each other in everyday life. Unlike most enslaved women, they did not have a chance to bond while working in the fields. Yet they may have found community with each other because of their similar situations. Perhaps with the limited freedom they were allotted, they passed each other on Fifteenth on their way in and out of their enslavers' properties. Maybe they ran into each other at the market on Seventeenth Street, where they could strike up friendships beyond the prying eyes of the men who enslaved them.

The women may have been permitted to visit each other at their enslavers' respective homes and slave jails, and perhaps they shared access to enslaved people who did chores for them. They may have savored the chance to interact with other women who walked the same fine line between free and enslaved, between Black and white. In their world, those who were free and those who were enslaved were not so easily distinguishable.

Perhaps Corinna Hinton Omohundro told the others that she had persuaded Silas Omohundro to allow her to move around the city freely to run errands and was sometimes mistaken for a white woman. She may have gone to shops to purchase fabrics with the cash he gave her to buy clothing for her children. Perhaps she took her watch to the watchmaker to have it repaired, and maybe she went to the tailor to be fitted for a dress.

Did Mary Lumpkin and Ann Banks Davis ask permission to do the same, telling Robert Lumpkin and Hector Davis about the freedoms that Silas Omohundro permitted Corinna Hinton Omohundro? By interacting with each other and swapping stories, did one woman's limited freedom begin to extend to the next?

Corinna Hinton Omohundro may also have shared how much she did to run Silas Omohundro's business. She was responsible for clothing all of the enslaved people who came through the jail. She also managed his boardinghouse, serving meals and drinks. She was provided with her own money for the work she did. Mary Lumpkin and Ann Banks Davis surely must have wanted a similar arrangement with their enslavers.

Silas Omohundro kept enslaved people to work in his jail and to serve him, one less chore Corinna Hinton Omohundro had to do. He even hired another enslaved woman to nurse one of her infants, as white enslavers often did for their white wives. Were the other enslaved women envious when they learned how Corinna was treated, or did her account of her life encourage them to ask their enslavers for the same kind of treatment?

Perhaps the women developed common ground and were able to talk intimately, telling stories about their children and sharing gossip they had heard from other enslaved people. Did they speak ill of the men who enslaved them? Did they dare share their dreams of leaving the slave jail compounds for better lives?

Corinna Hinton Omohundro and Mary Lumpkin, who were literate, may have encouraged Ann Banks Davis to learn to read and write. Maybe they talked about how they could ensure their own children were well educated. By interacting with each other, perhaps they dreamed bigger and hatched plans to use their relationships with their enslavers to create better lives for themselves and for their children.

Maybe the name Louisa Tandy Omohundro, who had left Virginia for Ohio more than a decade earlier, crossed their lips. Did they dare hope to follow in her footsteps to live free from enslavement and the slave trader who had owned her?

By the early 1850s, they may have already been plotting to get their children—and themselves—to a free state. Mary Lumpkin took a trip to Ohio in the late 1840s to meet with an attorney, suggesting that Robert Lumpkin was thinking about freeing her then. Mary may have already been considering schooling for her children in Massachusetts. Who among them was the first to mention Pennsylvania as a possible destination?

Mary Lumpkin's relationships with these other women probably had a positive impact on her mental health, making her feel less isolated. These friendships probably empowered her too. While staying focused on the larger goal of moving to a free state, the women may have encouraged each other to be braver in their interactions with their enslavers and perhaps even to demand more freedoms in Richmond.

AFTER LUCY ANN Cheatham was taken to New Orleans, she stayed in touch with Mary Lumpkin. The friends wrote letters back and forth to each other, and Lucy Ann asked Mary to address future letters to her in care of "her husband," John Hagan.

"When she left it was Lucy Ann Cheatham, when she returned it was Lucy Ann Hagan," Mary Lumpkin recalled.

Their in-person friendship had been brief but intense. The two women had a connection. They trusted each other, which may not have come easily for them with most other people. Lucy Ann Hagan sent packages containing money or clothing for her mother and half-sisters, and she entrusted their delivery to Mary Lumpkin.

They wanted to spend time together, to be in each other's presence. Lucy Ann Hagan returned to Virginia every other year with John Hagan and her children. Although John Hagan may not have given Lucy Ann a choice in where they stayed, Mary Lumpkin, in later court testimony, made it sound like Lucy Ann's decision to routinely stay at the Lumpkin compound. "She always stopped with me," Mary Lumpkin recalled with pride. "She never stopped with her mother."

Mary Lumpkin would have looked forward to these visits and the chance to reconnect with her friend. What must it have meant to them to have their connection renewed by regularly spending time together? Their deep bond may have helped sustain them.

Were they able to get time alone to talk about the immoral and depraved slave traders who imprisoned them and made them mothers? There were most likely few people Mary Lumpkin could complain to about Robert Lumpkin, and perhaps Lucy Ann Hagan was one of them.

Mary must have wanted to know how John Hagan treated her, what her friend's life was like in New Orleans, and how it differed from her own.

They knew each other's children and probably shared similar joys and frustrations of motherhood. Two of Lucy Ann's children had died, and perhaps they talked about those losses. Mary had also lost two children when they were very young.

Did they talk about what it was like to give birth to children without their own consent, without the freedom to choose to be mothers? Perhaps they shared what it meant to them to be able to stay with their children when so many enslaved women could not. They had both witnessed terrible atrocities and lived through multiple traumas themselves. Were they able to talk about what those experiences had been like and how they had been impacted? Did they discuss with each how to prevent the same traumas from happening to their children?

Through their interactions, both women had gained some level of independence that they would not otherwise have had as enslaved women. They certainly both craved freedom. Lucy Ann Hagan had brazenly named her daughter after the Swedish writer Fredrika Bremer, who wrote critically of the sales of enslaved people she witnessed in Louisiana and the slave jails she visited in Richmond. Perhaps they spoke often of attaining freedom and discussed what it would mean for them and their children. Maybe Mary Lumpkin told her friend she would demand money from Robert Lumpkin to make it happen.

The two women were surely able to understand each other's lives better than most anyone else, and they must have been a great comfort to each other. Maybe their sisterhood was not just a balm for mutual sadness but a tool for survival.

In lives that were traumatic and difficult on many levels, lives that spanned from enslaved girlhood to free womanhood, their friendship was a form of resistance.

The 1854 arrest and trial of Anthony Burns, an enslaved man from Virginia, under the Fugitive Slave Act captivated Boston and the nation. When the twenty-four-year-old Burns was returned to slavery in Virginia, he was held captive and tortured in Lumpkin's Jail, where he was visited by Mary Lumpkin. (Library of Congress)

5

Anthony Burns and the Fugitive Slave Act

AN ENSLAVED MAN WHO HAD ESCAPED RICHMOND SLAVERY ONLY TO BE captured in Boston was delivered to Lumpkin's Jail in 1854. Robert Lumpkin was to ensure that the man, Anthony Burns, paid a steep price for escaping and for embarrassing the South.

After a trial that captivated the American public, Robert Lumpkin saw to it that Burns, a tall, dark-skinned man with a scar on his face and an injured hand, would feel the South's wrath. He locked Burns in a tiny attic room, his feet and hands chained. The jailer gave Burns old water to drink and rotting meat to eat.

The mother of Robert Lumpkin's children took another tactic. Mary Lumpkin developed an interest in the young man whose trial had locked the nation in heated discussion about whether slavery should continue. Perhaps she had attended church with him before he escaped slavery. She may have gone to Burns in his attic room, showing him compassion by sneaking him a Bible and a book of hymns after learning that, like her, he was literate. Burns had "found a friend," writes his biographer, Charles Emery Stevens.

"Upon most slaves these gifts would have been thrown away; fortunately for Burns, he had learned to read, and the books proved a very treasure," Stevens wrote.

After Mary visited Burns, she may have questioned the conditions under which he was held and voiced her concern to Robert Lumpkin. Did she sometimes come to the defense of enslaved people who were being mistreated, or did she know better than to interfere with the will of her violent enslaver?

Burns, in turn, viewed Mary Lumpkin as Robert Lumpkin's "wife," describing her as a "yellow woman" who was permitted to move around inside various areas of the jail complex. Robert Lumpkin may not have known that Mary visited Burns. She may have been able to do so without being detected.

Perhaps she was curious about his experiences, and if she didn't know him, perhaps she had seen him around Richmond before his escape. Burns may have captured her imagination, making her think in new ways about securing freedom. Maybe it was Burns who sparked the idea that Massachusetts, where he had spent several months living as a free man before he was arrested, would be a good place for her daughters to be educated.

What would her attention to Burns mean to him at this low point in his life? Mary Lumpkin, perhaps risking her own safety, had chosen to use her small amount of autonomy in the jail to extend kindness to another enslaved person who had been stripped of his dignity and humanity.

BORN INTO SLAVERY in Virginia, Anthony Burns was one of thousands of enslaved people in Richmond who were leased from enslavers and moved around from odd job to odd job.

By the 1850s, Richmond's tobacco factories were almost exclusively staffed by enslaved people, as was Tredegar Iron Works. Enslaved people who were hired out had some limited freedom, living away from their enslavers in substantial communities of other Black people in their situation.

Burns's enslaver, Charles F. Suttle, a prominent Stafford, Virginia, merchant, had hired him out from the age of seven, and as a teenager, Burns had worked in mills. A piece of bone jutted out from the side of his hand, the result of an injury in a sawmill when a machine crushed his hand. Burns found his own jobs, and by 1854 he landed one at the Richmond docks, loading and unloading ships. He paid out half of his weekly wages to Suttle and kept the rest.

Since he was ten years old, Burns had dreamed of freedom. "I began to learn that there is a Christ who came to make us free; I began to hear about a North, and to feel the necessity for freedom of soul and body," he recalled in a March 1855 speech. "I heard of a North where men of my color could live without any man daring to say to them, 'You are my property'; and I determined by the blessing of God, one day to find my way there."

While working on the Richmond waterfront, the twenty-year-old Burns hatched a plan for escape: he befriended a sailor who hid him in the hold of a ship bound for Boston.

YEARS EARLIER, IN 1847, sixty-seven Black men, women, and children who had been freed by the Virginia enslaver Carter Edloe had also chosen Boston as their destination.

In his will, Edloe, a Prince George County plantation owner, instructed his executor to set free all the people he had enslaved. Edloe had put aside $8,000 for Harriet Barber, "my female slave," and the children he had fathered with her. His will provided $50 for each of the other people he enslaved to move.

When Edloe died in 1844, his executor, John A. Selden, forced the enslaved people to continue working, reasoning that they were required to earn the money Edloe had left them. One of the enslaved men, Peter Randolph, who could read and write, found a magistrate to assist him in filing a lawsuit against Selden in the chancery court in Petersburg, claiming that the people Edloe enslaved had been kept in "unlawful bondage" for three years and thirty-five days. An 1847 court ruling required Selden to set them free.

Edloe had purchased Barber and the children he had fathered with her from his brother-in-law, Richard Griffin Orgain. Did he sexually abuse her while she was in Orgain's care or had Barber chosen to have children with him, as Harriet Jacobs did with an unmarried white neighbor, Samuel T. Sawyer? By partnering with Sawyer, a lawyer, Jacobs had hoped to escape abuse by her brutal enslaver, James Norcom.

While Edloe did not recognize any of the children he had with Barber as his in his will, he had instructed his executors to take funds from his estate and invest it in "good stock" so that the interest might be paid to Barber annually. "Should there not be a sum sufficient to pay this legacy," the will read, "either in stock or money, I direct my Executors to sell my land in Southampton"—another Virginia county. "Should that not make up the deficiency, other land must be sold, or horses and cattle, as my Executors may think best," the will directed.

Edloe left the bulk of the estate to his nieces, and it's unclear how much money Barber ultimately received. She had moved with her children to Philadelphia by 1847, and it seems likely that she knew someone there, perhaps a sibling or a parent. She remained illiterate and would later operate a boardinghouse and work as a housekeeper.

A few of the other people Edloe had enslaved wanted to go to Ohio, but the group ultimately agreed to go to Boston. The magistrate secured free papers for them and hired a ship to transport them. Randolph reported that they were given only $15 of the $50 that Edloe had left for them. "All our money was taken from us, because we were black people," Randolph wrote in his biography.

The group of sixty-seven Black men, women, and children—ranging in age from twelve months to seventy-five years—left for Boston on September 5, 1847, on the *Thomas H. Thompson*. When the formerly enslaved Virginians landed in Boston ten days later, they were met at the wharf by notable abolitionists, including the writer William Lloyd Garrison, future Massachusetts governor John A. Andrew, the attorney Wendell Phillips, and the Reverend Samuel J. May, who assisted the enslaved families in finding housing and work around the region.

Peter Randolph described his arrival as a "new birth" and went looking for a church. He met the abolitionist Leonard A. Grimes, a free Black man born in Leesburg, Virginia, who had worked as a carriage driver in Washington, DC. Arrested in 1839 and convicted of helping enslaved people escape, Grimes had served two years of "hard labor" in the Virginia Penitentiary in Richmond.

In Boston, Grimes would become the first ordained pastor of a new activist church called Twelfth Baptist, which became known as "the Fugitive Slave Church" for its membership comprising formerly enslaved people, including many of the new arrivals from Virginia. Randolph would become a minister there too, as well as a leader among the city's free Black residents.

His experience in Boston was not as bad as Virginians had warned. "We came in 1847," Randolph wrote, "and have not been eaten up."

ANTHONY BURNS WAS stowed inside the bowels of the boat bound for Boston, a trip that normally took seven to ten days. This time, however, the ship encountered storms, and the trip lasted three weeks. Surrounded by cargo, Burns shook with cold and hunger in the dark.

Within weeks of docking in Boston, he found a job at Mattapan Iron Works in South Boston and made his way to Twelfth Baptist Church, where he likely met the Black abolitionist Coffin Pitts, who owned a clothing shop on Brattle Street. Pitts invited Burns to stay at his home and employed him at his store.

Burns had learned to read and write as a child by listening when his enslaver's sister taught the alphabet to white neighborhood children. When he wrote a letter to his brother in Virginia to let him know that he had arrived safely in Massachusetts, his enslaver intercepted the message and immediately set out for Boston to bring Burns back.

Four years earlier, the Fugitive Slave Act had been amended by Congress as part of the Compromise of 1850 between the South and the North. The original law, enacted in 1793, authorized local governments to capture enslaved people who had run away and return them to their enslavers. It also imposed penalties on anyone who helped enslaved people escape. It was among the most controversial laws of the early nineteenth century because white people were empowered to take into custody Black men and women they merely suspected were escaped enslaved people, denying them a trial and the right to defend themselves. The law resulted in countless free Black people being captured and sold into slavery, including Solomon Northup.

Incensed by what they perceived as a failure by the North to adhere to the original Fugitive Slave Act, Southern lawmakers argued for updates to the law. Senator James M. Mason of Virginia introduced a new measure in 1850 to strengthen the existing law, claiming that no one had "a right to interpose between the claimant and the fugitive, or to inquire whether the slave be his, or whether he is a slave at all, far less to molest or hinder him in the capture."

For the South, passage of a revised Fugitive Slave Act was "indispensable to the security of their property and the integrity of their institutions." In Georgia, preservation of the United States was dependent on the act's "faithful execution." The *North Carolina Standard* wrote that a revised law was "a simple act of justice." Addressing the North, the paper threatened that if the Fugitive Slave Act was not updated to reinforce the property rights of enslavers, "we leave you."

Henry Clay—a US senator from Kentucky who owned enslaved people and may have had children with one or more enslaved women—stepped forward as a "champion of compromise." He claimed to believe that slavery was immoral but felt that calling for its abolition was extreme. Clay proposed a new version of the Fugitive Slave Act as part of a group of bills known as the Compromise of 1850, which aimed to quiet calls for Southern secession. Since the 1840s, proslavery forces had talked of dissolving the United States by seceding.

Clay's proposal expanded the reach of the act, giving federal officers the authority to respond to claims of enslavement and to grant "certificates of removal." A response to Southerners' fears that new states would harbor enslaved people, the proposal also increased penalties for anyone who interfered with an enslaver trying to reclaim an enslaved person he owned and imposed a $1,000 fine or six months' imprisonment. It empowered the courts to levy payments to enslavers of $1,000 per enslaved person who escaped and increased the number of officials who were authorized to hear claims from enslavers and to grant certificates of removal. The new proposal said that "all good citizens" were "commanded to aid and assist in the prompt and efficient execution of this law, whenever their services may be required."

The compromise also allowed New Mexico, Nevada, Arizona, and Utah to become territories without deciding whether they would be free or slave states, and it enabled California to become a free state. In exchange for these concessions from the South, the Fugitive Slave Act was amended to the South's liking.

While Southerners opposed Northerners' attempts to add protections for free Black people, such as the right to trial by jury and *habeas corpus*, Northerners countered that Clay's proposal was not a true compromise, as it paid federal commissioners to return enslaved persons to Southern enslavers. "Every guarantee, every security in the new law was for the 'rights' of slave owners," writes the historian Thomas D. Morris.

"A tissue of more heartless and cold-blooded enactments never disgraced the legislation of civilized people," Representative George W. Julian of Indiana, a free state, told the House of Representatives on September 25, 1850.

Widespread resistance to the original law had been centered in Boston, the North's abolitionist and intellectual center and home to some of the nation's most important writers, including Ralph Waldo Emerson and Henry David Thoreau. Emerson told his neighbors, "I will not obey it, by God."

Some Northern communities passed "personal liberty laws," which mandated that anyone accused of being an enslaved person who had escaped receive a jury trial before being taken south. Other communities outlawed the use of local or state resources to arrest Black people. In some cases, juries declined to convict Black men and women indicted under federal law. Many Northerners saw the passage of the compromise as evidence that the South was conspiring to spread slavery through coercion and force, regardless of the will of Northern voters. Its impacts were wide-ranging. "This law . . . brought untold suffering," wrote Peter Randolph. "Many were pursued, hounded down, and carried back into slavery."

Harriet Jacobs, who had left her grandmother's attic and escaped to New York by 1842 where she was living as a free Black woman, said that the amendment of the Fugitive Slave Act was "the beginning of a reign of terror to the colored population."

Charles Suttle planned to use the newly revised Fugitive Slave Act to reclaim Burns as his property. After arriving in Boston, he went to the downtown federal courthouse and secured a warrant for Burns's arrest. On May 24, US marshal Asa Butman headed out to arrest Burns. Concerned that Boston's abolitionist community would rally to help Burns if they learned about his arrest, Butman lied about why Burns was being stopped, taking him into custody on the pretense that he had stolen items from a silversmith's shop.

Burns assumed that he was being arrested in a case of mistaken identity, but after he was locked in a jail cell on the third floor of the federal courthouse, Suttle entered and confronted him. He "doffed his hat, bowed, and said with mock politeness, 'How do you do, Mr. Burns?'"

"I called him as we do in Virginia, 'Master!'" Burns recounted later.

Suttle, who lived in Alexandria, Virginia, then asked Burns why he had escaped, portraying himself as a benevolent enslaver with the question. "Haven't I always treated you well, Tony?"

Burns resisted. He refused to respond.

Two DAYS EARLIER, the US House of Representatives had approved the controversial Kansas-Nebraska Act, which would further divide the North and the South. The act repealed the 1820 Missouri Compromise, which had admitted Maine as a free state and Missouri as a slave state, and it gave the territories of Kansas and Nebraska popular sovereignty— the ability to decide whether to allow slavery within their borders.

Many Northerners were outraged. "It annuls all past compromises with Slavery, and makes all future compromises impossible," said Senator Charles Sumner of Massachusetts. "Thus it puts Freedom and Slavery face to face, and bids them grapple."

To Massachusetts Democrats, passage of the Kansas-Nebraska Act in the House was evidence that the West would soon be opening up to slavery. On the evening of Burns's arrest, Democrats poured out of the Custom House on State Street, dragging cannons onto Boston Common and setting them off. The next day Burns appeared in court in Boston and the Kansas-Nebraska Act was approved by the US Senate. The confluence of these events would transform Anthony Burns into the "most famous slave in America" and inspire "a pocket revolution" in Boston.

The city had an extensive, organized network of people working to help enslaved people escape. One group in particular, the Boston Vigilance Committee, whose members included free Black people and white abolitionists, had sent at least forty groups of people fleeing slavery to Canada, England, and other parts of the United States. Its mission was to protect enslaved people who had escaped from being captured and returned to slavery under the 1850 Fugitive Slave Act.

For years, committee members housed enslaved people seeking freedom, helped them get legal representation, and provided clothing, furniture, medical assistance, and loans. They also warned of the arrival of slave catchers—men who came to the North to find an enslaved person who had escaped and take them back south. Committee members quickly learned of the arrest of Burns, the first enslaved person taken into custody under the act since 1851, when the committee had freed Shadrach Minkins in a brazen courthouse rescue. Abolitionists who helped Minkins, a Black man who had escaped slavery in Virginia and worshiped at Twelfth Baptist in Boston, had hoped that the fugitive slave law wouldn't be tested in the city again.

By the time Burns went before the court the day after his arrest, offers to pay for his legal defense had already come in to Suffolk County probate judge Edward G. Loring, who was acting as a federal commissioner. One came from the abolitionist Amos Adams Lawrence, who was helping found the city of Lawrence, Kansas, with settlers sent by the New England Emigrant Aid Company. Lawrence had written to Boston mayor Jerome Smith that he "would prefer to see the courthouse razed rather than [Burns] should be returned to slavery."

Meanwhile, members of the Boston Vigilance Committee were attempting to delay Suttle. Among them was Lewis Hayden, a formerly enslaved man whose first wife, Esther Harvey, and son were sold to Henry Clay; after their sale, Hayden never saw them again. He escaped enslavement in Kentucky with his second wife, Harriet Hayden, and son Joseph and set up a clothing store in Boston. Committee members swore out a complaint against Suttle and William Brent, another Stafford merchant and friend of Suttle who had accompanied him on the trip from Virginia. The complaint alleged that the pair had conspired to kidnap Burns.

The committee members hoped to make reclaiming Burns time-consuming, costly, and difficult enough that Suttle would give up and return to Virginia, leaving Burns behind.

WALKING PAST THE courthouse the morning after Burns was arrested, Vigilance Committee member Richard Henry Dana, an attorney, was informed that a Black man was in custody for escaping slavery.

Dana immediately went inside the courthouse and offered to represent Burns. "It is of no use," Burns told Dana. "I shall fare worse if I resist."

Commissioner Edward G. Loring granted Dana's request for a delay, against the objection of Suttle's Boston attorney Edward Griffin Parker. After Burns met with Leonard A. Grimes, Coffin Pitts, and Wendell Phillips, they hired Dana to represent him, and Dana recruited Charles M. Ellis as co-counsel. The pair began preparing Burns's defense.

Meanwhile, abolitionists plastered fliers on city buildings that read: "The Kidnappers Are Here!" Some antislavery advocates from outside Boston happened to be in town for an abolitionist convention and a gathering of women's rights groups. Among them was Harriet Beecher Stowe, whose novel *Uncle Tom's Cabin*, published two years earlier, had helped radicalize white Northerners against slavery. As other abolitionists heard about Burns's arrest, they made their way to Boston.

On May 26, some five thousand white abolitionists gathered at Faneuil Hall to devise a plan to free him. Phillips called for a group to gather at the courthouse the next morning. He compared the Kansas-Nebraska Act to "knocking a man down" and said that the use of the Fugitive Slave Act to arrest a formerly enslaved man was "spitting in his face after he is down."

A smaller group of mainly Black abolitionists met at the Tremont Temple, a church and gathering place, and decided to attempt to free Burns that night. They marched to the courthouse, which had been fortified after abolitionists rescued Shadrach Minkins from the building. Still, Boston abolitionists led by Lewis Hayden and Thomas Wentworth Higginson, a white Vigilance Committee member and minister, believed that it was worth trying to free Burns.

After two hundred men arrived at the courthouse that night, the crowd grew to about two thousand, yelling, "Rescue him!" Officers closed the main courthouse doors, and the crowd attacked one door. When a gun went off, they moved to another door and, using "a stout beam" guided by a dozen people, violently rammed it, creating an opening large enough for Higginson and a Black protester to squeeze through. Thirty to forty shots were fired, killing federal marshal James Batchelder and wounding several people, and the abolitionists were forced out by deputies. Thirteen people were arrested, and military troops arrived on the scene.

That was the last attempt to spring Burns from his holding cell.

While work was under way to prepare for the trial, Reverend Leonard A. Grimes attempted to buy Burns's freedom.

Some forty members of his congregation had fled to Canada after the passage of the Fugitive Slave Act. Hoping to keep Burns in Boston, Grimes offered Suttle $1,200, and the enslaver agreed to the price. A deadline had been established for the sale, but court officials blocked it, perhaps because federal officials had sent word that they did not want Burns freed. Grimes was bitterly disappointed and tried after the deadline passed to talk with Suttle, who backed out of the agreement and instead promised to sell Burns to him after he was returned to Virginia.

A trial before Loring began on May 29 and lasted three days, with hundreds of federal guards stationed inside the Boston courthouse. A crowd of thousands was gathered outside when Loring delivered his June 2 ruling: he ordered that Burns be returned to Virginia. "The decision was a grievous disappointment to us all, and chiefly to the poor prisoner," Dana recalled.

Bells tolled around Boston, and as word spread by telegraph to other communities bells tolled around the entire Commonwealth of Massachusetts. Dana and Grimes stayed with Burns while the courtroom was cleared. Burns worried that he would be sold to New Orleans, and Grimes, trying to keep his spirits up, pressed a piece of paper with his address into Burns's hand and asked him to write from Virginia.

Wendell Phillips solemnly informed Burns, "You must go back. There isn't humanity, there isn't Christianity, there isn't justice enough here to save you."

Dressed in a top hat and tails, as enslaved men for sale in Southern markets sometimes were, Burns was escorted by some two thousand officers, including Massachusetts soldiers, Boston police officers, and federal troops, on his march from the courthouse down State Street to a waiting ship at Long Wharf.

Store windows on the route were draped in funereal black crepe paper and flags hung upside down in a distress signal. An enormous coffin marked with the word LIBERTY was suspended across State Street. Boston newspapers released freshly updated editions hourly, selling them on the streets. Back in Richmond, the news probably spread quickly as well. Robert Lumpkin must have read reports of the trial outcome and talked about it with other slave traders and with the enslavers boarding with him. Mary Lumpkin may have whispered about it with her friends. Perhaps they already knew that Burns would be returned to Lumpkin's Jail.

In Boston, Burns passed some fifty thousand people who closed businesses and left work and school early to line the streets. The crowd filled in around him, hissing and howling at his escorts, "Shame! Shame!" and screaming "Kidnappers!" Military officers passing by taunted the crowd by singing "Carry Me Back to Old Virginny." Someone launched cayenne pepper into the crowd.

At the wharf, officers loaded Burns onto the *John Taylor*, an American vessel typically used to enforce customs regulations. President Franklin Pierce had chosen to make an example of Burns in order to prove that he would uphold the Fugitive Slave Act, and he did so at "an exorbitant price" to taxpayers—as much as $100,000.

The ship left the wharf that afternoon, with Burns aboard, "amid a storm of groans and hisses," weaving its way through little boats that had anchored in Boston Harbor to witness the event. Once at sea, Burns was transferred to the revenue cutter *Morris*, a US Coast Guard boat commissioned in 1847 and armed with a cannon, muskets, and pistols to enforce customs regulations.

Thousands of people who had gathered on the Boston streets filled train cars to return home to other city neighborhoods and the leafy suburbs. The poet John Greenleaf Whittier, a Quaker and abolitionist, jotted down his feelings about the day:

As I thought of Liberty
Marched hand-cuffed down the sworded street,
The solid earth beneath my feet
Reeled fluid as the sea.

THE *RICHMOND ENQUIRER* issued a white supremacist response to Burns's return to Virginia: "He is a young and tall black negro who would be very useful in a cotton field," the paper opined.

Burns arrived in Norfolk before being transferred to Richmond. Suttle's friend William Brent delivered Burns to "one Robert Lumpkin himself," who escorted Burns to his jail. Perhaps his arrival created a spectacle, with onlookers gathered on the streets of Richmond to watch the man who had been briefly free returned to slavery.

When Robert Lumpkin met up with him, he ordered Burns "to put his hands behind him; this done, the jail-keeper proceeded to fasten them together in that position with a pair of iron handcuffs," as noted by Charles Emery Stevens. "Then, directing Anthony to move on before, he followed him closely behind until they arrived at his jail." Perhaps Mary Lumpkin was there to witness his arrival.

Robert Lumpkin would see to it that Burns paid for his escape. He had built a reputation for breaking enslaved people. Mary Lumpkin may have already had an idea of what Burns was about to endure.

"Here he was destined to suffer, for four months, such revolting treatment as the vilest felons never undergo, and such as only revengeful enslavers can inflict," writes Stevens.

The US marshals who escorted Burns from Boston then attended a banquet hosted in their honor by Richmond residents.

"Slavery, being the sum total of all villainy, this dinner of course, was the sum total of all happiness to the Prince of Darkness," wrote Frederick Douglass in an editorial in his *North Star* newspaper. "Why did not the prison walls shake and the jailer tremble? I fear nothing can arouse. The nation is so deeply encrusted in its own shame, as to be lost to all sense of degradation."

Inside Lumpkin's Jail, Burns was isolated in an unventilated garret room that was "six or eight feet square." The room was meagerly furnished with a bench fastened to the wall instead of a bed. Even though bone jutted out from the side of one of Burns's hands, Lumpkin kept him handcuffed in irons, with both hands behind his back, and he left Burns's feet shackled with fetters. The irons were so tight that "they wore the flesh through the bone," the *Anti-Slavery Bugle* reported.

At the jail, Anthony Burns was abandoned on the attic floor. We don't know if Mary Lumpkin or her children knew how bad the conditions were for him, nor whether she attempted to talk with Robert Lumpkin about the way he kept Burns.

"His room became more foul and noisome than the hovel of a brute; loathsome creeping things multiplied and rioted in the filth," Charles Emery Stevens wrote. "The indecency resulting from such a condition is too revolting for description, or even thought."

Burns was only taken outside so that he could be ogled by Richmond residents and passersby, a regular event that Mary Lumpkin and her children may have witnessed. "He became an object of curiosity to all who had heard of his case, and twenty or thirty persons in a day would call to gaze upon him," Stevens writes.

Robert Lumpkin made an example of Burns outside the jail, and inside he attempted to prevent Burns from interacting with other enslaved people because "the taint of freedom was upon him, and infection was dreaded," Stevens wrote.

Burns noticed that Robert Lumpkin was unfaithful to Mary Lumpkin with a dark-skinned woman, whom he described as Robert Lumpkin's "black concubine." It is unclear what Mary Lumpkin knew of this other woman, or how she felt about Robert Lumpkin's abuse of her. Perhaps she saw it as a betrayal. Robert Lumpkin may have also felt betrayed when he noticed the enslaved woman, imprisoned near Burns, interacting with him.

"From one of the upper windows the girl contrived to hold conversations with Anthony, whose apartment was directly opposite," writes

Stevens. "Her compassion, it is not unlikely, changed into a warmer feeling."

Robert Lumpkin did not like what he saw, and he had the woman moved. "What he overheard roused his jealousy," according to Stevens, "and he took effectual means to break off the intercourse."

Burns found ways to talk with other enslaved people being held in the jail and, at the same time, to contest his detention. Using a spoon, he carved a hole in the wood floor so that he could talk with the men imprisoned in the room below the attic, and he shared stories of his brief freedom in Boston. Burns also snuck letters out of the jail that he wrote using writing paper and a pen that he had concealed on his body when he arrived at the jail. Other prisoners provided him with ink.

To send a letter to a friend, Burns would attach it to a brick he had dug out of the jail wall, then watch out the attic window until he saw a Black person passing on the street outside. If he could get the person's attention, he would throw the brick with the letter attached out the window and over the jail fence, a tactic that apparently worked in a few cases.

His letters to supporters in Boston described the conditions of the jail. He told them that enslaved people were packed into small rooms, chained to one another, nearly starved, and often whipped.

"I am yet bound in jail and am wearing my chains night and day . . . I am for sale," he wrote to Richard Henry Dana, his attorney. He asked Dana to buy his freedom, suggesting that his enslaver would take $800 for him.

He also wrote to Charles Suttle, his enslaver, describing how sick he was, and Suttle sent his friend William Brent to the jail for an explanation from Lumpkin. During his imprisonment, Burns's irons were removed for a few weeks—perhaps after Suttle's visit—when he had "a violent fever, and the irons were taken off by order of the physician," Dana recalled.

When Brent asked Burns how he had been able to mail letters, Burns enjoyed witnessing Brent's astonishment when he described how he had done it. Brent may have informed Robert Lumpkin that Burns was to be punished, not killed, as Burns was worth nothing to Suttle dead. Perhaps Mary Lumpkin had already suggested this to him, recommending that the jailer treat the young man better, if not to respect his humanity then at least to protect the investment.

After several months, Burns was nursed back to health to be sold.

BURNS'S CASE OUTLINED the vast differences between the views of slavery held by white Northerners and white Southerners.

In its aftermath, more Southerners began to find the idea of secession from the United States palatable. They realized that enforcing the Fugitive Slave Act in the North would be virtually impossible because some vocal Northerners opposed it and refused to support it. Newspapers across the South had reported every detail of Burns's trial, and their editorial writers were incensed by Northerners' behavior. "Such an execution of the Fugitive Slave law as that which we witness in Boston is a mockery and an insult . . . it must awaken the South to a sense of its position and the necessity of an independent and exclusive policy," opined the *Richmond Examiner*. "A few more such victories, and the South is undone."

The trial also fueled antislavery sentiment across the North. After Burns was returned to Richmond, Thomas Wentworth Higginson of the Boston Vigilance Committee delivered a sermon at his Worcester church calling for the end of apathy toward slavery. Pointing out that people who escaped slavery were not safe in Massachusetts, Higginson urged his parishioners to act by taking a stand.

The North burned with anger. New Englanders who had passively accepted slavery turned against it. "We went to bed one night old-fashioned, conservative, compromise Union Whigs"—members of a political party that believed in a strong federal government—"and waked up stark mad Abolitionists," wrote Amos Adams Lawrence.

In response, Massachusetts abolitionists founded the Anti-Man-Hunting League, which vowed to help enslaved people escape and to resist the Fugitive Slave Act. Five hundred white and Black male members pledged to use any means necessary, even kidnapping slave catchers.

At an 1854 Fourth of July abolitionist rally in Framingham, Massachusetts, William Lloyd Garrison burned copies of both the 1850 Fugitive Slave Act and the court's decision to send Burns back to Virginia. He also lit on fire the US Constitution, calling it "a covenant with death, and an agreement with hell."

Sojourner Truth, the outspoken abolitionist and women's right advocate who had been enslaved in New York, warned the crowd that God "would yet execute his judgments upon the white people for their oppression and cruelty."

Henry David Thoreau told those gathered that Massachusetts and the rest of the Northern states were guilty of complicity in the sins of slavery, adding that Burns's trial was "really the trial of Massachusetts." The "law will never make men free," Thoreau said. "It is men who have got to make the law free."

"The only remedy," William Lloyd Garrison concluded, was "*a dissolution of the Union.*"

AFTER BURNS HAD been in Lumpkin's Jail for four months, he was put up for sale.

In November 1854, Suttle sold him for $905 to David McDaniel, a North Carolina slave trader. Perhaps Mary Lumpkin had continued to visit him during his confinement at Lumpkin's Jail. Did she have mixed feelings about seeing him leave? Had his stay inspired her to secure freedom for herself and her children?

In Rocky Mount, North Carolina, Burns served as McDaniel's coachman and stable keeper. When he drove McDaniel's wife to the home of a neighbor, a visitor recognized Burns as "the slave whose case excited such commotion throughout the country." Through her pastor, she informed Leonard A. Grimes, the Massachusetts pastor, of Burns's whereabouts, and the pastor wrote a letter to McDaniel asking to buy

Burns. McDaniel agreed to a price of $1,300, and Grimes took up the task of trying to raise the money. He got donations totaling $676, and a bank cashier loaned him the rest.

In February 1855, McDaniel took Burns via train to Norfolk and then boarded a steamer for Baltimore, where he planned to meet Grimes. When passengers realized Burns was on board, they became hostile, and McDaniel "had to stand at the door for 3 hours with his revolver loaded and capped," attorney Richard Henry Dana recalled.

At the Barnum Hotel in Baltimore, Grimes gave McDaniel the funds that his Twelfth Baptist Church had raised to free Burns, and he and Burns quickly departed. "The train then whirled off," Burns's biographer writes, and "the land of bondage was forever left behind."

Grimes, formerly imprisoned in Virginia, and Burns, a formerly enslaved Virginian, made their way back to Boston, where a few weeks later a thousand people attended a reception held in Burns's honor at the Tremont Temple. Once settled into life in Boston, Burns went on a speaking tour in Massachusetts and New York and published a book about his experiences.

In the protocol of the time, Burns wrote to the Baptist church that he had attended in Stafford, Virginia, asking to be dismissed from membership so that he could join a Boston church. The church wrote a newspaper article announcing that it had excommunicated Burns for the "sin" of stealing himself from his master and "disobeying the laws of God and men."

Stunned, Burns responded, "I was stolen and made a slave as soon as I was born." He continued, "That manstealer who stole me trampled on my dearest rights. He committed an outrage on the law of God . . . God made me a man—not a slave."

Burns later moved to Ohio to attend Oberlin College, the first college in America to admit Black students. He studied for the ministry but did not complete his degree, leaving school to preach in Indianapolis before making his way to Ontario to lead a congregation. He died in 1862 of complications from the injuries sustained at Lumpkin's Jail.

The citizens of Massachusetts made sure that Burns was the last enslaved person to be captured under the Fugitive Slave Law in Massachusetts. After his trial, legislators asserted states' rights and vowed not to comply with the Fugitive Slave Act. Boston became a sanctuary city for enslaved people escaping slavery. Yet the misery inflicted on enslaved people at Lumpkin's Jail would continue for another decade.

Mary Lumpkin, also religious, had shown compassion toward Burns and may have done so for other enslaved people being held at the jail. Yet she was not likely in a position to interfere with how they were treated. She could not stop families from being separated, women from being raped, men from being starved, or children from being beaten. She could not put an end to the torture that Anthony Burns endured.

The only ways she could help Anthony Burns must have been visiting him and comforting him with the books that she brought. Perhaps she said little to Robert Lumpkin about his treatment of Anthony Burns in order to secure the best outcome for herself and her children.

In 1826 this building was constructed in Ipswich, Massachusetts, and two years later the Ipswich Female Seminary was opened. Robert Lumpkin and Mary Lumpkin's daughters would attend from 1856 to 1858. (Courtesy of the Ipswich Museum)

6

Leaving the South

Robert Lumpkin and Mary Lumpkin's two daughters were approaching puberty, a dangerous time in the lives of enslaved girls.

For years Mary Lumpkin had undoubtedly worried about them, knowing from her personal experience what could happen to a young enslaved girl. Robert Lumpkin may also have wanted to protect them from the fate he imposed on Mary—being sexually abused and forced to have children. Worried that a financial misstep would result in them being taken from him, he knew that he needed to get them to safety before they were childbearing age.

Enslaved people had long been utilized as assets by enslavers who wanted to borrow money. Offering up enslaved people as collateral enabled enslavers to borrow significant amounts of cash and obtain credit, often through neighbors and friends. Thomas Jefferson mortgaged 150 of the people he enslaved in order to build Monticello.

Enslaved people were easier to sell than land. In some Southern states, more than eight in ten mortgage-secured loans utilized enslaved people for collateral. The historian Bonnie Martin notes that "slave owners worked their slaves financially, as well as physically," by mortgaging the enslaved people they owned to buy more enslaved people.

Credit was widely available at banks. Citizens Bank and Canal Bank in Louisiana, two subsidiaries of JP Morgan Chase, accepted as collateral some thirteen thousand enslaved people from 1831 until the end of the Civil War in 1865. As a result of that practice, banks had to take ownership of enslaved people when the loan recipients defaulted. After foreclosures, one bank owned an estimated 1,250 enslaved people for a period of time, and on occasion a bank would seize a whole plantation, including the enslaved people who lived there. To liquidate these "assets," some banks relied on slave traders to sell the enslaved people. Banks were also forced to search for enslavers who absconded with the people they enslaved—and had offered as collateral—while they were trying to foreclose on these defaulters.

Mortgages for enslaved people were required to be recorded just like mortgages for homes. An enslaver had a mortgage drawn up by a notary, listing the enslaved person's name and age, and then recorded the mortgage at a city or county courthouse.

When creditors made claims on the estate of Tennessee enslaver David Logue, he sold the people he enslaved, including his son Jarm Logue, later known as Jermain Wesley Loguen, along with his siblings and their mother, the enslaved woman renamed Cherry after she was kidnapped from Ohio as a girl.

David Logue had treated young Jarm as a pet, caressing him and sometimes allowing him to sleep in his bed, and he had promised Cherry that he would give his son freedom. Later, when liens were placed on his property, David Logue determined that he could not keep his word to Cherry and also become solvent.

"He was deeply grieved; but not so much grieved that he was willing to adopt the only expedient that would avert it," Loguen wrote of his father in his autobiography, *To Set the Captives Free*. Rather than declare bankruptcy, David Logue's pride "compelled a determination to convert his slaves, and even his own flesh and blood, into money to pay his debts."

He described how his father's financial distress played out for him, his mother, and his siblings. "In the dead of night, when they were locked in sleep, the negro quarters were surrounded by stout men, armed with revolvers and shackles," Loguen wrote. His mother awakened and realized that she was shackled, her infant sleeping beside her, and she shrieked in fear. When she inquired about David Logue, who had promised to protect her, "she was told that . . . she no longer belonged to him."

If Robert Lumpkin had used Mary Lumpkin or his children with her to secure a loan, he knew that they could be seized—with or without his sign-off—if he failed to pay a debt. Even if he hadn't used the children as collateral on loans, he may have worried that they could be taken from him if he fell upon tough financial times. They were property in the eyes of the state.

Perhaps he feared a scene like the one that unfolded in Georgia when creditors arrived at an enslaver's property to seize the child of an enslaved woman who had died. The enslaver told them that the girl was his daughter. "True, but she is also your slave as well," the creditors informed him. In another instance, an enslaved woman's son with her enslaver was light-skinned and educated, and he believed he was free. When his father died, creditors decided that the boy was part of the estate, and he was sold to a slave trader who applied a cream to his face to make him look darker.

Perhaps, like Hilton Waddell, the white father of two enslaved daughters who moved from Virginia to Lexington, Missouri, Robert Lumpkin cared for his children and never denied that they were his. Waddell's daughter, Harriet Ann Daves, recalled that "my father was good to me. He would give me anything I asked him for." When a white relative mocked her, Waddell told the relative that his daughter was just as good as she was.

Annie and Martha Lumpkin may have been adored by their white father, hugged, kissed, and "petted" like the enslaved daughters of John Hemphill, a Texas supreme court justice and US senator, and Sabina, a woman he enslaved. Hemphill "treated them as his children, taking them in his arms . . . in his carriage to ride with him; and . . . fondled and kissed them." He may have bought them candy and apples, as Silas Omohundro did for his children.

Lumpkin worried about the welfare of his daughters, and he knew he had options. He had seen his peers in the slave trade sending their children with enslaved mothers to freedom. Moving his girls out of Richmond was the best way to protect them, and Mary Lumpkin demanded it.

FOR YEARS AFTER the 1841 mutiny aboard the *Creole*, Robert Lumpkin and the other slave traders who had lost people they enslaved sought reimbursement, but to no avail.

In 1842, British foreign secretary Alexander Baring, also known as Lord Ashburton, traveled to America to negotiate a dispute over the border between America and Canada. As part of the Northeast Boundary Treaty negotiations, Lord Ashburton and Secretary of State Daniel Webster broached the subject of the *Creole*. In the discussion, Baring promised Webster that Britain would avoid future "officious interference" with American ships and agreed to pay enslavers for the enslaved people that had been freed. The Webster-Ashburton Treaty also ended the threat of war with Britain.

Thirteen years after that meeting, the claims commission for the two countries found that Nassau officials had violated international law by interfering with America's legal slave trade and declared that a slave revolt was "an uncontrollable occurrence." In 1855, the British government reimbursed the enslavers for the enslaved people who had been set free after the *Creole* landed in the Bahamas. Robert Lumpkin and the other slave traders were greeted with a windfall, receiving a combined $110,300.

The decision was welcomed in the South. "News of a cheering character for some of our citizens has been received here, and several fortunes have been unexpectedly realized," Vermont's *Spirit of the Age* reported.

"Every effort has been made to obtain indemnity for these slaves, but without success until the present time," reported Richmond's *Daily Dispatch*.

Robert Lumpkin had owned forty-one enslaved people aboard the *Creole*. He had already been reimbursed for four of the enslaved people by the American Life Insurance and Trust Company Principal. The commission paid him and Edwin Lockett, a trader he partnered with in New Orleans, a total of $20,000—worth more than $627,000 today. George Apperson, a slave trader who was also the proprietor of the York Town Saloon, received $15,000. William H. Goodwin, the trader who held Solomon Northup in his jail, got $20,000, while John Hagan, the New Orleans trader, was paid $8,000.

"The judgment of the commission is a just one and in an international point of view highly important and gratifying," wrote the *Daily Dispatch* in January 1855.

The payment apparently came too late for a man identified as "G. H. Lumpkin," who was probably Robert Lumpkin's distraught brother, Wilson. He may have had an ownership stake in some of Robert Lumpkin's enslaved people. For him, the financial loss that resulted from the mutiny was devastating and life-altering. Upon hearing of the mutiny on the *Creole* in 1841, he "became deranged" and was checked into the "Eastern Lunatic Asylum," later known as Eastern State Hospital, in Williamsburg, Virginia, one newspaper said. Other records show that Wilson Lumpkin was imprisoned in a Richmond city jail in January 1848 to wait for a vacancy at the state hospital, and that seven months later he was admitted to the psychiatric hospital.

The fourteen-year-old claim to the commission "had been considered hopeless," *The Spirit of the Age* concluded in 1855. The payout was welcomed by slave traders, as the next few years proved to be difficult ones. The Panic of 1857, an economic depression caused by Europe's declining interest in American agricultural products, showed the vulnerability of banks and left those in agriculture less prosperous. The panic followed a period of prosperity and surely left slave traders feeling financially vulnerable.

With the panic fresh in his mind and the financial windfall from the *Creole* in his pocket, Robert Lumpkin worked to move his daughters out of the slave jail and out of slavery. He and Mary Lumpkin would make sure they were educated and living in a free state.

RICHMOND SLAVE TRADER Bacon Tait already had found a way to move his children and the Black mother of his children out of Virginia. In 1852, he bought a house in Salem, Massachusetts, where he moved with Courtney Fountain, a free Black woman from Winchester, Virginia, and their four children, who were also born free.

Before he created a family with Fountain, Tait had complained for years about not being married. In Virginia, Tait stated in legal papers that Fountain "held to him the relation of house-keeper," but in the North he presented her as his legal wife.

Fountain had both Black and white abolitionist roots, and some of her family had migrated north as restrictions on free Black men and women increased in Virginia in the aftermath of Nat Turner's rebellion. Tait set up his family near Fountain's brother and sister in Salem, which had a vibrant free Black community and integrated schools. It was also home to the Salem Female Anti-slavery Society, established in 1832 as the first antislavery group in America organized by Black women.

Tait lived in Salem half the year and spent the other half in Richmond, where he continued to trade in enslaved people at the jail he had built on Cary Street. In 1858, Tait would eventually set free the last person he enslaved, Henry Banks, who had helped him operate the jail.

After Tait moved his family to Massachusetts, several Richmond slave traders followed in his footsteps, taking action to free their children and the children's enslaved mothers by moving them north. Seventeen years after Silas Omohundro moved Louisa Tandy Omohundro and their son Littleton to Ohio, Silas Omohundro was preparing to send his two oldest children with Corinna Hinton Omohundro to the North too. By 1857, eight-year-old Silas Jr. and seven-year-old Alice Morton were living in Lancaster, Pennsylvania. They were cared for by Eliza Cheatham, whom Silas Omohundro referred to as Corinna's sister. It is unclear whether she was related to Lucy Ann Cheatham.

The children probably either attended school or were taught at home by a tutor. Silas Omohundro also bought a house and land in the county, which was a busy thoroughfare for enslaved people seeking freedom in the North due to its location on the border of Pennsylvania and Maryland, a slave state.

The slave trader George Apperson made a different choice for his children with Louisa Girard, a Black woman he may have enslaved: he sent them to school in a city where slavery was allowed. In 1857, Apperson enrolled his daughters Tarquina and Leonede in the St. Francis School for Colored Girls, founded in Baltimore in 1828 to serve enslaved and poor Black girls and run by the Oblate Sisters of Providence, who were free women of color. The girls' "racial identity qualified them for enrollment in the Oblate school," and they attended until 1860.

Robert Lumpkin was surely influenced by his fellow slave traders, and Tait may have suggested Massachusetts as a free state where his daughters could get an education. Slavery had been outlawed in the commonwealth since 1783, and school segregation had been banned in 1855. Tait may have pointed out that he and his family could provide assistance if Martha and Annie went to Massachusetts for their education.

Before enrolling his daughters at the Ipswich Female Seminary, Robert Lumpkin had visited Massachusetts, traveling north in 1842 to meet Bill Robinson in Boston and during the Anthony Burns trial in 1854. Lumpkin had enslaved Robinson from childhood and used him as an overseer and jail supervisor after he grew up. Robinson had been freed by British authorities when the *Hermosa* crashed off the shore of the Bahamas in 1840 and had made his way to Boston.

When Lumpkin tracked him down, Robinson agreed to meet with him at the Tremont House hotel, where Lumpkin acknowledged to others that Robinson "is a free man." More than a decade later, when Burns's trial was under way, Robert Lumpkin was asking for him, and Robinson worried that he was at risk of being taken south. Richard Henry Dana advised Robinson that if Robert Lumpkin made a claim on him, "he would be delivered up," Dana wrote.

Bacon Tait, who was also exploring options to educate his children, may have been able to advise Robert Lumpkin about Northern schools that would be welcoming to his daughters. In 1859, Tait would send his fourteen-year-old daughter Constance Rosalie "Connie" Tait to the College Institute for Young Ladies, or Spingler Institute, founded in 1843, in Union Park, New York City. Eleven-year-old Marie Josephine Tait attended the Moravian Seminary for Girls in Bethlehem, Pennsylvania, from which she would graduate in 1865.

Perhaps Bacon Tait knew of the Ipswich Female Seminary and recommended it to Robert Lumpkin. Maybe he mentioned the possibility that Robert Lumpkin's daughters would pass as white in Massachusetts, as Tait's did. Like Robert Lumpkin, Tait was "very fond of his children, especially of his daughters, and seemed to be, as he well might be, proud of their beauty and accomplishments." As a doting father, Tait would have been a good person to advise Robert Lumpkin about how to give his daughters a better life.

Mary Lumpkin may have been enthusiastic about this plan for her daughters. Perhaps, in some small way, she had been influenced by Anthony Burns. Maybe the fact that he lived in Massachusetts made it appealing to her. Or perhaps when Burns spoke with her while confined at Lumpkin's Jail he had suggested that her daughters might be educated or find freedom there. Mary Lumpkin may have known that scores of people formerly enslaved in Virginia had started new lives in Massachusetts.

Regardless of how Robert Lumpkin and Mary Lumpkin decided on Massachusetts as the destination for Martha and Annie, their daughters would soon be living in a free state—a land more foreign than they could have dreamed.

BY THE TIME Mary Lumpkin's daughters arrived in Massachusetts to attend school, her dear friend Lucy Ann Hagan had been set free.

After Lucy Ann Hagan left Richmond aboard a slave ship in 1849, she had given birth to four children with John Hagan. Only two survived—a son, William, and their daughter Frederika, or Dolly.

By the time William was born in 1855, John Hagan may have known he was dying. In Richmond, a John Hagan—perhaps the trader from New Orleans—placed an advertisement to sell his carriages "on account of my prolonged indisposition," adding that he was "compelled to retire to improve health." In New Orleans, John Hagan wrote his will and then petitioned a Louisiana court for the freedom of twenty-six-year-old Lucy Ann Hagan and their children. The petition was granted less than two weeks later, on May 23, 1856.

Within weeks of the court decision to free Lucy Ann Hagan and her two children with John Hagan, he was dead. His will referred to her as "the woman" and "my slave," and it did not acknowledge their children as his own, instead referring to them as "her children." Yet John Hagan left their children "the property on Esplanade Street purchased by me of Hope H. Slatter"—the slave trader—and $5,000 to maintain the land. His decision to leave them property may also have paved the way for Robert Lumpkin and other Richmond slave traders to provide for their own children at death.

Knowing that he was deeply indebted, John Hagan noted in his will that if there was no cash left at the time of his death, he wanted everything—"all I may possess"—left to his mother, Rosanna Hagan, with the exception of "the woman Lucy Ann Cheatham, and Dolly (child or children) who I wish set free as soon as possible." The will, written before Lucy Ann Hagan and their two children had been granted freedom by the court, noted that she had paid him "in ready cash a sufficient sum to pay for her freedom."

Four years after his death, Lucy Ann Hagan, by then thirty years old, was operating a boardinghouse in New Orleans. She was among nearly a hundred Black and brown women in the city who made a living by keeping "comfortable and attractively decorated rooming and boarding houses." Single, older white women dominated the boardinghouse industry, but free and enslaved Black women also operated them.

Lucy Ann Hagan had quickly transitioned from enslaved to enslaver. In 1860, she owned four enslaved people: a twenty-six-year-old woman, a twenty-one-year-old woman, a sixteen-year-old boy, and a four-year-old girl. She became complicit in the trade, finding a way to rationalize keeping Black women and children enslaved after all she had endured.

Frederika Hagan, who may have passed as white, would attend Mount St. Vincent Academy on the Hudson, located in the Bronx—the first institution to offer higher learning for women in New York. William remained in New Orleans and became a bookkeeper.

Once Lucy Ann Hagan was free, Mary Lumpkin may have been able to ask her for advice about how to achieve freedom for her children and herself. Perhaps she could already envision what that life would look and feel like.

IPSWICH, MASSACHUSETTS, a sleepy, snowy hamlet with a curious history of abolitionism, would become a temporary home for Robert Lumpkin and Mary Lumpkin's daughters.

The community had been known as Agawam by the Indigenous people who made it their home for thousands of years. In 1633, it was settled by white farmers, fishermen, shipbuilders, and traders, but remained a small, rural town. Ipswich became known for the production of lace, and stockings were produced in the town in the 1800s.

One of the first Black Americans to successfully sue for her freedom—and the first to do so using a jury trial—had been enslaved in Ipswich. Jenny Slew, the child of a free white woman and an enslaved man, had lived as free before John Whipple Jr. enslaved her. She took him to court in 1765, saying that because the status of the child follows the mother, she should be free. She lost her first attempt, but the second time she filed suit, in 1766, the jury found in her favor, ordering Whipple to free her and awarding her money in damages and court costs.

In the fall of 1856, Martha and Annie Lumpkin, about eleven and nine years old, traveled 575 miles to attend the town's seminary, which trained young women as missionaries. Perhaps Robert Lumpkin paid someone to escort the girls, or maybe he took them himself, as John Hemphill would do for his two enslaved daughters in 1859. Hemphill transported Theodora and Henrietta, about twelve and ten, from Texas to Ohio's newly opened Wilberforce University after the death of their enslaved mother, Sabina. Hemphill, a signatory of the Confederate Constitution, paid for his daughters' tuition, board, clothes, and books. After dropping them off at school, founded on the grounds of the former Tawawa Springs health resort, he corresponded with them regularly, writing letters and sending presents.

In Ipswich, the Lumpkin daughters must have felt isolated, being so far away from their parents and everyone they knew, with the exception of their father's slave trader contact, Bacon Tait. They probably lived with a local family or a widow, as most of the students did. Perhaps their mother and father also wrote them letters and sent them packages. Even though they surely missed their parents and siblings, on some level it must have been a relief not to be in the slave jail compound anymore. How did they make sense of the life they left behind? And how did freedom feel to them?

For much of the year Ipswich was difficult to reach, not only because it was far from Richmond but because of its long, cold winters. New England was snowed in for nearly half the year. But by 1840, after Ipswich got train service, access to the seaside town improved.

The population of just over three thousand was nearly all white. The town was also home to a strong antislavery contingent, but it was not led by Quakers, who were persecuted there for being heretics.

When the Lumpkin girls arrived in Ipswich, schools for enslaved people were prohibited in Virginia, which had passed statutes in 1831 that instituted a fine of $10 to $100 for those who educated enslaved people. In response to these laws, Nancy Lewis Ruffin, a free Black woman in Richmond who had hired a tutor, moved her eight children to Boston so that they could attend school while her husband George stayed behind to work as a barber. Their son George Lewis Ruffin would become the first Black man to graduate from Harvard Law School, the first Black man to serve on the Boston City Council, and the first Black judge to sit on an American court.

In Boston, three schools for Black girls had been funded by philanthropists by 1827. By the 1830s, larger cities offered public schools for Black children, but in smaller towns private schools remained the only option. Across the commonwealth, public schools had been integrated in 1855, so by the time the Lumpkin daughters arrived in Massachusetts, Black children had been attending public school with white children for a year.

In the aftermath of Anthony Burns's arrest, Massachusetts legislators determined that the commonwealth would no longer enforce the Fugitive Slave Act, as they "no longer believed in the sanctity or priority of the federal law," writes Thomas D. Morris. They began considering their responsibility for protecting Black citizens. In January 1855, Massachusetts governor Henry Gardner asked the legislature to pass new laws to ensure that Black residents were afforded the right to trial by jury and the writ of *habeas corpus*—the requirement that an imprisoned person be brought before the court to determine if his detention was lawful. "Weave every safeguard you justly may round these primal birthrights, older than our national birthday, and dear as its continued existence," Gardner wrote.

A bill designed to protect free Black people from being seized passed the Massachusetts Senate and the House and was "without a doubt, the most involved Personal Liberty Law ever passed," notes Morris. It provided Black residents with a variety of protections and called for the removal of any state official who helped capture enslaved people seeking freedom. In 1858, a new governor removed Judge Loring from the bench for his role in deciding Anthony Burns's case.

After Burns's trial, free Black people had more protections in Massachusetts. And the enslaved children of the slave trader who had tortured Burns in Virginia were safer in Massachusetts because of him.

THE IPSWICH FEMALE Seminary was first established in 1826 as a coeducational school by a group of the town's wealthy residents. Two years later, the longtime educator Zilpah Polly Grant took over as principal and shifted the school's focus to girls. She named Mary Lyon as her assistant principal.

At the time, the education of women was mostly limited to grammar school, but the Ipswich Female Seminary offered girls both secondary and college-level education. The school provided instruction in chemistry, grammar, botany, astronomy, theology, and moral philosophy. By 1833, an average of 142 students enrolled each semester.

The school was "a very powerful influence on the development of education of women in America," said Ipswich's late town historian Mary Conley. "Women finally had the opportunity to get an education in fields similar to those men were studying."

The two-story building, located on a hill near the center of town, was equipped with maps, blackboards, and chemistry sets and also had a well-stocked library. "The primary objective of the school seems to be to provide faithful and enlightened teachers; but the course of instruction is such, as to prepare the pupil for any destination in life," a visitor wrote in 1833.

At the time, the operation of women's schools was dependent on male benefactors. Grant and Lyon asked the town investors to provide "a seminary building free of rent," and they also wanted to build "a boarding house with conveniences for 120 boarders furnished as to give ladies as favorable a situation as is afforded to young men at our colleges."

When they were unable to persuade the founders to establish an endowment, Lyon began fundraising to open a new school devoted to the liberal education of women, and in the process she became a pioneer in the field. In 1835, she left the Ipswich Female Seminary to charter the Mount Holyoke Female Seminary in South Hadley, Massachusetts. At the time, there were 120 colleges for men in the United States, but none for women. Mount Holyoke became the first of the "Seven Sisters"—the female equivalent of the Ivy League institutions, which at the time admitted only male students—and female education entered a new era.

Zilpah Grant left the Ipswich Female Seminary three years later, forcing its temporary closure in 1839. Ipswich residents worked to revive the school by recruiting a former student and her educator husband to lead it. Eunice Caldwell Cowles was born in Ipswich and had worked at the Ipswich Seminary as a teacher after completing her education there. At twenty-four years old, she had served as principal of Wheaton Academy, later known as Wheaton College, in Norton, Massachusetts, and as Lyon's associate principal at Mount Holyoke Female Seminary. When she married Reverend John P. Cowles, a professor of Hebrew at Oberlin College, the couple had moved to Elyria, Ohio, to establish a school. In 1844, they agreed to return to Ipswich, and "for the next 33 years they ran the Ipswich Female Seminary with an iron hand and turned out a most brilliant array of students," wrote the *Peabody Times*.

About the same time the Cowleses came back, Ipswich resident Lucy Caldwell—who was probably a distant relative of Eunice Caldwell Cowles's by marriage—founded the Ipswich Female Anti-Slavery Society with other women who lived in town. Lucy Caldwell's husband, Josiah Caldwell, chaired the Ipswich Anti-Slavery Society. The female society met in the parlor of the couple's home, where they often hosted antislavery speakers traveling across New England.

There are some indications that the seminary leaders also had abolitionist leanings. John Cowles had been engaged in the antislavery society in Oberlin, some sources claimed that abolitionist fliers were handed out on the Ipswich Female Seminary campus, and an Ipswich Seminary teacher reportedly published poetry in an antislavery magazine. Was part of the school's mission supporting enslaved girls?

MARY LUMPKIN SURELY wanted her children to achieve more than she had, and she saw to it that they were well educated.

As children, Martha and Annie Lumpkin and their brothers probably had a tutor teaching them reading, writing, and arithmetic. In Richmond, Martha had learned French and the girls likely received music lessons, as the family later acquired a piano. They must have been fairly accomplished, as gaining admission to the Ipswich Female Seminary in itself seems to have been a difficult feat.

On campus, students attended rigorous classes in a disciplined atmosphere designed to prepare them to serve as missionaries across the United States and around the world. School officials kept a log of absences from class and church, as well as tardiness reports. Semester bills were accompanied by the student's grades and a tally of how many minutes late she had been to classes, to her room at night, and to the table at mealtime.

When Martha and Annie Lumpkin were enrolled at the Ipswich Female Seminary, most of the students came from Ipswich and nearby Massachusetts communities or other New England towns. Students from Southern locales, such as Mississippi, Florida, and Georgia, were the exception. A pair of Indigenous girls from an area of Canada that is now Minnesota had attended the school, but it is unclear whether any other Black students attended.

Ipswich Female Seminary leaders either were not aware of the Lumpkin girls' family life or did not make note of it in their surviving files. It's impossible to know whether the seminary had been a destination for other children of enslaved women and their white enslavers. Perhaps the girls kept their racial background, their father's work, and their mother's enslaved status as closely guarded secrets.

That was the route taken by Harriet Jacobs's enslaved daughter, Louisa Jacobs, a multiracial girl who in 1859 attended Young Ladies Domestic Seminary School in Clinton, New York, after her white father moved her north to work as a house servant without emancipating her.

"They did not know her history, and she did not tell it, because she had no desire to make capital out of their sympathy," wrote Harriet Jacobs.

Yet when school leaders eventually learned that Louisa Jacobs and her mother had been enslaved, "every method was used to increase her advantages and diminish her expenses," Harriet Jacobs later wrote.

If they did not know for sure, the Cowleses may have suspected that Martha and Annie Lumpkin were the daughters of a slave trader. Their last name would have been a tip-off for anyone who read abolitionist papers or had followed the Anthony Burns case. They might have remembered that he was housed in Lumpkin's Jail after he was returned to Virginia.

Yet measures were taken to conceal their background. Though they did not change their last name on school papers, Martha and Annie Lumpkin were identified as being from Philadelphia and may have gone there during breaks in the school year. Once they had left Richmond, it is unlikely that they ever returned. The risk of them being kidnapped and enslaved by someone else may have been considered too great.

Mary Lumpkin must have helped shape their school experience. "For years before the war . . . this slave-mother of the white jailer's children united with Lumpkin in sending their children to the North to school, winter after winter," wrote James B. Simmons, an administrator with the American Baptist Home Mission Society who would meet them after the war.

The young women were perceived as white. "These girls, though born of a slave mother, were so white that they passed in the community as white ladies," recalled Charles Henry Corey, who also met them later.

Some light-skinned Black men and women achieved this by moving to a new area, particularly the North or the West, and simply allowing neighbors and coworkers to assume their race—a tactic that the Lumpkin daughters may have used later in life too. For some multiracial people, the act of passing as white was effortless, but the emotional costs of denying their Blackness, and sometimes their families, were high. For others, displaying multiple racial identities enabled them to "possess more fully their own lived, perceived, or implicit sense of selfhood," wrote Martha J. Cutter, a professor of English and Africana studies. Some passed only part of the time, and this may have been the approach taken by the Lumpkin girls when they were young. Others passed in order to get the privileges that came with being white, such as staying in nice hotels, eating at good restaurants, attending the theater, or landing higher-quality and better-paying jobs. In the Lumpkin girls' case, perhaps they passed in order to attain an excellent education.

Mary Lumpkin may have warned them not to speak of their father's slave trading business or the jail where they had been raised when they were outside of Richmond. Perhaps Robert Lumpkin agreed with this approach too. With antislavery sentiment alive at the school and across Massachusetts, and the name of their slave trader father in the mouths of many abolitionists, the sisters surely kept hidden from most people not only their racial background but the nature of their home life.

WHILE MARTHA AND Annie Lumpkin were attending the Ipswich Female Seminary, Mary Lumpkin and Robert Lumpkin were in the process of ensuring that she and all five of their children could live in freedom for good. Perhaps she had sent Robert and Richard away too. Herron said the oral history passed to her indicated the children went to three different locations.

In March 1857, the US Supreme Court ruled in *Dred Scott v. John F. A. Sanford* that the US Constitution was not written with the intention of providing citizenship to Black Americans. In its decision about whether Dred Scott, born enslaved in Virginia, should continue to be enslaved after being moved by his enslaver to free states, the Court declared that Black people were not, and would never be, citizens. It also overturned the Missouri Compromise, which had outlawed slavery in some territories, finding it unconstitutional. The *Dred Scott* decision revived efforts to marginalize free Black people, such as the renewal of debate among Virginia legislators about whether free Black men and women should be re-enslaved.

That year, Mary Lumpkin traveled to Pennsylvania, a free state, to purchase a home. Perhaps Robert Lumpkin went with her to arrange the purchase or appointed someone to act on his behalf. The road to freedom in Philadelphia was a well-trodden path for enslaved women.

In 1832, Hertford, North Carolina, enslaver James Cathcart Johnston freed Edy Wood, an enslaved woman, and his four daughters with her, including Mary Virginia Wood. He set them up in Philadelphia, arranging for a wealthy Black barber, Frederick Augustus Hilton, to rent a house and secure bank accounts for them. The Pine Street home where they stayed belonged to Sarah Allen, the widow of the prominent Black leader Richard Allen, who had been bishop of Bethel Church. Once they were settled in, Mary Virginia Wood became a charter member of both the interracial Philadelphia Female Anti-Slavery Society and the Female Vigilance Association, which raised money to help enslaved people who had escaped to Philadelphia.

When Mary Lumpkin bought the home in Philadelphia, she may have already known Harriet Barber, who had moved to Philadelphia from Virginia with her children a decade earlier, after the death of her enslaver Carter Edloe. Perhaps they were related. Or maybe Robert Lumpkin knew her. Years earlier, he had leased a young enslaved woman named Ann Matthews from her Richmond enslaver, Edward Matthews, and allowed her to go to Philadelphia about 1850 to give birth to a child. In Pennsylvania, Ann Matthews's child lived as free, but it's unclear who cared for the child when Ann Matthews returned to Robert Lumpkin's charge in Richmond, where she lived at his slave jail. Perhaps the child was left with Harriet Barber, who was caring for a girl with the last name Matthews in 1860. Could she have been Robert Lumpkin's child?

Robert Lumpkin continued to allow the young "yellow woman"—as the *Daily Dispatch* described the light-skinned, probably multiracial Matthews—to regularly travel to Philadelphia to see her baby. Another indication of his leniency with Ann Matthews was her arrest in 1853 in Richmond on the charge of "remaining in the commonwealth contrary to law," which required free Black people to leave the state within a year of being set free. She was not allowed to go "at large if a slave."

When Ann Matthews appeared in court, Edward Matthews testified that he was her enslaver and said that he had threatened to sell her multiple times. Richmond's mayor, Joseph C. Mayo, who was responsible for handing down punishments for enslaved people, had announced his intention when he took office that year "to make all negroes and mulattoes know their places and obey the laws." Mayo determined that Ann Matthews was, in fact, enslaved, and informed Edward Matthews and

Robert Lumpkin that she "should not be allowed the privileges of a free woman," the *Enquirer* reported.

If Ann Matthews's child, by then three years old, belonged to Robert Lumpkin, perhaps he had traveled to Philadelphia to meet and visit the girl. Maybe Robert Lumpkin, feeling comfortable in that Northern city and knowing his way around, entrusted his children with Mary Lumpkin to Harriet Barber too.

She lived in the Seventh Ward among Philadelphia's elite mixed-race community and may have introduced Mary Lumpkin to influential neighbors. Perhaps Barber pointed her to someone selling a nearby house. Mary Lumpkin ultimately purchased a home just a block from the one where Barber lived.

Silas Omohundro had already moved his two oldest children with Corinna Hinton Omohundro to Pennsylvania's Lancaster County, which sat on the Mason-Dixon Line demarking the border between slave states and free states, with Delaware and Pennsylvania on one side and Maryland and Virginia (now West Virginia) on the other. Located on the banks of the Susquehanna River, Lancaster County had a large population of Black residents and abolitionists. It was also home to organizations that both protected enslaved people escaping slavery and helped them get to Philadelphia and beyond, making it a hub of what would become known as the Underground Railroad.

Philadelphia had been built and settled almost entirely by Quakers in 1682, and like Ohio, Pennsylvania would become a destination for the formerly enslaved people freed by Virginia enslavers. In 1804, a Virginia enslaver freed fifty-six people who arrived at the Lancaster County town of Columbia in wagons. A year later, in 1805, Sallie Bell, a Quaker from Virginia, emancipated about one hundred enslaved people who also settled there, as did many other enslaved people who escaped.

Soon after the people Bell had enslaved landed in Columbia, a rumor circulated that enslaved people were escaping from Virginia by way of Wright's Ferry, where the Quaker William Wright, Lancaster County's architect of the Underground Railroad, had begun helping enslaved people escape as early as 1804. He dressed the men in women's clothes and sometimes put them in a wagon with a false bottom, sending them six miles east to his brother-in-law, Daniel Gibbons, who asked enslaved people to choose new names before continuing their journey. Two Black businessmen, William Whipper and Stephen Smith, who had built a successful lumber company and real estate business in Columbia, owned a boxcar with a false end that they used to hide people escaping by train.

Silas Omohundro and Corinna Hinton Omohundro traveled at least twice to Lancaster to visit their children. While there, the Richmond trader introduced Corinna Hinton Omohundro as his wife and Eliza Cheatham, who was caring for their children, as his sister-in-law. On one trip, they stayed in Lancaster at least a week before returning to Virginia. A few years later, Silas Omohundro bought a house in Philadelphia, and Silas Jr. attended boarding school there. Both children reportedly passed as white.

Mary Lumpkin may have talked with Corinna Hinton Omohundro about what life in Pennsylvania was like for her children. Maybe Mary suggested to Robert Lumpkin that she too would like to move there with their children. Harriet Barber may also have been urging her to seek freedom in Philadelphia. She may have used her experience navigating the city as a newly free Black woman to pave the way for Mary Lumpkin and her children to build a new life in Philadelphia.

At the end of 1857, Mary Lumpkin purchased a home under the name Mary F. Scott, using what was presumably either her birth surname or the name of a previous enslaver. The decision to put her name on the deed as the sole owner of the tidy brick home was surely made by Mary Lumpkin and Robert Lumpkin together, reflecting both her desire for autonomy and financial independence and his willingness to go along with her wishes. He surely recognized that putting her name on the deed was the most efficient way to protect the asset for her and their children. Robert Lumpkin and Mary Lumpkin were not married, and by law they could not have been.

Putting the home in her name would save her from hardship down the road.

PHILADELPHIA WAS THE southernmost city in the free state of Pennsylvania, located only a few miles from the slave states of Delaware and Maryland, and it had a large population of multiracial residents by the 1850s. Long the destination for free Black people and fugitive enslaved people headed north through its borders, Pennsylvania was a natural place for Richmond slave traders' children to land.

"Philadelphia became a leading example of black freedom in the nation," writes the historian Erica Armstrong Dunbar.

Perhaps Harriet Barber introduced Mary Lumpkin to some of the influential people who would become her neighbors, such as Morris Brown, a shoemaker whose father, also named Morris Brown, had helped found the country's first African Methodist Episcopal Church in Philadelphia. The elder Brown had been held in police custody in Charleston in 1822 after word leaked out about a planned slave revolt led by Denmark Vesey, a free Black man.

Born to free Black parents in Charleston, the elder Brown traveled to Philadelphia in 1816 to help establish Bethel Church with Richard Allen, who was born enslaved. In 1787, Allen had founded the Free African Society in Philadelphia with Absalom Jones, a prominent Black preacher who had been born enslaved in Delaware. The elder Brown then returned to Charleston to found the African Methodist Episcopal Church of Charleston, later named Emanuel AME. Upon Allen's death in 1831, the elder Brown became Bethel Church's second bishop.

In 1850, Harriet Barber also lived next to two multiracial families from South Carolina—carpenter John Venning and his wife Mary Venning, and tailor Robert Houston and his wife Charlotte Houston, as well as their respective children. Nearly eight hundred free Black people relocated from Charleston to Philadelphia between 1858 and 1862.

Another of Harriet Barber's neighbors was Thomas J. Bowers, a Black opera singer known as "The Colored Mario" and "The American Mario" for the similarity of his voice to that of the Italian opera tenor Conte di Candia Giovanni Mario. A human rights activist, Bowers refused to perform in venues that barred Black audience members or segregated them from white guests. In 1860, the German grocer Henry Edrich, his Black wife from South Carolina, and their multiracial children lived near Harriet Barber. A multiracial cobbler, Daniel Glover, and his family also lived on the street.

In this neighborhood, Mary Lumpkin could make vital connections with respected Black people who had been living as free for years, had made connections around the city, and had already achieved some success. She didn't have to hide who she was. But as a light-skinned woman, she may have been able to move in and out of Black and white worlds in other parts of the city with more ease than many formerly enslaved people. She may have needed to be perceived as white in order to find work in white people's homes.

Despite the large number of Black men and women living in Philadelphia and the city's perceived acceptance of these new residents, there were plenty of roadblocks there and even dangers. The Fugitive Slave Act kept Mary Lumpkin and her children at risk of being kidnapped, transported to the South, and re-enslaved. Moreover, Pennsylvania residents did not necessarily greet them with open arms. Frances Ellen Watkins Harper, a Black poet born free in Baltimore, described Pennsylvania as "the meanest of all" of the states she had traveled in "as far as the treatment of colored people is concerned."

"The shadow of slavery," she wrote in 1858. "Oh how drearily it hangs."

Although Philadelphia was in some ways a welcoming place for free Black people, the Abolition Society building, Pennsylvania Hall, was destroyed by angry white mobs days after it opened in 1838. (Library of Congress)

7

Richmond Families
in Philadelphia

AFTER MARTHA AND ANNIE LUMPKIN COMPLETED TWO YEARS OF
study in Ipswich in 1858, they headed for Philadelphia in order to maintain their freedom.

"The father, fearing that some financial contingency might arise
when these, his own beautiful daughters, might be sold into slavery
to pay his debts, kept them, after their education had been completed,
in the free State of Pennsylvania, where they would be safe," Corey
wrote.

A city with a long history of Black progress, Philadelphia by then had
the largest Black population in America outside of the slave states, with
more than twenty thousand Black residents. There Martha and Annie,
then about thirteen and eleven, moved in with Harriet Barber. They
may have joined up with two of their brothers, ten-year-old Robert and
five-year-old Richard. It's unclear if the boys had come straight from
Richmond, or if they had they been living as free in other places.

Family oral history suggested the children went to three different locations—Massachusetts, Ohio, and New Orleans. By 1860, they were all under Barber's roof. Perhaps she had reached an agreement with Robert Lumpkin about when she would be allowed to move to Philadelphia to be with them. She would also take her fifth child, John, who was born about 1857.

Barber had moved to Philadelphia with her four daughters and one son, who ranged in age from seven to fifteen. Even as the family secured freedom, life remained relentlessly tragic. Each of Barber's four daughters died in the 1850s, and likely by the time the Lumpkin children arrived, only her son William was still alive.

While boarding the four eldest Lumpkin children, Barber also housed three young women from Virginia: Ann Smith, Dorothy Smith, and Susan Thompson. The women worked as cooks and servants and either assisted with Barber's boardinghouse or were employed locally. Also living with her were two school-age girls from Virginia. Perhaps Harriet Barber had found a way to make a living by housing children fathered by enslavers with enslaved women—children like her own, children she could help free.

One of the girls, Louisa Matthews, may have been the daughter of Ann Matthews, the enslaved woman whom Robert Lumpkin had leased and allowed to give birth in Philadelphia. The other girl, Ella Jones, had a common last name, like the Richmond slave trader Thomas M. Jones, who was living with Silas Omohundro at the time. Could she have been his daughter?

Barber's home, once filled with the sounds of her daughters, was now full of the sounds of other people's children, all of whom had been separated from their parents. Perhaps she hugged and kissed the Lumpkin children, giving them love and affection. Maybe they were able to feel the change in their lives as newly free people. Or maybe, as children, their lives were so restricted and their longing for their parents so great that freedom was not yet a gift they could truly appreciate.

Annie and Martha Lumpkin were learning to navigate a bustling city after living in Ipswich, the Puritan white enclave. In Philadelphia, they were in the heart of a vibrant Black neighborhood, where, like them, many of their neighbors were multiracial.

Adapting to this new world must have been challenging, but their mother would be arriving soon to help them navigate it. After two years in Massachusetts, maybe they had their own ideas about the kind of lives they wanted to live.

IN 1860, MARY Lumpkin joined her older four children and some fifty-seven thousand Black residents in Pennsylvania, long a magnet for formerly enslaved people who had been freed and for those seeking freedom.

After so many years of trying to protect her children, she was finally free. What did it feel like to her? Harriet Tubman recalled her escape from slavery in Maryland to Pennsylvania this way: "When I found I had crossed that line, I looked at my hands to see if I was the same person. There was such a glory over everything; the sun came like gold through the trees, and over the fields, and I felt like I was in Heaven."

What was it like for Mary when she arrived? Was the reality what she expected? Tubman recalled that when she made her way to Philadelphia, "I was free, but there was no one to welcome me to the land of freedom. I was a stranger in a strange land."

The neighborhood where Mary Lumpkin and her children lived, the Seventh Ward, would later be memorialized by the American sociologist W.E.B. Du Bois as the heart of Philadelphia's vibrant and economically diverse Black community. When Mary Lumpkin arrived, fewer than one-third of the Black men and women living in the Seventh Ward had been born in Philadelphia. After Pennsylvania natives, Virginia-born residents made up the majority of the neighborhood's Black population.

Du Bois referred to Pennsylvania as "the natural gateway between the North and the South." Free Black men and women and enslaved people escaping slavery crossed its border as they headed north, and many of them made their way to Philadelphia via Lancaster County. At the same time, enslaved people and free Black people were being kidnapped there and shipped south to be re-enslaved. Despite its inherent risks, many enslaved people believed that Philadelphia offered more opportunities to hide than most Eastern cities.

As early as the 1700s, there were so many multiracial people living in Philadelphia that one neighborhood was nicknamed "Mulatto Hall." Some white people perceived the growing multiracial population as threatening, however, prompting Pennsylvania leaders in 1725 to enact a law prohibiting interracial marriages. It would not be repealed until 1780.

As the size of the multiracial population skyrocketed in Philadelphia and wider Pennsylvania, their numbers were decreasing in Maryland, Delaware, and Virginia. Black and multiracial people tended to live in separate wards, and the largest concentration of wealthy multiracial people was found in the Seventh Ward, where over 11 percent of the residents were Black or multiracial. The population included descendants of refugees of the Haitian Revolution, formerly enslaved people from the South, and a generation of children born from mixed-race marriages in Philadelphia.

The Lumpkin children probably attended school in Philadelphia with children who looked like them and who had similar life stories. The 1860 Philadelphia census identified all four as white—a designation made by the census enumerator, not the person being counted.

PART OF PHILADELPHIA'S attraction for Black refugees was the city's potent history of abolitionism.

The first wave of abolitionists in the city were Quakers. Presbyterians also played a role in making the city hospitable to Black men and women by freeing the people they enslaved by the 1760s. Some seventy-five enslaved people were emancipated in Philadelphia through wills between 1741 and 1770, and hundreds more were freed in the 1770s by Quakers and other Philadelphians inspired by their actions. In 1775, a group of mostly Quaker men established the Pennsylvania Abolition Society in a Philadelphia tavern, and it became the most famous abolitionist society of the eighteenth and nineteenth centuries.

As the American Revolution came to a close, antislavery sentiment spread further, the result, in part, of abolitionists appealing to people's religious convictions and comparing the enslavement of Black men and women with Britain's hold on the colonies under its rule. In 1780, Pennsylvania became the southernmost state to abolish slavery when the Pennsylvania Congress passed the Gradual Emancipation Act in response to lobbying by Anthony Benezet, a French Huguenot who had emigrated from London and become a Quaker activist.

The act, intended to grant free Black men and women equal legal status, prohibited the importation and sale of enslaved people, but it did not free anyone who was already enslaved. The Gradual Emancipation Act also stipulated that all children born to enslaved people after March 1, 1780, though they would not be enslaved, would be indentured servants until they turned twenty-eight years old.

Enslaved Black men and women living in Pennsylvania learned the details of the law and figured out how to use it to their advantage. The act required that enslavers register all enslaved people with the state; any unregistered enslaved person would automatically become free. Enslaved people brought into the state would become free after six months. Enslavers could convert the enslavement to indentured servitude or remove the enslaved people from Pennsylvania before the six months ran out. George Washington routinely took the people he enslaved out of Philadelphia, where the US capital was located during his presidency, in order to keep them enslaved.

In 1796, one of the women Washington enslaved ran away from the executive residence in Philadelphia. Born at Mount Vernon around 1774, Ona Judge was the daughter of Betty, an enslaved seamstress, and was assigned to wait on Martha Washington, bathing and dressing her. With the help of free Black friends, Judge escaped while the Washingtons were packing to return to Virginia for the summer, and much to George Washington's frustration, he was never able to recapture her.

Enslaved people whose enslavers failed to register them appealed to authorities and were freed. Enslavers from out of state sometimes learned that the people they enslaved had been set free by law when it was already too late to register them. Other enslaved people negotiated with their enslavers in order to become indentured servants.

In the wake of the act, an organized network for helping enslaved people escape had begun to take shape. George Washington referenced it in two letters in 1786. He claimed that an enslaved person escaped to Philadelphia and that "a society of Quakers in the city, formed for such purposes, have attempted to liberate" the man.

About the same time, in 1787, Pennsylvania developed antikidnapping laws. Gradual emancipation was ineffective in some ways because it was difficult to differentiate between a free Black man and an enslaved one, and the laws could be manipulated by white men. Yet the act resulted in profound change for many Black residents and reduced the number of enslaved people in Pennsylvania from 6,855 in 1780 to 3,760 a decade later. As enslavers set free the people they enslaved in the 1780s, Philadelphia boasted the largest urban free Black population in the nation, with nearly 2,000 free Black men and women living there by 1790.

Some hearts and minds were changing. The enslaver Benjamin Franklin, who had published advertisements for slave sales in his *Pennsylvania Gazette*, became an opponent of slavery after the US Constitution was ratified in 1787. He was named president of the Pennsylvania Society for Promoting the Abolition of Slavery and the Pennsylvania Abolition Society, which worked to abolish slavery and integrate free Black men and women into American society, and in 1790 he sent the first Congress a petition asking for slavery to be abolished nationwide and for an end to the slave trade. Congress took no action before he died that year.

Black children also had access to education in Pennsylvania that they didn't have in other states. In 1750, Anthony Benezet, who taught white children during the day, began teaching Black children at his home in the evenings. He encouraged the Quakers to start a school for Black children, and they opened their first one in 1770. The Bray Associates, an Anglican philanthropic society founded in 1724, opened a small school in 1758 to educate both free and enslaved Black children.

In 1793, the Pennsylvania Abolitionist Society opened another school for free Black children and hired Eleanor Harris, an African-born woman, as schoolmistress. The Pennsylvania Abolition Society's education committee decided to build its own school for Black children that could accommodate 130 students. Clarkson Hall, named for the British abolitionist Thomas Clarkson, opened in 1813 with an enrollment of ninety-four boys of elementary school age. A female teacher, Elizabeth Clendenin, operated a school for girls with help from the Pennsylvania Abolitionist Society.

At the turn of the century, slavery was beginning to fade away in Pennsylvania. By 1808, some of the children born in Pennsylvania to enslaved people had become free through the Gradual Emancipation Act. These newly free Black men and women made their way to Philadelphia, along with a steady stream of immigrants. Between 1820 and 1830, the state's Black population would grow 25 percent, to 15,600. That year, only eleven Black men and women were enslaved in Philadelphia.

A NEW WAVE of Pennsylvania abolitionism coincided with the growth in the Black population. Black men and women turned their focus to assisting enslaved people in other states who were trying to get free. A more aggressive form of antislavery action, this wave of abolitionism attracted many Pennsylvania Abolition Society members.

Black women were also playing a role in the antislavery movement. When the Philadelphia Female Anti-Slavery Society was founded in 1833, ten of its forty-two charter members were Black, making it the first integrated female abolitionist group in America. Charlotte Vandine Forten, wife of the wealthy Black abolitionist James Forten, who financed the publication of Garrison's *Liberator*, and their three daughters, Margaretta Forten, Sarah Louise Forten Purvis, and Harriet Forten Purvis, were among its members.

Amy Hester "Hetty" Reckless and Mary Virginia Wood Forten, the mother of the poet Charlotte Forten, were two of the members who had been enslaved. In Philadelphia, Reckless set up a safe house that served as a stop on the Underground Railroad. She also promoted school and vocational training for enslaved people and established a Black women's shelter. Grace Bustill Douglass was the daughter of Cyrus Bustill, who had baked bread for George Washington's army during the Revolutionary War. Bustill, born enslaved, was a founding member of the Free African Society, and in 1803 he had established a school for Black children in his home. Grace Bustill Douglass's daughter, Sarah Mapps Douglass, joined the organization and would open a school for Black children in 1820.

The Quaker minister Lucretia Coffin Mott, a white friend of the Purvises and a suffragette, was a founding member who is credited with organizing the society. Another member was Angelina Grimké, a wealthy white woman who was among the first women to speak publicly against slavery. Her brother fathered three enslaved sons with an enslaved woman, Nancy Weston, whom Grimké would acknowledge. The society circulated abolition petitions, held public meetings, and raised funds. Members provided food, clothing, and shelter to enslaved people who were escaping slavery and helped them get to the next location on their way to freedom.

William Purvis, a wealthy English cotton merchant, had moved his family from Charleston to Philadelphia in 1819, seeking more opportunity for his three sons, who had been born to a free Black woman, Harriet Judah. She was the daughter of Dido Badaracka, who had been kidnapped in Morocco as a girl. Purvis and Judah's sons attended the Clarkson School. When he died in 1826, he left his children a great fortune.

In 1833, William's son Robert Purvis, husband of Harriet Forten Purvis, helped William Lloyd Garrison found the American Anti-Slavery Society in Philadelphia, which called for immediate abolition. Four years later, Robert Purvis joined with other Philadelphia Black men and women to form the Vigilant Association of Philadelphia to help people escaping slavery. The Purvis home had a secret room for hiding enslaved people who were escaping slavery.

By the early 1850s, the group had been reborn as the Vigilance Committee, and William Still, perhaps the most important figure in the Underground Railroad, became its chairman. The organization helped hundreds of Black men and women who had escaped slavery get farther north, including Henry Box Brown.

Tensions with whites rose as Philadelphia's Black population grew and Black men and women established community groups and businesses. Free Black people had trouble landing jobs, and educational opportunities were limited. Because most churches and owners of meetinghouses refused to rent their facilities for antislavery gatherings, white and Black abolitionists teamed up to build a large meeting hall. More than two thousand people invested in a joint stock company to build Pennsylvania Hall, while others donated materials and labor. When construction was completed on May 14, 1838, the facility housed abolitionist offices, a produce store, an antislavery reading room, the antislavery newspaper, and several meeting and lecture rooms.

Residents who blamed abolitionists for the city's growing Black population and the competition for jobs spread rumors of racial "amalgamation" and inappropriate behavior at the hall. Days after the opening, a meeting of women at an antislavery conference inside the hall was about to begin when a crowd gathered outside threw bricks through the windows. The attack escalated, and the doors were broken down by a white mob that entered the hall and set it on fire. Firefighters who arrived on the scene only sprayed water on the surrounding buildings. The $40,000 Pennsylvania Hall was destroyed in the ensuing race riot, one of five in Philadelphia between 1828 and 1849 that also ruined Black homes and businesses.

The night after the destruction of Pennsylvania Hall—a place designed to discuss the evils of slavery—mobs of white people burned an orphanage for Black children under construction by Quakers ten blocks away. They also damaged Bethel Church, assaulted Black men and women, and looted homes.

In the aftermath, some white residents claimed that those responsible for the damage and violence were "strangers." Pennsylvania Hall managers also asserted that "the destruction of our Hall by a mob is not a true exponent of the sentiments of the citizens of Philadelphia." The practice of white people explaining away violence against their Black neighbors has been utilized throughout American history, notably during the civil rights era of the mid-twentieth century and the Black Lives Matter movement. Those who burned Pennsylvania Hall included local laborers, professionals, and merchants, yet the police report blamed abolitionists, claiming that their views and encouragement of "race mixing" had incited violence.

Black men and women continued to move to Philadelphia, in spite of the race riots, and some Black residents were prospering. There was an increase in Black ownership of real estate, including churches and benevolent societies, libraries, building and loan associations, insurance companies, labor unions, and branches of fraternal organizations.

Yet while some Black men and women were prospering, there was a huge divide between the wealthier Black residents and the newly free people who had escaped slavery. Nearly half of the city's Black population—45 percent—were illiterate. Many women worked as domestics, seamstresses, fruit huskers, or laundresses, while Black men worked as mariners, day laborers, carpenters, shoemakers, and tailors.

Officials sought equality for the newly free Black people, some of whom had little personal freedom as indentured servants. By 1847, Pennsylvania secured the right of judicial inquiry for its citizens, enabling Black people to complain about misconduct. As Mary Lumpkin was buying her home in Philadelphia, Pennsylvania residents were working to get a law passed to "put an end to all slaveholding." A bill was introduced on February 14, 1859, but it was never brought to a vote, perhaps because John Brown's raid on the federal arsenal at Harper's Ferry, Virginia, intervened that October.

Some free Black people had become more radicalized in the aftermath of the Supreme Court's *Dred Scott* ruling. The decision had convinced abolitionists that slavery would not be ended by legislative or court action. They were ready to resort to violence to secure freedom for enslaved people.

In 1859, just as the Lumpkin children were settling into Philadelphia and abolitionists in the state were working to pass a strong personal liberty law, the white abolitionist John Brown was preparing to raid a Virginia town 170 miles away.

The struggle between the North and the South about extending slavery to the new territories left proslavery advocates in the South frustrated by what they considered "repeated unconstitutional aggressions" by Northern state governments on the rights of enslavers. Brown, with the help of his sons and a small group of supporters, including free Black men, planned to create a new free state in Virginia governed by a constitution he would write. He reasoned that if slavery could be driven out of a single state, the system of slavery would be weakened.

Brown spent more than a decade planning the action, using Chambersburg, Pennsylvania, as his staging ground. He posed as the owner of a mining operation so that shipments of guns could be sent to him. Brown also spent time in Philadelphia, working to help free enslaved people and living in the home of the Black artist David Bustill Bowser, the grandson of Cyrus Bustill.

Brown and his sons moved to Kansas in 1855 as part of the Free-Soiler movement, which was working to keep it a free state. In May 1856, Charles Sumner, the abolitionist senator from Massachusetts, gave a five-hour speech on the Senate floor, railing against the proslavery views of two fellow senators. Two days later, Sumner was savagely beaten in the chamber by House member Preston Brooks of South Carolina. It would take him years to recover from the serious injuries. A few days after Sumner was attacked, founders of the antislavery town of Lawrence, Kansas, were attacked by proslavery fighters in the "Sacking of Lawrence." Brown and his sons retaliated, killing five men in Pot-tawattomie Creek in Franklin County, earning the territory the nickname "Bleeding Kansas."

Brown chose Virginia's mountains as the passageway in and out of Harper's Ferry. The Underground Railroad operator Harriet Tubman had traveled this route when she escaped enslavement, and she would help others do the same. To find financing, Brown traveled north in May 1858 to meet with abolitionist supporters known as the "Secret Six," a group that included Thomas Wentworth Higginson, the minister who had tried to help Anthony Burns escape. At least one member of the group believed that Brown's plan was doomed to failure, yet the group set out to raise money to support him. While they attempted to distract authorities who had learned of his plans for a raid on the artillery, Brown went to Kansas, and later that year he attacked two proslavery settlements in Missouri. He freed twelve enslaved people and then escorted them to freedom, marching thousands of miles and putting them on a ferry to Canada.

Brown worked to create bonds with radicalized free Black people by meeting with members of Masonic lodges, attending Black churches, and connecting with Underground Railroad sources. In Philadelphia, he met with potential allies from the Frank Johnson Guards, a militia company formed by Black men. During the summer of 1859, the night before a parade was scheduled in Philadelphia, one of Brown's lieutenants gave a speech commending "the Negroes of Philadelphia for organizing a military company and stated that there was a grand project on foot to invade the South with an army of northern Negroes and free the slaves." This speech set off alarm bells among authorities, and John Brown urged local leaders to hold off talking about his raid on the day of the parade for fear that his plans would be uncovered.

A few months later, Brown met with Dangerfield Newby, a Virginia-born, formerly enslaved man. Newby's white father, Henry Newby, had moved to Ohio in 1858 with his children and their enslaved mother, Elsey Pollard, in order to free them all, but Dangerfield Newby's wife,

Harriet Newby, and his children with her were still enslaved in Virginia. Dangerfield Newby worked as a blacksmith to save money to free them, but when her Warrenton, Virginia, enslaver refused to sell her, he joined Brown's "black raiders"—a group of Black men supporting Brown's efforts.

In a series of letters to her husband, Harriet Newby expressed her love for her husband and described her fears of being sold. "Dear Dangerfield, come this fall without fail, money or no money, I want to see you so much," she wrote, "that is one bright hope I have before me nothing more at present but remain your affectionate wife."

Other Black men joined Brown's effort, including John Anthony Copeland Jr. from Oberlin and Osborne Perry Anderson, a free Black man living in Canada. Lewis Hayden tried to recruit more Black men in Boston, but only one of them, John Anderson, arrived in Harper's Ferry in time for the action. In August 1859, one of Brown's supporters, Henry Watson, a barber in Chambersburg, Pennsylvania, who had helped enslaved people get free, arranged a meeting at a quarry between Brown and Frederick Douglass. Shocked by Brown's focus on attacking the federal arsenal rather than on liberating enslaved people, Douglass would not support the raid. After the attack, Douglass fled to Canada and then England, where he had planned to do a series of lectures, in order to avoid being arrested and charged as an accomplice.

On October 16, 1859, Brown and his followers—including three of his sons—marched silently down a country road and, crossing a bridge at the Potomac River, seized the arsenal and occupied Harper's Ferry. A group of at least eighteen men rounded up hostages, including a few enslaved people. The revolt by enslaved people that Brown had anticipated would follow on these events never happened.

US Marines led by Brevet Colonel Robert E. Lee, who would become a Confederate hero during the Civil War, rushed to the site from Virginia. The following morning they surrounded Brown and his men, who were holed up inside the arsenal's firehouse, a small brick building. Dangerfield Newby, sent outside to guard the fort's entrance and fend off attackers, was shot by a sniper from the second floor of an adjacent building and became the first of Brown's men to die. His wife's desperate yet hopeful letters were found on his body. Just as she feared, she and her children were sold south to Louisiana, perhaps by Robert Lumpkin, Silas Omohundro, Hector Davis, or one of their Richmond slave trader colleagues.

When Brown refused to surrender following Lee's conditions, Marines descended on the building, arresting Brown and killing two of his sons. A total of sixteen men died in the raid—ten of them John Brown's men. Five escaped, including Osborne Anderson, who walked through the Virginia mountains to Pennsylvania and then took trains to Canada.

Brown was sentenced to death, and Virginia governor Henry Wise chose to carry out the sentence, ensuring that Brown would become a martyr. Thomas Wentworth Higginson, one of Brown's Boston supporters, considered but ultimately did not attempt to kidnap Wise to save Brown. On December 2, 1859, Brown was executed on the gallows in Charles Town, in front of fifteen hundred armed guards. "I, John Brown," he wrote in a note left behind in his cell, "am now quite certain that the crimes of this guilty land will never be purged away but with blood."

As the country inched closer to civil war, Northerners and Southerners were already killing each other over slavery. While some historians have considered Brown's raid a failure, he did accomplish one of his goals—working together with Black abolitionists. At a speech at the HBCU Storer College in Harper's Ferry in 1881, Frederick Douglass cast Brown as a champion of liberty.

"If John Brown did not end the war that ended slavery," Douglass said, "he did at least begin the war that ended slavery."

Sixteen months after the uprising at Harper's Ferry, a war between the North and the South was under way.

WHEN MARY LUMPKIN arrived in Philadelphia with her youngest child in the summer of 1860, she joined a community of women in a similar position—women she already knew who were the mothers of mixed-race children of Virginia enslavers and slave traders, and who were probably friends.

Silas Omohundro bought a house about a mile away from Mary Lumpkin's and relocated Silas Jr. and Alice Morton from Lancaster in about 1858. The children were being educated, either attending school or being privately tutored. A piano teacher, Mary G. Davis, lived with the Omohundro children. Corinna Hinton Omohundro apparently moved there or stayed sometimes.

The next year, Hector Davis had purchased a brick house on Lombard Street, around the corner from Mary Lumpkin's. By June 1860, Ann Banks Davis was living in the house with three of their four young children: Audubon, Matilda, and Victoria. It's not clear where Virginia, or Jennie, was when the census was conducted. Ann Banks Davis couldn't read or write, but the children were enrolled in school, possibly a Quaker one.

The Davis and Lumpkin children lived steps apart and may have attended school together or been taught by the same tutor. They took music lessons, perhaps using the piano the Lumpkins acquired, and the children likely played in the same parks. Perhaps the women and their children gathered in each other's houses, sharing meals and swapping stories about their new lives.

Perhaps Robert Lumpkin and Hector Davis had enough resources that the mothers of their children did not have to work. In 1859, Hector Davis's slave trading business had sold enslaved people with a market value of $2.67 million—more than the value of all the flour shipped out of Richmond that year. Maybe the women joined Black churches, which set expectations about how they should behave and provided shape to their lives as they sought to remake the image of Black men and women into one of upstanding citizens.

In Philadelphia, they were alone together navigating a new city and newfound freedom. Harriet Barber, although illiterate, may have been able to provide some advice as they tried to find ways to fit in and build better lives for themselves and for their children.

What must it have been like to live in a neighborhood surrounded by other multiracial people, some of whom had similar origin stories? They may have wished to keep their relationships with white slave traders to themselves. Perhaps feeling that they couldn't tell anyone else about what had happened to them, they erased pieces of themselves in order to make life work in the North.

But around each other, they could be their true selves, confiding in one another and commiserating about their shared experiences. They knew what it was like to be chosen by a slave trader and have his children. And now they were finding out what it was like to be freed by him.

BLACK WOMEN MADE up the majority of Philadelphia's Black population, and they outnumbered Black men 11,300 to 8,400 in 1859. A good many of them may have been in the same situation as Mary Lumpkin—sent north alone by white men who impregnated them and wished to protect their children. In Pennsylvania, their lives were particularly regulated.

Without inherited family wealth or reputation, most Black women in Philadelphia worked. Erica Armstrong Dunbar notes that "freedom arrived by degrees" for Black men and women in Pennsylvania, and that women were among its last recipients.

Black men and women in Philadelphia had worked strenuously to be perceived as reliable and respectable neighbors, and they considered these hard-won reputations crucial to succeeding in the city. They were suspicious of the goals of the American Colonization Society, established in 1816 in Washington, DC, to promote Black migration to western Africa and to Liberia in particular. The society suggested that Black men and women would never be full citizens in the United States, foreshadowing the *Dred Scott* decision.

In the early 1800s, as more Black schools were being founded in Philadelphia, Black women formed mutual aid societies to help each other move from enslavement to freedom. The first one in America was Richard Allen and Absalom Jones's Free African Society of Philadelphia, which welcomed as members men and women who led "orderly and sober" lives. By the 1820s, free Black women had begun to adopt "Christian ideals of piety, sobriety, and industry," values that were important to white women. Reform movements of the early nineteenth century worked to improve morals, as interpreted by whites, within the Black community.

As Black life in Philadelphia was centered on churches and denominational affiliations, aid societies were connected to churches, and they provided social networks for Black women as well as financial support. The associations assisted Black women, many of whom were new to freedom after a lifetime of enslavement, enabling them to provide food for their families, help sick family members, and pay for burials of children and spouses.

More than sixty of the organizations were founded in Philadelphia, and many women belonged to more than one. Perhaps Mary Lumpkin, through her social connections in her neighborhood, was able to join at least one. The organizations required members to pay dues, which blocked poor Black women from joining, but Robert Lumpkin may have provided enough funds for Mary Lumpkin to afford membership.

The mutual aid organizations were designed "not only to assist the community, but also to chaperone it," writes Dunbar. While helping Black women by providing them with education and financial support, these organizations also monitored the activities of their communities. They expected Black women to behave properly in public—an expectation that surely extended to newly free Black women like Mary Lumpkin.

Women were instructed to avoid cursing, fighting, being drunk in public, and adultery. At Mother Bethel, Richard Allen and several male church leaders headed a disciplinary committee that met to listen to members discuss troubles at home. Their beliefs set the values that regulated the lives of Black females.

Both Black women and men were worried about not meeting the organizations' standards and feared social isolation and disconnection from any mutual aid or social associations. Little public assistance was offered to Black residents, and anyone pushed out of their church could land in poverty.

The Female Benevolent Society of St. Thomas, the Daughters of Africa, and the African Female Band ostracized those who didn't meet their expectations for ethical behavior. Those who drank or got in public fights "were not welcomed or supported," Dunbar writes. The Free African Society monitored the personal lives of all of Philadelphia's Black residents but paid special attention to its members. A Committee of Monitors made surprise visits to members' houses to ensure that they acted morally at home.

Belonging to one of these organizations provided a path for Black women to reach respectability and gave them an opportunity to mother Philadelphia's Black community. Though enslavement had robbed Black women of the chance to raise their own children as they would have wanted, they could take on mothering roles in their churches and social organizations, redefining themselves, Dunbar argues.

"Black women attempted a large task to transform the image of Black Philadelphia, with the desire of attaining respectability and the rights of citizenship," she writes.

What might it have meant to Mary Lumpkin, a religious woman, to practice her faith with other Black people, without the oversight of a white preacher who looked the other way when members of his congregation were sold? What did it mean to be part of a community of Black women?

MARY LUMPKIN IS listed in the 1861 Philadelphia city directory as Robert Lumpkin's widow, which may have been the story she told people. In fact, Robert Lumpkin was in Richmond, still running his slave jail.

That year, Hector Davis, an auctioneer, was in Richmond living with the Kentucky slave trader Newton M. Lee, who ran a slave jail on Franklin Street, and his wife, Maria Jane Lee, and their family.

Silas Omohundro was boarding the slave traders Leonard T. Slater and Thomas M. Jones, who were in business together. The census enumerator surmised that "Corinna Hinton, 32," lived next door with her sons, five-year-old Colon and one-year-old Riley Crosby, but it is likely that she and Silas Omohundro lived together. A sixty-year-old Patsy Clark, whom Silas Omohundro may have hired or enslaved to help Corinna Hinton Omohundro, also lived with her.

Robert Lumpkin and Hector Davis were preparing to found Traders' Bank of the City of Richmond, probably to help finance their slave trading. Davis was elected president, and Lumpkin was a superintendent. The state legislature approved the establishment of the bank in 1860, and the *Richmond Daily Dispatch* declared that Traders' Bank and other new banks "will add considerably to the banking capital of Richmond, and give a new impulse to trade and our manufacturing enterprises."

In February 1860, the state legislature incorporated the Traders' Bank of the City of Richmond. The commissioners of the bank included many of the traders in Lumpkin's circle, including Thomas M. Jones and William H. Betts, who once owned Lucy Ann Hagan.

The bank was organized in Richmond in April and had capital of $1 million. The *Daily Dispatch* reported in May 1860 that one-quarter of the subscriptions to the stock of another new banking enterprise, Bank of Richmond, had been made by people living outside of Virginia, many of them in New York. The Bank of Richmond was also predicted to open soon.

"We see that capital is coming from abroad to be employed in commerce in Richmond, and we see, moreover, that through these subscriptions to our bank stock a number of citizens residing elsewhere are to become interested in the prosperity of this place," the *Daily Dispatch* reported.

Perhaps these Northern investors were less interested in Richmond's prosperity than in its investments in slavery. In August 1860, Virginia governor John Letcher authorized Traders' Bank to begin operations, noting that it had raised $301,100 in subscriptions through $100 shares.

The bank issued $50 banknotes that featured an enslaved man carrying a basket of cotton. The $20 banknotes depicted an enslaved man picking cotton, a woman spinning thread, and Henry Clay, the US senator from Kentucky.

Less than a year later, the Civil War was under way. In March 1861, the Confederate States of America would begin printing its own money. Both its bills and the Traders' Bank notes would be worthless when the war was over.

President Abraham Lincoln visited Richmond on April 2, 1865, two days after the Confederacy evacuated its capital. Newly free Black Richmonders flocked to him as he toured the still-smoldering city, as depicted in a drawing by J. Becker. (Library of Congress)

8

Capital of the Confederacy

By the time Abraham Lincoln was elected president on November 6, 1860, and the Southern states were amping up talk of secession, Mary Lumpkin and her five children were safely ensconced in Philadelphia.

Robert Lumpkin may have visited them there. Perhaps he even considered moving north to be with Mary Lumpkin and his children, as Bacon Tait had done. Robert Lumpkin may have wanted to follow the model of the traders Isaac Franklin and John Armfield, who in 1836 walked away from their slave jail while their slave trading business was still enormously profitable. But it is unlikely that Robert Lumpkin had made anywhere near the money Franklin and Armfield had.

Although Virginia had gone from holding 45 percent of enslaved people in the country in 1790 to 12 percent in 1860, it still had the largest population of enslaved people in the country. Over the years, however, the state had lost its position of power as the center of Southern politics. Plantation owners and farmers had migrated south, and enormous numbers of enslaved people had been sold to other states.

Leaders in the Lower South didn't want to be subject to the Lincoln administration and had for years considered whether they could count on Virginia to support their position. In 1857, the *New Orleans Delta* warned that "Virginia is not fully awake as she should be to the great question of Southern interests."

"The Slave South proper—the Cotton States—must look to themselves alone for defense," wrote the *Charleston Mercury*.

What exactly were they defending? The right to continue purchasing and selling children.

Virginia had acquired great wealth when the value of its enslaved citizens rose as they became the backbone of the cotton states' economy. The power dynamic shifted when enslavers in the Lower South accumulated more wealth—and enslaved people—than the Upper South. Suddenly, the Lower South found it was more independent.

In December 1860, the legislature of South Carolina met and voted to secede from the United States of America. Six others states—Mississippi, Florida, Alabama, Georgia, Louisiana, and Texas—soon decided to join South Carolina, and their representatives met in Montgomery, Alabama, in February 4, 1861, to establish a separate government, the Confederate States of America.

When Virginia's Secession Convention occurred nine days later in Richmond, most Virginia delegates opposed secession at first, because they believed that slavery would be protected if the United States stayed together. As talk of secession heightened, some leaders in Virginia, as well as in North Carolina, Arkansas, and Tennessee, began to recognize the benefits of aligning with the Lower South and determined that it was better to leave the United States than to risk the collapse of their slave-driven economy. Property owners in the Upper South relied on the traffic of enslaved people to fund the operation of their farms and plantations, which they dreamed of making profitable again, and they worried about losing the people they enslaved.

The newly formed Confederacy attacked the federal Fort Sumter in Charleston, South Carolina, on April 12, 1861, beginning the Civil

War. After it fell, Jefferson Davis, the provisional president of the Confederacy, sent his vice president, Alexander H. Stephens, to Virginia to urge the commonwealth to secede. Stephens gave a version of his "Cornerstone Speech," explaining that the new government was the first to be founded on the idea that Black people were inferior to whites.

Following months of debate, the Secession Convention voted to secede on April 17, 1861. A few weeks later, on May 23, 1861, Virginia voters ratified the ordinance of secession.

AFTER VIRGINIA SECEDED, officials offered Richmond as the capital of the Confederacy. It was clear to Confederate leaders that Montgomery—too small and too isolated—would not be an effective capital.

Richmond was a hub for military and government operations, as well as hospitals and prisons, and its industrial powers made it a good fit. By then, the city had more than fifty tobacco manufacturers, a dozen flour mills, a distillery, and a brewery. It was the iron center of the South, with four rolling mills, fourteen foundries, and fifty iron and metal works lining the James River. The Confederate government would need these Richmond companies to manufacture heavy ordnance and iron cladding for naval vessels and bullets. It would also need plenty of enslaved labor, which was abundant in Richmond.

While Richmond's location a hundred miles from Washington, DC, put it at risk of attack and capture, it was also clear to Confederate leaders that Richmond's resources needed to be protected.

Even before the Confederacy decided on May 24 to relocate its capital to Richmond, volunteers poured into the city. John B. Jones, a clerk in the War Department of the Confederacy, noticed as he approached Richmond that "every hour there are fresh arrivals of organized companies from the country." Jones wrote in *A Rebel War Clerk's Diary*: "Martial music is heard everywhere, day and night. . . . The ladies are sewing everywhere, even in the churches." While they were busy making uniforms, Northern merchants took to Richmond streets, collecting debts that were owed to them.

Before the war, Richmond had a population of thirty-eight thousand. More than eleven thousand of them were enslaved. The city's population quickly ballooned to as many as one hundred thousand as ten thousand to fifteen thousand troops poured into the city. Government officials came to work in the War Department, and others arrived seeking jobs that war would bring, among them free Black people from all over the South. The city was transformed into an enormous camp, with hotels and boarding-houses filled to capacity. Visitors slept anywhere they could, including on top of billiard tables. The arrival of so many men brought shootings, fights, and prostitution. Soon, injured soldiers would be arriving in the city too, filling up local hospitals created to treat them.

Jane Arrington, enslaved in North Carolina, recalled learning that the North was fighting the South because Northerners had determined that enslaved people had to be free. "De papers said if dey could not be freedom by good men dere would be freedom by blood," she recalled.

The day after Virginia seceded from the United States, federal troops swarmed Alexandria. As the troops took control of the city, they seized the old Franklin and Armfield slave jail and the slave trader Joseph Bruin, its owner since 1844. On the floor of the jail, troops found letters written between slave traders from 1837 to 1857, excerpts of which were published in the *New-York Daily Tribune* on July 15, 1861. Thomas Boudar of New Orleans wrote to his partner George Kephart: "You ask . . . for information about little boys and girls," Boudar wrote. "All I can say is that they are always ready sale, but they must be purchased right or they do not pay much profit."

In Alexandria and St. Louis, slave jails were converted to prisons for Confederate soldiers and civilians, leading one inmate to complain about being held in "a horrible place." The "Forks of the Road" slave market at Natchez, Mississippi, became a gathering place for Black men and women seeking freedom and the protection that Union soldiers could provide. In Richmond, slave jails met a variety of fates. Bacon Tait's jail operated as a Confederate jail for punishing enslaved people. Another slave jail on Lumpkin's Alley, the thirteen-room McDaniel's

Jail, became known as "Castle Godwin" and was used to house Union prisoners.

Robert Lumpkin's jail did not get converted. He continued working in the slave trade, seemingly unabated, selling enslaved people through the jail. "FOR SALE PRIVATELY_A No 1 HOUSE BOY. Apply at LUMPKIN'S JAIL," read an advertisement in the *Daily Dispatch* in 1861.

He was also holding runaways for other enslavers. George W. Parker placed a newspaper advertisement in December 1861 requesting help finding a twenty-one-year-old man he had enslaved. Parker asked that "my boy Frederick," who had run away from coal mines in rural Virginia, be taken to Lumpkin's Jail if he was recovered, "so that I get him again." Parker offered a $25 reward.

Once the war was under way, life for enslaved people in Richmond became more restrictive. For years, many of them had been allowed to choose their employers, live independently, and socialize with free Black people. Confederate government officials, however, feared that Black men and women would plan a rebellion and revoked many privileges in order to more closely monitor their activities. Leaders passed ordinances prohibiting enslaved people from living away from their enslavers, which effectively ended informal hiring practices.

These rules would soon be relaxed because the Confederacy needed the labor of enslaved people. The Confederate War Department also hired out some enslaved men, paying the enslavers for work, not the enslaved. They labored in government warehouses, tanning yards, and hospitals, and Black women did laundry and cooked in government hospitals. Many enslaved people had to take on more jobs and responsibilities—a cook also became a washwoman and an ironer.

Lumpkin and other slave traders may have agreed to rent to the Confederacy any enslaved people who were available. Others were taken, or impressed, to do jobs the Confederacy needed done. Even from the early days of the war, the Confederacy did not have enough workers, and it seized enslaved people from farms to dig trenches and build reinforcements. The Richmond mayor's police force picked up Black people from city streets for pass violations and then turned them over to Confederate authorities. By 1862, the Confederate government was the largest "employer" of enslaved people.

During the war, slave traders were still brazenly dealing in children too. Hector Davis placed advertisements in 1862 announcing the sale, at auction, of "a very likely young WOMAN and child, a qualified house servant. Also, a small GIRL, seven or eight years old." On December 12, 1862, multiple advertisements for the sale of children were published in the *Daily Dispatch*. One described an auction in a Charlottesville public square of "about 35 valuable SLAVES, consisting of Men, Women, Boys, and Girls."

The "Trustees of Buffalo Congregation" in Prince Edward County advertised a "SALE OF VALUABLE SLAVES" the same year on Christmas Day. That "One Man, three Lads, three Women, and ten Children under 12 years of age" were being sold away from their families by a church on the day of Christ's birth speaks to the church's level of culpability.

In the bedlam of war, many enslaved people saw an opportunity to escape and took it. They sought the protection of Union troops or headed to Hampton's Fort Monroe, the only federal military instillation in Virginia that was under Union control throughout the war. Union general Benjamin F. Butler referred to the first three escaped enslaved people to arrive as "contraband of war" and refused to return them to their enslavers, a decision that resulted in an enormous influx of enslaved people seeking freedom. The Union Army adopted a policy of providing wages, food, and clothing to formerly enslaved people in "contraband camps" throughout the Confederacy. Fort Monroe was transformed into "Freedom's Fortress," the heart of a Black revolution. Mary S. Peake, a free Black woman, started a school near the fort in September 1861, teaching fifty-three Black students during the day and twenty at night on land that would become the grounds of the HBCU Hampton University.

One of the enslaved boys working for Hector Davis escaped. His enslaver, N. F. Bowe, placed an advertisement offering a $50 reward for sixteen-year-old Joshua. The boy had "a variety of clothing but will probably put on soldiers' old clothes," and was "aiming for the Yankee camps," the *Daily Dispatch* advertisement read.

Mary Barbour's father saw his chance to free his family when Union troops raided the farm of his Avery, North Carolina, enslaver. He took the wagon and mules and headed for the nearby farm where his wife Edith and their young children were enslaved by Jefferson Mitchel, who had sold away twelve of the couple's children. Only Mary and her younger siblings, Henry and twins Liza and Charlie, remained. She remembered her dad waking her in the middle of the night, dressing her in the dark, and telling her to "keep quiet" as the family made its way to a Union camp.

Enslaved people also escaped from work at the Richmond and Danville Railroad Company. "It is supposed that these Negroes are employed in some of the camps, cooking for the soldiers," read an advertisement placed in 1862 by Chas. G. Talcott, the railroad superintendent.

Even children took the opportunity to run away. One advertisement from December 1862 sought a "bright mulatto girl, SALLY, about 13 years old; had on a dark blue dress." The girl may have had much in common with Mary Lumpkin and Robert Lumpkin's daughters, then free in Philadelphia.

WITHIN A YEAR of the war's beginning, the Union had entered the Mississippi River at its mouth in order to choke off Confederate shipping routes to New Orleans, suffocating the Southern economy and its largest site of cotton exportation.

The Union's April 1862 seizure of New Orleans, home to 168,000 people, was a significant blow to the Confederacy. "The rebels, in losing it, lose the most important and flourishing city in the South," reported a Northern paper.

As Confederate soldiers evacuated New Orleans, enslaved people began to flee their enslavers. Black women and their children were harassed but were prepared to defend themselves. They ran away from enslavers, refused to be beaten, and reclaimed their enslaved children.

General Butler, who had termed these escaped enslaved people "contraband" in Virginia, had a great need for Union troops, and he found employment for some of the Black people in New Orleans, where he was then stationed. Brigadier General John Wolcott Phelps, an abolitionist from Vermont, established Camp Parapet a mile upriver from New Orleans, and it welcomed several hundred formerly enslaved people, who arrived by summer. Phelps began to arm the Black men, laying the groundwork for the establishment of the first unit of the United States Colored Infantry, the 73rd Regiment.

President Abraham Lincoln issued the Emancipation Proclamation on January 1, 1863, a decision that allowed him to turn the newly free Black men into Union soldiers. The proclamation freed enslaved people in states that had seceded from the Union, but it allowed slavery to continue in border states. "All persons held as slaves" within the rebellious states "are, and henceforward shall be free," it read. Over the next two years, he would work to pass the Thirteenth Amendment to the Constitution, which ended slavery and involuntary servitude in the United States, "except as punishment for a crime." It was approved by the Senate in April 1864 and the House in January 1865, and Lincoln signed off on it February 1, 1865. He submitted the proposed amendment to state legislatures for ratification, and the required number of states ratified it in December 1865.

In the North, Frederick Douglass had long urged Lincoln to allow Black soldiers to enlist, in the hope that when Black troops were successful in battle it would undermine the belief held by some whites that Black men and women were inferior. Pennsylvania governor Andrew Curtin refused. When John Mercer Langston, a former Virginian who was an elected official in Ohio, encouraged Governor David Tod to recruit Black soldiers, Tod responded, "When we want you colored men, we will notify you."

The 54th Massachusetts Infantry, the first Black regiment in the North, was created in 1863 by abolitionist governor John A. Andrew. Lewis Hayden recruited Black men to join, and two of Frederick Douglass's sons, Charles and Lewis, enlisted. Sojourner Truth's grandson, James Caldwell, served in the 54th and would become a prisoner of war at James Island, South Carolina, between 1863 and 1865.

James Fountain Jr., a barber and relative of Courtney Fountain, the mother of Bacon Tait's children, enlisted in September 1864, was immediately transferred to the 55th Massachusetts Infantry, another Black regiment, and served in South Carolina. Langston and Leonard A. Grimes recruited for the unit, and volunteers came from New York, Indiana, Ohio, and Canada. In Ohio, John Malvin, an abolitionist who was born free in Virginia and, as a boat captain, helped many enslaved people escape, organized a Black military company that joined the 54th and 55th Massachusetts regiments.

Henry Watson, the Pennsylvania barber who helped enslaved people escape, served as a private in the 29th Connecticut Volunteer Infantry, Company E, as did James L. Saunders, the son of Warrenton, Virginia, slave trader Jourdan Saunders and Mary Wilkins, a free Black woman.

Osborne Anderson, who had survived as a volunteer in John Brown's raid, enlisted and served as a recruitment officer in Indiana and Arkansas. Thomas Wentworth Higginson, the white pastor who had attempted to free Anthony Burns, served as a captain in the 51st Massachusetts Infantry, and then later as a colonel in the First South Carolina Infantry Regiment, or Volunteers. Black men from the South Carolina and Georgia Sea Islands enlisted in this first regiment of enslaved men in the South. Harriet Tubman and Susie Baker King Taylor, a fourteen-year-old girl who escaped slavery, both served as nurses for the unit, and Taylor wrote a book about the experience.

By the time the war came to an end, one in ten Union troops was Black.

ONCE THE CIVIL War was under way, Silas Omohundro's children with Louisa Tandy Omohundro, who had lived as free in Ohio for years, enlisted in the Union Army to fight against their father's interests.

At the start of the war in 1861, Littleton J. Omohundro was working as a salesman and living with his mother. That year, when he was about twenty-three years old, he joined the Pearl Street Rifles, an Ohio regiment nicknamed "Neff's Detachment" for its leader, Colonel Peter Rudolph Neff. It did not face combat. His younger brother, twenty-year-old Sidney, joined the Fourth Ohio Volunteer Calvary after completing school in August 1862. His regiment was composed almost exclusively of young businessmen from Cincinnati and was known as the Union Dragoons or the Cincinnati Union Dragoons. It participated in the main battles of the West, as well as in General William T. Sherman's 1864 "March to the Sea" from Atlanta to Savannah. During the march, soldiers destroyed railroads, burned houses and barns, and ransacked farms for food and supplies while attempting to frighten Georgians into abandoning the Confederacy.

Both men joined white volunteer Union regiments before Lincoln allowed Black soldiers to enlist, an indication that they had probably been passing as white for years. The United States had not maintained a large army, and because many West Point–trained officers and cavalry had left to fight for the Confederacy, Lincoln had to seek seventy-five thousand volunteers for a three-month surge.

Thomas Jefferson's grandson with Sally Hemings also passed as white and fought against the Confederacy. John Wayles Jefferson, the oldest child of Eston Hemings, who had changed his last name to Jefferson, joined the Eighth Wisconsin Infantry Regiment as a major and fought in Mississippi and Louisiana. When he was promoted to colonel, he begged an acquaintance from Ohio who knew him as Black "not to tell the fact that he had colored blood in his veins, which he said was not suspected by any of his command." It's also possible that Harriet Barber's son, William H. Barber, and Mary Lumpkin and Robert Lumpkin's oldest son Robert enlisted.

Silas Omohundro had freed his enslaved son and the boy's mother only to see the young man and his brother, born free in Ohio, fighting against the values their father represented, against the beliefs that had resulted in their enslavement. Back in Virginia, dozens of Omohundros—both close and distant relatives of Silas Omohundro—fought with the Confederacy to preserve slavery.

WHILE LITTLETON OMOHUNDRO was fighting for the Union at the start of the Civil War, his half-brother Silas Omohundro Jr. contracted typhoid fever and died on December 4, 1861.

Three years earlier, Corinna Hinton Omohundro and Silas Omohundro had sent their nine-year-old son Silas Jr. to Pennsylvania to be educated and live as free. Silas and his younger sister, Alice Morton Omohundro, had not seen their father in years. "On account of pressing business engagements the father was unable to visit his offspring," read Silas Omohundro Jr.'s obituary in *The Star of the North*.

"Time wore on, the breaking out of the Southern rebellion cut off all communication between parent and children," the newspaper continued.

A. W. Rand, an attorney who served as the children's guardian, sent word to Union major general John E. Wool at Fort Monroe, asking that Silas Omohundro be informed of his son's death, but Rand did not receive a response to his letter. "It is not known whether the message was received or not, as no reply has yet been returned," the obituary read.

Two weeks after the death of Silas Omohundro Jr., the *Richmond Dispatch* ran a story noting that the boy was the son of a Richmond merchant but did not specify that the father was a slave trader and made no mention of the boy's mother. Rand "felt deeply pained at the death of his youthful ward, and adopted every proper means to pay the last tribute to the deceased," hiring an undertaker and buying multiple coffins to preserve the boy's body. One of the coffins "was rendered perfectly air-tight in order that the remains might be preserved, in case the father should at any time succeed in reaching this city."

The newspaper reported that none of the boy's relatives attended his funeral. His sister may have been deemed too young to go, or perhaps the newspaper wasn't aware of her presence. Reverend Henson, a Virginia acquaintance of Silas Omohundro who worked as a pastor at a Philadelphia Baptist church, attended the service after reading about the boy's death in the newspaper. Did Mary Lumpkin and Ann Banks Davis go to the funeral, and were they accompanied by any of their children?

The Philadelphia newspapers noted that "the funeral was very largely attended, which no doubt was caused by the peculiar circumstances of the case." Philadelphians would probably have found the case even more peculiar if they'd been informed that the deceased's father was a slave trader. The city's Black and abolitionist populations would surely have been interested to know that the boy had been born to an enslaved woman. But those details did not make it into the newspapers.

Silas Jr.'s body was interred at Laurel Hill Cemetery, a rural burial ground for elite Philadelphians where mayors, congressmen, and Army generals lay at rest. His body was placed in a vault owned by the doctor who cared for him.

It is unclear when, or if, Corinna Hinton Omohundro arrived in Philadelphia to visit her son's grave and to comfort Alice Morton, who would stay in Philadelphia and marry a white man. Perhaps Mary Lumpkin and Ann Banks Davis took the girl under their wing, supporting her through her loss until she could be reunited with family again.

DURING THE WAR years, Mary Lumpkin witnessed the courtship of her daughter Martha Lumpkin and George Edward Kelsey, a young man from South Carolina who had landed in Philadelphia by 1861.

Kelsey lived near the Lumpkin home, worked as a bartender, and would later be employed as a clerk. He may have arrived in Philadelphia by way of Boston, where an eighteen-year-old student named George Kelsey had been living six years earlier. Born about 1837 in South Carolina, the student George Kelsey boarded with the family of Thomas P. Knox, an abolitionist doctor from Ireland. Knox lived next door to the

Home for Aged, Colored Women, of which Leonard A. Grimes was a founder. Knox also helped enslaved people escape to Canada in 1855 via the Boston Vigilance Committee, and in 1857 he provided medical care for another enslaved person escaping slavery, allowing the woman to stay with his family.

Kelsey may have been the light-skinned son of an enslaver and an enslaved woman. Maybe he had been sent north to attend school, like the Lumpkin daughters, or perhaps he had fled enslavement. It's also possible he was white.

When Martha Lumpkin met Kelsey, her mother witnessed her daughter being courted—an experience she had never been able to have. Educated and free, Martha Lumpkin had the opportunity to choose who she would marry and who would be the father of her children. She may have been encouraged by Mary Lumpkin and others to marry someone as light-skinned as she was in order for her children to pass.

On November 2, 1862, as the Civil War raged, twenty-five-year-old Kelsey wed Martha Lumpkin, who, at sixteen, was marrying at a fairly typical age for women at the time. The couple must have passed as white, at least under some circumstances, because they were wed by a white pastor, Daniel March, from Massachusetts, at the white Clinton Street Presbyterian Church, which later joined with Immanuel Presbyterian Church. Marriage documents refer to her as white but do not mention Kelsey's race.

Was Mary Lumpkin able to attend the wedding or would her presence have given away that Martha Lumpkin was not white? Robert Lumpkin most likely was unable to travel north. It's unclear how much he knew about his daughter's union and whether he had worked to maintain a relationship with her after she left home.

Lewis Bonner, whose wife's father was her enslaver, recalled that her father stayed in touch with her and frequently sent money. "Before he died, he put her name in his will and told his oldest son to be sure and keep up with her. The son was sure true to his promise, for till she died, she was forever hearing from him or he would visit us," Bonner recalled.

The Kelsey newlyweds lived in Mary Lumpkin's house with her and her other children. The year after they married, they had a son, George—a child they soon had to bury. In death, at least, the family was Black. The boy's body was interred in 1864 at Olive Cemetery, a burial ground for Black Philadelphians, including the abolitionists James Forten and William Still and some four hundred soldiers in the US Colored Infantry. Harriet Barber's daughters were also buried in Olive Cemetery. When she died in 1864, she would be buried there too.

In the next decade, Martha Kelsey would have four more children, a daughter Anna, son Horace, daughter Aileen, and finally, another son named George. I traced some of Mary Lumpkin's descendants through Horace and Aileen. Martha Kelsey and at least one of her brothers, possibly Richard, made it possible for her family line—and that of Robert Lumpkin—to live on.

WHEN NEW ORLEANS fell, the domestic slave trade to its major port came to a halt. Perhaps Robert Lumpkin's trade became more local.

He is likely to have also taken in renters, as Richmond by then was "crowded to suffocation, with hardly standing room left." Hospitals were packed with injured soldiers, and thousands of Union soldiers were held as prisoners in tents year-round on Belle Isle, an island in the middle of the James River.

There were shortages of all kinds across the South, including clothing, medicine, and paper, but the food shortage, which extended to even the most common food items, was particularly alarming and "became increasingly serious as the war years dragged on," writes the historian Mary Elizabeth Massey.

The South's normal crops were in short supply because of drought and flooding during the war years, and farms east of Richmond that once provided food to the city were destroyed in battle. Because the Confederacy had impressed enslaved people, they weren't available to work the land. Tilling the soil was difficult because the farmers' horses and oxen had been stolen by both Union and Confederate troops. There wasn't even enough food to sustain cows and pigs. As one historian notes, "The Confederacy was always hungry."

The limited supply of food was depleted by the Confederate government, which confiscated produce from farmers and merchants to give to troops. Richmond merchants stockpiled food or dramatically marked up the prices. Some free Black residents were so desperate and hungry that they risked their freedom stealing food. By then, rats were in many people's diet.

"Everything is being so cleanly consumed that no garbage or filth can accumulate," one man wrote, adding that Richmond residents were "such good scavengers" that there was "no need for buzzards."

Richmond's food shortage lasted longer and was more severe than in any other Southern city because of its exponential population growth. Had it been able to access the amount of produce normally available, there still would not have been enough to feed the increased population.

Famine set in after a massive snowstorm made the roads into Richmond impassible and further limited food supplies to city markets. In response, a group of women led bread riots on April 2, 1863. The riots came on the heels of a March explosion at Tredegar Iron Works, which produced artillery for the war. Sixty-nine workers were killed, all but seven of them women. A mob of one hundred women and boys grew to more than one thousand as it left Capitol Square for the city's business district, breaking down doors with axes and stealing bacon, ham, and coffee.

Some interpreted the bread riots, which occurred in other Southern cities as well, as evidence that the Confederate people were turning on their government and as "a good omen of the end being nigh."

Yet years of war and suffering remained.

DURING THE WAR, both Hector Davis and Silas Omohundro died in Richmond.

Hector Davis died in January 1863, at the age of forty-seven. It's unclear when Ann Banks Davis learned of his passing. His will, prepared in 1859, legalized the freedom he had given her and their children by allowing them to relocate to Philadelphia. The will did not acknowledge that her children were his.

"I give to a servant-woman, Ann, of mine, her freedom, to be removed out of the State, with her four children, Jennie, Audubon, and Victoria, and Matilda, and after their removal the sum of $20,000, she, Ann, to have the interest on one-fifth of the amount, and the interest of the balance to be expended in raising the said children till they become of age; then the principal to be given them."

In 1860, Hector Davis had told census enumerators that his real estate was valued at $20,000 and his personal estate at $100,000. Hector Davis's sister sued his executor to obtain what she could for her children. Ann Banks Davis sued her and her brother-in-law, but received nothing because the funds invested for their benefit were worthless after the war. Her son, Audubon, became a journalist, and she lived with him and his family in Philadelphia. When he died young, she lived with her grandson, named Hector Davis.

In 1864, Silas Omohundro died in Richmond. His will set free "my woman" Corinna Hinton Omohundro and their children, whom he named and also acknowledged as his own. The will also left her his estate, which his daughter Alice Morton Omohundro would allege in a lawsuit years later was worth between $60,000 and $100,000 at the time of his death. In 1860, he had told census enumerators that he owned real estate valued at $3,000 and had a personal worth of $75,000, presumably consisting almost entirely of enslaved people.

"I do absolutely emancipate and forever set free from all manner of servitude my woman Corinna Omohundro, and her five children . . . who are also my children," he wrote.

Silas Omohundro left Corinna and their children his entire estate, with the exception of another enslaved woman, Agness, and her two children, whom he freed, raising the question of whether he had fathered those children with her. Corinna received his Richmond residence and slave jail, but the will allowed her to keep the Philadelphia house instead if she preferred. Silas Omohundro even made sure that if Corinna married after he died, she would be able to keep the property in her name. He ensured that it would not be for a future husband's "use or benefit" and that it wouldn't be "subject to his debts, contracts or control." He also provided for the property to be sold after she died, and for the profits to be split among their children.

He left her furniture as well as the silver, china, and glassware they may have used to entertain. And he made sure that she kept the jewelry she had become accustomed to wearing—including a gold watch, a gold chain, two diamond rings, and a diamond cross. His gold watch and chain would go to Colon Omohundro, his eldest living son with Corinna Hinton Omohundro. The will also stipulated that the interest on his investments should be paid to her twice a year to help support the children.

Louisa Tandy Omohundro and her five children were completely left out. About 1866, Littleton Omohundro sued Silas Omohundro's estate, claiming that when the Civil War broke out his father had been building a house in Cincinnati for Louisa Tandy Omohundro, his "wife." The suit claimed that Silas Omohundro visited Ohio regularly until the war began, a claim supported by the birth of four children by Silas Omohundro after Louisa moved to Ohio.

The circuit court ruled in favor of Littleton Omohundro, who was seeking $4,391 plus interest for money he advanced his father to pay for the construction work. Silas Omohundro's executor, Richard Cooper, appealed that decision and brought it to the state supreme court, claiming that the circuit court's finding had been in error. Cooper argued that the Civil War made Silas Omohundro and his son in Ohio "alien enemies" and therefore the contract between father and son was null and void. In 1874, the supreme court upheld the lower court's decision, ruling that signed receipts from Louisa Tandy Omohundro and the contractor building the house proved that Silas Omohundro owed money to Littleton Omohundro.

Corinna Hinton Omohundro filed her own lawsuit in order to claim her inheritance of Silas Omohundro's two homes in Pennsylvania, which would not legally recognize her marriage to Silas Omohundro. She apparently made her way back from Philadelphia, where she may have been staying, to claim the Richmond estate, valued at $84,060. As part of the settlement, she became an enslaver herself, just as Lucy Ann Hagan had done, taking possession of three enslaved women and one boy—Lavenia, Polly, Mariah, and Tom. Perhaps she worried that they would be sold and wanted to protect them. Maybe some of them were related to her, or maybe she wanted help maintaining the Richmond slave jail.

Most of the money she inherited was tied up in litigation, and she never got much of it. After Silas Omohundro's death, she paired up with Nathaniel Davidson, a white soldier turned journalist from Maine who would operate a wood and coal shop on Fifteenth Street while Corinna Hinton Omohundro ran a bakery next door. She also took in boarders and grew vegetables to sell at a market. In 1874, when she was known as Corinna Davidson, she would move with her sons to Washington, DC, for Nathaniel Davidson's job at the *Washington National Republican* newspaper.

Silas Omohundro's home in Lancaster, Pennsylvania, also became the subject of a supreme court decision that required Corinna Hinton Omohundro to pay an inheritance tax because, in the court's determination, she and Silas Omohundro were not married.

The Lancaster auditor had found that Pennsylvania wasn't entitled to collect an inheritance tax, finding "that Silas Omohundro and Corinna Omohundro were married, and that she is the lawful widow," and the state's orphans court confirmed the auditor's finding. The state supreme court found on July 7, 1870, however, that "the auditor made a plain mistake in inferring a marriage between Silas Omohundro and Corinna his slave from the testimony of those who heard him declare her to be his wife while on their visits to Pennsylvania."

The decision found that "the fact of marriage is contradicted by the will and by all the circumstances." The state supreme court decision noted that "nowhere in the will is she denominated his wife, or is it intimated that she sustained such a relation to him." Corinna Hinton Omohundro was referred to as his "woman," the decision noted, adding that the will emancipated her and her children and used similar language in respect to Agness and her two children, who were also enslaved.

The state supreme court wrote of Silas Omohundro: "It is evident that he knew that Corinna and her children sustained no legal relation to him, which could entitle them to his estate without a will."

"That he should call her his wife in this state is not strange," the court concluded. "He could not indulge in the practice of concubinage with her in this state, as he had done in Virginia, without subjecting himself to reproach, and perhaps to banishment." The court found that "there is no probability . . . of a prior emancipation and actual marriage." The state supreme court reversed the orphans court decision, and the state collected the inheritance tax.

To settle his estate, an enslaved "likely girl"—perhaps not too different from Louisa Tandy Omohundro and Corinna Hinton Omohundro—was put up for sale at public auction. Her name was lost to history, her story erased.

THE END OF the war came the following year, in 1865, and with it the end of Robert Lumpkin's world.

On April 2, Robert E. Lee, a high-ranking officer in the Confederacy, sent a telegram to the Confederate War Department, recommending that Jefferson Davis, the head of the Confederacy, evacuate Richmond. "I see no prospect of doing more than holding our position here till night. I am not certain I can do that," Lee wrote from Petersburg. "I advise that all preparation be made for leaving Richmond tonight."

Davis was at St. Paul's Episcopal Church near the State Capitol when the telegram arrived, and an official walked down the aisle to hand it to him. Though Davis remained in deep denial about the imminent loss of the war, he ordered the Confederate government's evacuation. The news spread quickly.

Calvin Fairbank, the abolitionist pastor who had been arrested in Kentucky and jailed for helping enslaved people escape slavery, was in New York when he heard that Richmond had fallen. He rushed to Sullivan Street African Methodist Episcopal Church, founded in 1819 after Richard Allen sent a representative from Philadelphia to organize an independent church in New York.

"Richmond has gone up!" Fairbank yelled. In response, "a wail—a shout—a shriek of 'Hal-Lelujah!' swept through the house into the street and through the city like the shout of victorious armies."

In Richmond, the announcement kicked off a mass departure from the city by officials and wealthy citizens, who fled on horseback, in carriages, and on boats. Others made their way to the train depot to board a train out of town.

Among them was Robert Lumpkin, who had "made up a coffle of fifty men, women and children in his jail yard . . . and hurried them to the Danville Depot. 'This sad and weeping fifty, in handcuffs and chains, was the last slave coffle that tread the soil of America.' On that Sunday afternoon . . . all were hastening to get away from the doomed city. . . . But there was no room for Mr. Lumpkin and his slaves."

He was turned away from the train station, and "so ended the slave trade in Richmond."

"The last slave coffle that the United States would ever see walked on, trudging atop a carpet of Confederate bonds that had been underwritten by their sweat and that now lay abandoned, worthless and blanketing the muddy streets of the panic-ridden capital of Virginia," the *New York Times* reported. Lumpkin took the people he enslaved, marched them back to his jail, and locked them up again.

Jefferson Davis spent the afternoon with aides packing papers at the White House of the Confederacy. A carriage arrived about 7 p.m. to take him to the train station, and he "departed for station with newly lit cigar between his teeth." His train was scheduled to leave at 8:30 Sunday night, but he was not ready to abandon the city. He waited at the station for hours, hoping for some bit of good news. It was nearly midnight before the train pulled out of Richmond, bound for Danville. A few hours later, the railroad bridge would be set on fire.

That night local officials began emptying Richmond's alcohol supplies into the street, on orders from the City Council. "The gutters ran with a liquor freshet"—an overflow like a river flooding from rain—"and the fumes filled and impregnated the air," reported the *Richmond Whig*. "Fine cases of bottled liquors were tossed into the street from third story windows, and wrecked into a thousand pieces."

Exhausted and hungry Confederate soldiers, retreating through the city, drank it down. "From that moment law and order ceased to exist; chaos came, and a Pandemonium reigned," wrote the *Whig*.

The soldiers roamed the streets and used the butts of their guns to break glass doors on store windows, and thousands of drunken people stole jewelry, clothing, and food. Later that night, Confederate officials set fire to warehouses full of tobacco in order to prevent Union troops from taking the supplies, ignoring the pleas of residents to stop. The fires quickly spread to other buildings, and no one was there to put them out. "The entire business part of the city on fire, a sea of flame," wrote witness John Leyburn.

The "Evacuation Fire," as it came to be known, decimated Richmond's financial district. It took out the War Department, the courthouse, banks, hotels, newspapers, and mills. It destroyed railroad depots and the Mayo Bridge over the James River. By the time the fire burned out, it had destroyed about one-quarter of the city—more than eight hundred buildings, including homes. Residents who lost their houses were forced to sleep on the grounds of the State Capitol.

"The entire business portion of the city is a heap of smoldering ruins," reported the *New York Times*, "and nothing but the absence of wind saved the entire city from destruction."

The slave trading district, including Lumpkin's Jail, survived. Robert Lumpkin undoubtedly kept a close eye on the fires, but he may have kept the people he enslaved trapped there, knowing that they wouldn't be able to free themselves as the fire came close.

As morning arrived on Monday, April 3, "the air was lurid with the smoke and flame of hundreds of houses weltering in a sea of fire," reported the *Richmond Whig*.

BEFORE DAWN, NEWLY free people crowded the streets, where Black forces would soon liberate the city. "Liberation Day" would be celebrated by Richmond's Black residents for years to come.

One of the first reporters to enter the city, Thomas Morris Chester, a Black correspondent for the *Philadelphia Press*, credited the liberation of the city to Black soldiers of the 36th US Colored Infantry of General Draper's First Brigade, First Division, 25th Army Corps. The 36th had been organized in 1864 and was involved in siege operations against Petersburg and Richmond.

"GLORIOUS—FALL OF RICHMOND—CAPTURED BY THE BLACK TROOPS," reported the *Washington National Republican* in an extra edition on April 3, 1865.

Others credited the US Colored Infantry of the Fifth Massachusetts Cavalry, commanded by Colonel Charles Francis Adams Jr., the grandson of John Quincy Adams. They had been termed the "Brave Boys of the Fifth" for a series of battles in Petersburg from June 1864 to April 1865 that were crucial in defeating the Confederacy.

That morning, officers from the white 13th New York Artillery flew the US flag at the Virginia State Capitol. The 36th US Colored Infantry, many of whose members were formerly enslaved people who had enlisted from camps in Hampton Roads, Virginia, also made their way into Richmond.

Virginia resident Moble Hopson told of a Confederate soldier he called "Oncle" Shep Brown, probably a white neighbor, who witnessed Black troops seize the city.

Brown described his forty-man company hiding behind hay bales and tobacco bales and listening for Union troops, who arrived at daybreak, shouting, prancing, yelling, and singing. He described a "huge sea" of Black faces filling the streets from wall to wall.

After discovering Brown's unit, the Black troops waited for the arrival of white Union officers to seize the Confederate soldiers' guns and march the men to Libby Prison, which had over the duration of the war held more than one hundred thousand Union prisoners. By the time more Union troops arrived, the Black troops had taken the city, Hopson recounted.

Among the men streaming into Richmond that morning was Garland H. White. As an enslaved boy, he had been sold away from his Virginia family to Robert Toombs, who served as a US senator for Georgia before the Civil War, the first secretary of state for the Confederacy, and a high-ranking Confederate officer. White had escaped to Canada and upon his return to the United States made his way to Ohio, where he recruited Black soldiers for the 28th US Colored Infantry from Indiana—one of the first regiments to enter the city—and then served as its chaplain.

White marched through Richmond at the front of his unit, smiling at the newly free Black residents who lined the streets. "It appeared to me all the colored people in the world had collected," he wrote.

The officers and soldiers of his unit asked him to speak on Broad Street before the crowd of Black people. "I was aroused, amid the shouts of ten thousand voices, which proclaimed for the first time in that city freedom to all mankind," he recalled later.

Black men and women had gathered near Lumpkin's Jail, where still imprisoned people chanted, "Slavery chain done broke at last! Broke at last! Broke at last! Slavery chain done broke at last! Gonna praise God till I die!" The crowd joined in as Union soldiers opened the jail, freeing Lumpkin's captives.

"The doors of the slave pens were thrown open, and thousands came out shouting," White recalled, although there may not have been that many imprisoned by that time. "I became so overcome with tears that I could not stand up against the fullness of joy that filled my heart."

That day, "there were parents looking for their children who had been sold South of this state in tribes, and husbands came for the same purpose," White recalled. He recounted how Union soldiers shook the hands of formerly enslaved people, who were now "breathing the air of freedom."

After White spoke briefly before the crowd, some of the men in his unit took him to an older woman "among the many broken-hearted mothers looking for their children" who wanted to speak with him. She peppered him with questions:

"What is your name, sir?" she asked.

"My name is Garland White," he responded.

"What was your mother's name?"

"Nancy."

"Where was you born?"

"In Hanover County, in this state."

"Where was you sold from?" she asked.

"From this city," he replied, and continued answering the woman's questions about his life after he ran away from Toombs.

Finally, she responded, "You are my son! Yes, indeed, you are my very son, Garland! It is your mother, Garland, you have been talking to, who has spent twenty years of grief about her boy!"

Mother and son embraced. Later, he recalled, "I cannot express the joy I felt, when my mother caught me and held me in her withered arms."

"God is on the side of the righteous," he shouted. "You are, you are my own mother!"

Their joyous reunion must have been one of dozens, perhaps hundreds, that day between family members who had been separated, some by Robert Lumpkin and other Richmond slave traders. After the war's end, reconnecting with family was a top priority of newly freed Black men, women, and children, and the reunions of people torn apart by slave sales would continue for years.

A Northern reporter in 1865 encountered a formerly enslaved man who had walked more than six hundred miles searching for his wife and children. A formerly enslaved woman, Mary Armstrong, recalled reuniting with her mother in a Texas refugee camp after the war. "Law me, talk about cryin' and singin' and cryin' some more," Armstrong said, "we sure done it."

Just as enslavers and slave traders had placed advertisements to sell enslaved people, once free, the formerly enslaved people took out ads looking for kin from whom they had been separated by sale. Formerly enslaved people continued placing advertisements for decades.

Mark Messer, a formerly enslaved man living in Danville, Virginia, took out an advertisement in the *Richmond Planet* in 1897 seeking information about his father, who had been sold away forty to fifty years earlier. Messer's father, Americus Valentine, was born in Currituck County, North Carolina, and sold in Lumpkin's Jail. The advertisement said that all of Messer's brothers had died except one, and it listed the names of his sisters and their spouses. Messer was apparently hoping to trigger the memory of someone who might have known Valentine or his children.

Messer was able to locate some of his father's family after placing the ad, and not long after, Messer's mother, Elizabeth Jones, placed an advertisement of her own. She noted that she had also passed through the Richmond jail when her Virginia enslaver, Batt Evans, sold her to speculators in Petersburg. "They carried me to Richmond and put me in Lumpkin's jail and sold me to a man named William Spears who lived in Alabama," her advertisement read. It's unclear if she made any connection.

Many other formerly enslaved people would not find the parents, children, or siblings they had been separated from in the name of white greed. After the war, Mattie Curtis's parents went looking for their fourteen oldest children, all whom had been sold away. They found only three.

On April 4, President Abraham Lincoln arrived in Richmond unannounced.

Twelve sailors delivered him ashore at Rockett's Landing on the James River. Crowds of Black men and women recognized Lincoln and his twelve-year-old son Tad, and they rushed toward the pair, shaking Lincoln's hand, touching his coattail, and kneeling to kiss his boots.

Lincoln told them, "You must kneel to God only and thank Him for the liberty you will hereafter enjoy."

From the wharf, "he walked through Shockoe Bottom in wonder, among throngs of people celebrating freedom on the very docks from which thousands of their kin had been shipped to the cotton country," writes the historian Edward Baptist.

The crowd following Lincoln grew as he visited the former Confederate White House, where he was hoping to meet with the Union's commanding officers. Instead, he found a delegation of Southerners, who encouraged him to end the war peacefully. After the meeting, Lincoln and his son rode a carriage through Richmond, touring the State Capitol and Libby Prison and witnessing the financial district still burning.

Lincoln did not give a speech in Richmond—or if he did, it was not recorded. When asked, he advised the Union commander, Major General Godfrey Weitzel, about how to handle the city. "If I were in your place," Lincoln told him, "I'd let 'em up easy. Let 'em up easy."

In the capital of the Confederacy, Lincoln wanted to rally his broken country around a promise to rebuild and a plan to reincorporate the South into the United States. He promoted inclusion and suggested not placing blame.

After his tour of Richmond, Lincoln spent the night docked on the warship USS *Malvern*. The next morning, on April 5, he resumed peace talks and then left Richmond for the last time. Ten days later, he was dead.

WHEN THE UNION took Richmond, Robert Lumpkin's luck ran out. As he stood at the threshold of his jail, smoke wafting through the air, perhaps he felt a fraction of the misery he had created for enslaved people. The people he enslaved had been set free. Fires downtown continued to smolder, and at about noon the bank he had founded blew up.

He had lost his business. But he had fared better than many, as he still owned the jail property and he had protected Mary Lumpkin and their children.

Although they had watched the war from the sidelines in Pennsylvania, they would not have been entirely insulated from death and destruction. In southern Pennsylvania, free Black men were captured and forced to work for the Confederacy.

For the four-year duration of the war, Philadelphia provided funds and soldiers for the war effort, staffing eleven Union regiments, and kept an eye out for attack by the Confederacy. Philadelphia trains transported soldiers and supplies to the South and returned with wounded men as well as Confederate prisoners. The region was home to some two dozen military hospitals, and patients also arrived by ship. After the Battle of Gettysburg in 1863, area hospitals couldn't accommodate all the wounded men, who had to be put up in fire stations and churches.

"Philadelphia assumed the appearance of an armed camp, a look it was to retain for four long and bitter years," writes the historian Winnifred K. MacKay.

Philadelphia men had been eager to enlist when the war began, and more than ninety thousand served. In the Seventh Ward where the Lumpkins lived, Octavius V. Catto raised a volunteer regiment of Black men to help defend Pennsylvania after it was invaded by the Confederacy in 1863. The Union rejected the unit because the troops were Black. Undeterred, Catto went on to recruit for other regiments of the United States Colored Infantry that were sent to the front lines.

Philadelphia women had supported the government by sewing uniforms for Pennsylvania troops. Volunteers had provided clothing and food, cared for the sick, buried dead soldiers, created homes for returning war veterans, and taken in orphaned children. Residents alarmed by the expense of the war and the mounting death toll had advocated peace talks. When the war finally ended, the city celebrated.

Staffers at the *Inquirer* were gathered around, reading dispatches from the South, and they shouted when news came around 9:30 p.m.

on April 9 of Robert E. Lee's surrender to Union general Ulysses S. Grant at Appomattox Court House, Virginia. Newspaper staff lit lamps around the building, and other downtown businesses lit up too, including the Chestnut Street Theatre. "God Has Grant-ed Us Victory!" read a canvas sign stretched across the building. Fire engines came out with bells and whistles, and residents poured onto the streets to join the celebration. People marched around playing fiddles, drums, and horns.

Perhaps Mary Lumpkin and her children awakened and joined in the celebration. Surely the life they had once lived in Richmond seemed far behind them at war's end and they would have been rejoicing in the freedom that all enslaved people would now enjoy. But perhaps the children also worried about their father and wondered about his fate. Mary Lumpkin surely thought about what it meant for her.

WHEN THE CIVIL War ended, four million enslaved people in the South were finally free, at least on paper. But what did freedom even mean for them?

They had no money, no land, no homes. Most had only the clothes on their back. How were they supposed to find a place to live? How would they clothe and feed their families? How would they get the education they had long been denied and the skills they needed in order to find work and buy property?

"After the war was over we was afraid to move," recalled W. L. Bost, who had been enslaved in North Carolina. He described being "like turtles" after emancipation, occasionally sticking "our heads out to see how the land lay."

Some formerly enslaved people did not even know they were legally free. A number of enslavers kept the war's end a secret from the people they enslaved. In May and June 1865, as US troops traveled the South, they continued to encounter Black people still being held in slavery.

"Some of the masters were very reluctant in giving up their servants, and tried to defraud and rob them out of their freedom, and many of the slaves had to run away from their masters to be free," wrote Peter

Randolph, the formerly enslaved Virginia man who became a Boston preacher.

Minnie Fulkes, enslaved in Virginia, said that her mother and siblings weren't freed until a month after the war ended. Her enslaver, Betsy Godsey, finally told Fulkes's mother that she could stay with her and continue to cook for her, as she had done during slavery, and in exchange Godsey would provide food and clothing for her and her children. "You see, we didn't have nuthin' an' no whar to go," Fulkes recalled.

She said that her mother, like many enslaved people, stayed on her former enslaver's property until she was able to find a way to leave. "But my God it wuz 'ginst our will, but, baby, couldn't help ourselves," she recalled decades later.

Fannie Berry, also enslaved in Virginia, said that she was free "a long time" before she knew it. Even after she knew she was free, things didn't look up. "Baby, all us wuz helpless an' ain't had nothing."

Some Black men and women refused to stay with their former enslavers any longer. "I lef' der minute I finds out dat I is free," recalled Cornelia Andrews, enslaved in North Carolina.

As soon as the war ended, Sarah Debro's mother retrieved her from her enslaver, Polly White Cain, who had made her a house servant. Cain asked to keep Debro, but her mother refused, telling Cain that she had taken her daughter away from her and didn't "pay no mind to my cryin.'" She wanted her child back.

"We's free now, Miss Polly," Debro's mother told Cain. "We ain't gwine be slaves no more to nobody."

As SOON AS the war ended, Peter Randolph departed from Boston to serve as a preacher to Richmond's newly free Black people.

On his way south, he learned of Lincoln's assassination at a stop in Baltimore, where flags had been lowered to half-mast. After the president's funeral, Randolph continued toward Richmond, arriving twenty-five days after the surrender.

"The colored people from all parts of the state were crowding in at the capital, running, leaping, and praising God that freedom had come at last," Randolph recalled. "It seems to me I can hear their songs now as they ring through the air: 'Slavery chain done broke at last; slavery chain done broke at last—I's goin' to praise God till I die.'"

Randolph described finding Richmond brimming with both Union and Confederate soldiers. "All hours, day and night was the marching of regiments, going and coming," he wrote. "The sight of some of these would bring tears to the dryest eyes, as they beheld men wounded, maimed in every possible shape and form that could be mentioned. And many of these, like the poor colored people, were truly glad that the war was over."

Newly free Black men, women, and children were huddled in temporary structures at Chimborazo Hospital, located on a high bluff overlooking the city. More than one hundred buildings had housed the largest Confederate hospital during the Civil War and treated some seventy-five thousand patients. The hospital was transformed into a refugee camp where clothes were made, food was served, and schools were opened. Richmond's Black population had doubled, and white people, viewing their new Black neighbors as a threat, pelted them with rocks. Yet the Black men, women, and children arriving daily were peaceful until they were forced to defend themselves.

"It had been argued by some that, if the Negroes were set free they would murder and kill the white people. But instead of that, they were praising God and the Yankees for life and liberty," Randolph noted.

He took a job with the newly formed US Bureau of Refugees, Freedmen, and Abandoned Lands, commonly referred to as the Freedmen's Bureau and established when Lincoln approved an act of Congress. Administered by the War Department, the Freedmen's Bureau was charged with providing assistance to formerly enslaved people as well as hundreds of thousands of poor whites.

The bureau had been formed before the war's end in order to implement a land distribution policy known as "forty acres and a mule," devised in response to a meeting between General William T. Sherman and Secretary of War Edwin M. Stanton and Black leaders in Savannah, Georgia, in January 1865, after Sherman's "March to the Sea."

"For the first time in the history of this nation, the representatives of the government had gone to these poor debased people"—representatives of Black men and women—"to ask them what they wanted for themselves," Stanton recalled.

"The way we can best take care of ourselves," said the group's formerly enslaved leader, Reverend Garrison Frazier, "is to have land, and turn it and till it by our own labor . . . and we can soon maintain ourselves and have something to spare. . . . We want to be placed on land until we are able to buy it and make it our own."

Sherman's Special Field Order No. 15, which Lincoln approved, called for the United States to take ownership of a strip of land along the Atlantic from Charleston, South Carolina, to St. John's River in Florida, including Georgia's Sea Islands, that extended thirty miles west from the coast. Black families would be settled on those 400,000 acres of land in 40-acre segments, and the Army would lend mules to the new settlers.

Some members of Congress, including Massachusetts senator Charles Sumner, had promoted land distribution in order to break up the power of Southern white landowners. But after Lincoln's death, President Andrew Johnson would overturn Sherman's Special Field Order No. 15 in the fall of 1865, returning abandoned lands to pardoned white Southerners, and Congress backed the decision not to provide any property for newly free Black men and women.

"Instead of forty acres and a mule, they had to return to their former masters barefooted, and hat in hand, and ask permission to work for 'victuals and clothes,'" said Randolph.

He described seeing "these hungry souls crowding in at my office to obtain the slips of paper that was to give them the necessities of life"—food, clothing, and access to housing, all of which was available at Chimborazo. The Freedmen's Bureau also helped settle disputes with former enslavers.

Sarah Harris, born enslaved in North Carolina, recalled enslaved people being turned out when white people freed them "with no homes and nuthin." As a four-year-old, Harris begged her father, Frank Walton, to return to their former enslaver because she didn't like the biscuit, white potatoes, and cured meat served by the Freedmen's Bureau.

"I cried every day at 12 o'clock to go home," Harris recalled. "I would say, 'Papa let's go home, I want to go home.'" Let's stay here, her father responded, they will send you to school. He would tell her, "Don't cry, honey."

The Freedmen's Bureau offices also became places where the formerly enslaved went to get information about husbands, wives, and children from whom they had been separated. In August 1866, a formerly enslaved Virginia man went to the Freedmen's Bureau office in Charlottesville, Virginia, looking for help finding his children. "Simon Fleming wishes to know what has become of his children. They were sold south in Richmond by Hector Davis," the Freedmen Bureau's notes read. Fleming tried to figure out how to locate his children, but whether he was able to find any of them is unknown.

The bureau was designed to be an economic driver to rebuild the South, but it was inadequately funded by Congress and opposed by President Johnson. Whites in the South greeted the bureau agents with hostility and violence and saw them as interfering in local matters when they offered help to Black Americans. Because the support provided by the Freedmen's Bureau was inadequate, newly free people were forced to choose between starving and returning to work for their former enslavers, some of whom continued to beat and abuse them.

"Is there a case in all history, that can be compared with this, where over four millions of people, ignorant and empty-handed, are turned loose into the world to seek for themselves homes in the face of every possible disadvantage?" Randolph asked.

Seemingly brokenhearted, he added, "The true condition of the colored people at this time will never be written."

By THE TIME Randolph arrived in Richmond, groups of Black men and women had already begun to take control of their churches and to establish schools.

Long overseen by a white preacher, First African Baptist Church, located on Broad west of Shockoe Bottom, served as the epicenter of Black social life in antebellum Richmond. Within two weeks of the war's end, a school had been set up in the church to teach more than one thousand pupils.

Women from the North, many of whom were Black, arrived to teach newly free Black children to read and write. "No children of the North look happier, and no books are dearer to a child's heart than the little green-back primer each one carries," the American Missionary Association reported. The textbook was probably a pro-Union publication meant to influence children's thoughts about the war.

After the war, Richmond officials sought to control Black residents and force them out of the city, implementing a requirement that Black residents and visitors show special passes that gave them permission to move around. More than eight hundred Black men, women, and children were arrested for not having a pass and held in Richmond jails and former slave pens during the first two weeks of the pass requirements.

Union soldiers stationed in the camps to protect the newly freed Black Americans instead abused them. "For the slightest provocation, and sometimes for no cause whatever, the butts of their guns and bayonets were used unmercifully upon them," Randolph wrote. Angry that enslaved people had been set free, the men "took the authority given them by the wearing of the blue to express it," he wrote, referring to the uniform color of the Union Army.

Black leaders responded with a court of inquiry into misconduct, and they filed affidavits by, or on behalf of, Black men and women in the Freedmen's Bureau court in Richmond. They detailed assaults by former Confederates and federal guards. Black residents reported being beaten and robbed, having their homes ransacked or burned, and being sexually assaulted in holding cells.

More than three thousand Black people attended a mass meeting on June 10 at the First African Baptist Church to discuss how they were being treated by Union soldiers. Six days later, representatives from each of the Black churches presented the findings to President Johnson at the White House and also lobbied for Black churches to be able to appoint their own pastors and own their church buildings. He listened to the men and offered his assistance. The president repealed the pass and curfew laws, removed the Richmond mayor, and replaced abusive Army officers.

Yet President Johnson proved less willing to help with larger systemic problems facing newly freed people.

EVEN BEFORE THE war ended, slave pens had become places to shelter and feed formerly enslaved people in Union-occupied towns like Washington, DC, and Alexandria, Virginia. After the war, the places where enslaved people had been imprisoned and sold were further transformed.

Nashville's slave pens "changed their inmates" after the war, noted Jermain Wesley Loguen, who became a noted abolitionist and ran the Underground Railroad in Syracuse, New York. He had escaped slavery in Tennessee in 1834 after his white father and enslaver sold him, his siblings, and his mother.

Loguen went to Canada for three years before returning to the United States. His aunt and new enslaver, Sarah Logue, had written to him, claiming that he had left her family in a desperate situation by escaping and taking "Old Rock, our fine mare." She informed him that because of his escape, she had been forced to sell his sister and brother, and told him that, if he gave her $1,000 and reimbursed her for the horse, "I will give up all claim I have to you." He replied, "I meet the proposition with unutterable scorn and contempt."

In Syracuse, Loguen had worked to help free enslaved people with Samuel J. May, the minister formerly of Boston, and had wed abolitionist Caroline Storum. A prominent AME Zion preacher who was appointed bishop in 1868, Loguen and his wife were said to have helped 1,500 people escape. Their daughter, Amelia, married Lewis Douglass, one of Frederick Douglass's sons, and another daughter, Sarah, became the first Black woman to graduate from Syracuse University's School of Medicine and one of America's first Black female doctors. Loguen returned to Nashville in 1865 to be reunited with his elderly mother.

In place of "the poor, innocent and almost heartbroken slaves" who for years had been held captive in Nashville's slave jail as they awaited sale to the Lower South, Loguen found that the new captives were "some of the very fiends in human shape who committed those diabolical outrages"—presumably enslavers and slave traders. "Their sins have found them out," he wrote.

In Lexington, Kentucky, a Black Congregational church gathered in a former slave jail operated by Lewis Robards, a dealer of "fancy girls." Considered "the most unscrupulous of the traders," he was known to buy enslaved and free Black people from kidnappers. Robards was also suspected of kidnapping people himself to sell and of trading in terminally ill enslaved people. In Lexington, he housed most enslaved people in "damp, unhealthy, eight-foot-square 'coops' with brick floors, seven-foot ceilings, and barred windows and doors," but kept "fancy girls" in parlors above his office. During slavery, one visitor saw "very handsome mulatto women, of fine persons and easy genteel manners, sitting at their needle work awaiting a purchaser."

In Savannah, one slave market became a place where free Black people could worship, engage in political activism, and attend school. A Black man led free Black people in prayer, followed by singing, in the same building. A Black educator taught one hundred Black children from the auctioneer's platform.

"I listened to the recitations, and heard their songs of jubilee," wrote a visitor from Boston. "The slave-mart transformed to a school-house! Civilization and Christianity had indeed begun their beneficent work." This was a site "from which had risen voices of despair instead of accents of love, brutal cursing instead of Christian teaching."

In Charleston, South Carolina, the war correspondent Charles C. Coffin removed the word "MART" from above a heavy iron gate in front of one of the largest markets for the sale of enslaved people in the South. He took the key to a guardhouse where "thousands of slaves had been incarcerated there for no crime whatever, except for being out after nine o'clock, or for meeting in some secret chamber to tell God their wrongs, with no white man present."

Coffin shipped the steps of the slave market to abolitionists in Massachusetts, and on March 9, 1865, William Lloyd Garrison stood on those steps to give a speech at Boston Music Hall. The audience raised "thunders of applause" and waved "hundreds of white handkerchiefs" to demonstrate their approval.

Robert Lumpkin also found a new use for his property. He rented out the jail building to Black men who planned to operate it as a hotel. He provided the men with a formal title of transfer, but it was blocked by the Richmond hustings court, which refused to transfer the hotel license to them. The court cited a Virginia law that prohibited Black men from keeping hotels.

When the Black men were unable to get a hotel license, Robert Lumpkin apparently ran the hotel himself, a business that agents of slave trader Rice Ballard had been known to pursue. Prior to emancipation, running a hotel had been considered working to support the slave trade. How successfully Robert Lumpkin converted a former slave property into a welcoming hotel is unknown, but it seems it would have been a near-impossible task.

An 1874 drawing by William Sheppard of First African Baptist Church, Richmond's first large all-Black church. Until the Civil War ended, it was required to have a white preacher. (Library of Congress)

9

After the War

WHEN THE WAR ENDED, MARY LUMPKIN RETURNED TO VIRGINIA, THE land where she had been born enslaved.

In April 1865, Mary Lumpkin made her way back to the broken and starving city of Richmond. She returned to Robert Lumpkin, his former slave jail, and its many ghosts. Regardless of how she felt about Robert Lumpkin, she and their children relied on him financially. He had enabled them to live as free and he had educated them. Perhaps she felt she owed it to him to go back. Perhaps her return was a contingency of a deal they had struck. Maybe she also hoped to find family from whom she had been separated.

The money Robert Lumpkin had been giving Mary Lumpkin and their children to support their life in Philadelphia had probably slowed significantly, if not dried up altogether. She may have also realized that it was in her own financial interest to help Robert Lumpkin figure out how to make a living in the aftermath of war.

For five years, she had lived with their children in the Philadelphia house she bought in her own name. Martha Kelsey's husband lived with them too, and soon there would be more grandchildren. Her youngest son, John, was about eight. It's unclear if he or any of her other children accompanied Mary Lumpkin when she returned to Virginia or if they stayed in Philadelphia.

The schooling that Martha Kelsey and Annie Lumpkin received in Ipswich before the war was considered sufficient at the time for women. Robert most likely was working. In 1867, Richard appears to have enrolled at the New York Hudson River Institute in Columbia County. John may have attended school in Philadelphia.

What did the children think when Mary Lumpkin went back to their father? Did they urge her not to go? Would any of them ever visit him again?

They may have missed him in their years apart. Perhaps they wanted to see him—or perhaps, with some distance, his way of life, and their enslavement, was unforgivable. Surely their feelings about him were complex and would have varied from child to child.

At the war's end, some enslaved women who had been in Mary Lumpkin's position left the white men who had enslaved them and forced them to have children. Among them was Mary Ann Collins, who had been enslaved by Hilton Waddell in Orange County, Virginia. "My mother told my father she was tired of living that kind of a life, that if she could not be his legal wife she wouldn't be anything to him," said her daughter, Harriet Ann Daves. Collins and Daves moved to Leavenworth, Kansas, and Daves was sent to school in Nebraska. She never saw her father again.

Once Mary Lumpkin was in Richmond, she and Robert Lumpkin transferred ownership of the Philadelphia home to George Kelsey. This decision seemed to indicate that Mary Lumpkin planned to stay in Richmond for some time, if not permanently. The next year, George Kelsey, who was working as a clerk, paid taxes on two watches and the piano at the house.

In Richmond, Mary Lumpkin's time was probably devoted to running the household and the new hotel business, as Robert Lumpkin no longer had enslaved people to do the work for him. Perhaps he had hired some formerly enslaved people to help out. Accustomed to having multiple income streams, Robert Lumpkin was probably looking for other ways to make money. Perhaps Mary Lumpkin offered to iron, cook, or clean for other families.

According to one account, Mary Lumpkin and Robert Lumpkin got married when she returned from Philadelphia. "After Richmond fell, he did the honorable thing of marrying her, and so legitimatized her and her children," wrote American Baptist Home Mission Society administrator James B. Simmons, who would meet Mary Lumpkin a few years later. He referred to Mary Lumpkin as the "lawful widow" of Robert Lumpkin, and after her marriage, he claimed, she "was admitted to membership in the First African Baptist Church." Yet it seems unlikely that Mary Lumpkin and Robert Lumpkin wed. Marriages between white and Black people had been prohibited since 1691 by Virginia law and would not be allowed until 1967, when the US Supreme Court handed down its *Loving v. Virginia* decision.

The Code of 1860 continued to prohibit marriage between a "white" person and a "negro" or "colored person." It was also a crime for any clerk of court to knowingly "issue a marriage license contrary to law," for anyone to "perform the ceremony of marriage between a white person and a negro," or for any "white person" to "intermarry with a negro."

Robert Lumpkin and Mary Lumpkin may have claimed that they were married when it was advantageous to them, as Silas Omohundro had done with Corinna Hinton Omohundro in Pennsylvania. But if Mary Lumpkin had been Robert Lumpkin's lawful wife, she would have been named as his wife in his will, which he penned in 1866. Instead, he referred to her in the legal document as a woman "who resides with me."

It is more likely, then, that Robert Lumpkin and Mary Lumpkin continued to live together under an agreement that they had made with each other, the terms of which we are unlikely to ever know.

MONTHS AFTER THE war ended, Robert Lumpkin sought and received a presidential pardon and amnesty from President Andrew Johnson.

Lumpkin's request, dated July 14, 1865, stated that during the war "he remained at home attending to his business and took no part in the war." He noted that he held no civil or military office in the Confederacy, and that he disapproved of the secession of the southern states. He also pledged allegiance to the newly united country.

He valued his property, including real estate, at $20,000—the threshold that required him to apply for an individual pardon if he wanted amnesty. On July 17, President Johnson issued his pardon on the condition that Robert Lumpkin take an oath of loyalty.

"Whereas, Robert Lumpkin, of Richmond, Virginia, by taking part in the late rebellion against the Government of the United States, has made himself liable to heavy pains and penalties; and whereas, the circumstances of his case render him a proper object of executive clemency," the pardon read. "Now therefore, be it known, That I, Andrew Johnson, President of the United States of America, in consideration of the premises, divers other good and sufficient reasons me thereunto moving, do hereby grant to the said Robert Lumpkin a full pardon and amnesty for all offences by him committed, arising from participation, direct or implied, in the said rebellion."

The pardon would be void if Robert Lumpkin acquired "any property whatever in slaves" or if he made use of "slave labor."

With the president's signature on that document, Robert Lumpkin's years of slave trading were written off by the federal government, his abuses of Black bodies forgiven. A long line of slaveholding, slave-abusing, and slave trading men throughout the South were pardoned in his wake, their many crimes overlooked. The impact of these pardons would define America during Reconstruction and beyond—and still defines it today.

Had he lived, Lincoln might not have been so generous to Confederates. During his annual message to Congress on December 8, 1863, he had outlined plans for rebuilding the South that included offering amnesty to most former Confederates but excluded government officials and people who had mistreated prisoners. President Andrew Johnson chose to pardon high-ranking Confederate government and military officials—powerful white people—and did very little to provide for Black Americans.

Because lawmakers refused to allow a policy of land redistribution to Black men and women, many formerly enslaved people were forced to continue working as sharecroppers for the same people who had enslaved them. The failure of the American government to provide land for formerly enslaved people after all they had done to establish the country was among the decisions most detrimental to Black Americans in slavery's immediate aftermath—and for all the years that have followed. It is an important element in the case for reparations for descendants of enslaved people.

The Amnesty Act of 1872, signed by Johnson's successor, President Ulysses Grant, allowed all but the highest-ranking Confederate leaders to hold public office and, as a result, make laws. These men were also permitted to own land and vote. Nearly every act of treason committed by Confederates against the country had now been forgiven by the US government.

President Grant also closed up the Freedmen's Bureau that year, ending its programs to support and educate newly free Black men, women, and children. In 1877, federal troops left the South. Confederate leaders who had fought to maintain slavery would adopt laws that further oppressed Black men and women. For them, slavery was not over.

ROBERT LUMPKIN DIED the year after the war ended, on October 25, 1866. His obituaries did not acknowledge his career as a slave trader or his ownership of Lumpkin's Jail.

The 1853 obituary for his peer Hope H. Slatter referred to him as "the notorious Slave Trader" and noted that Slatter "gained wealth and infamy from the trade in blood." Yet Robert Lumpkin, who owned one of the most notorious slave jails in the South, was referred to simply as "another old citizen."

His ownership and management of a slave jail that housed and tortured thousands of Black people were forgotten. The sale of people away from their families was erased. In death, his scandalous history was wiped clean. He was made new as "the proprietor of Lumpkin's Hotel."

"He was born and raised in this city, was sixty-one years of age, and was an honest man," the *Richmond Enquirer* wrote.

Burial records list typhoid fever as Robert Lumpkin's cause of death. The *Richmond Dispatch* reported that "he was attacked by cholera some ten days ago, and never recovered." He was buried in an unmarked grave in his mother's plot at Shockoe Hill Cemetery, the resting place of Chief Justice John Marshall and the future gravesite of the Union spy Elizabeth Van Lew.

Robert Lumpkin had outlived many of his slave trader colleagues. John Hagan had been gone for a decade. Silas Omohundro and Hector Davis had died during the war, along with William H. Goodwin. Bacon Tait was one of the few Richmond slave traders of some renown still living. Most of the young enslaved women with whom they had children would live for decades.

In Robert Lumpkin's will, he left everything to Mary Lumpkin, the woman "who resides with me." At the time, white women were lucky to get one-third of their husband's estate. Robert Lumpkin gave Mary Lumpkin all his real estate, including the Richmond jail parcels and what he described as "my house" in Philadelphia—the house Mary Lumpkin bought and whose title she transferred to George Kelsey when she had returned to Richmond the previous year.

He also left her a home in Huntsville, Alabama, that he had bought three years earlier for his brother Thurston Lumpkin, who was also a slave trader, and a $14,105 bond his brother owed him. The will stipulated that Thurston Lumpkin could continue to live in the Alabama house and that, if he paid the debt, ownership would be conveyed to him.

Robert Lumpkin also left Mary Lumpkin cash, stock in the Richmond and Danville Railroad, and fifteen shares from the bank he had founded, now worthless. In the will, he stipulated that if Mary Lumpkin married after his death, her inheritance would be "wholly void." If they had been married, he would have been attempting to sidestep Virginia's laws of coverture, which required a married woman's property and real estate to be transferred to her husband.

He also acknowledged his children with Mary Lumpkin in the will and stipulated that, if Mary Lumpkin married, her inheritance would go to "her children," naming all five—Martha, Annie, Robert, Richard, and John—"and any other child she may hereafter have by me." The will further stipulated that if Mary Lumpkin died before he did, the inheritance would be divided equally between their children. No other descendants were named.

Robert Lumpkin's will provided for the protection of his daughters' share of the inheritance from current or future husbands, just as Robert Lumpkin's stepfather had done for his stepsister, and as most wealthy white men of the time did for their white daughters. "The shares of the female children to be held in trust for their separate use, so that they same shall not be liable for the contracts, debts or engagements of any husband they may then have or thereafter take," the will read.

Because he died after the war, Mary Lumpkin's inheritance was valued at far less than it would have been during the peak slave trading years. Confederate dollars were worthless, and he had lost his investments in enslaved people when they were set free. His slave jail was a hotel, and his property was not ripe for commercial development. The value of his Shockoe Bottom land, once worth $6,000, had surely plummeted. Land in an area prone to flooding, located near an African burial ground, and tainted by a history of slavery was not desirable. Besides, the city was expanding westward.

"The Lumpkin property has become of little value comparatively, and is occupied wholly by colored persons with little prospect of being occupied in future by any better class," a racist real estate assessor wrote in 1872.

Despite the inheritance Robert Lumpkin left her, Mary Lumpkin found herself in a precarious position when he died. He had not appointed an executor to help her handle the estate, as Silas Omohundro had done for Corinna Hinton Omohundro. Perhaps that decision was a cost-saving measure, or maybe he had no friends left to ask. Instead, he made Mary Lumpkin the executor of his estate. She would have to figure out for herself how to pay the bills that came with an inheritance. Taxes would soon be due.

Maybe she continued to take in boarders at the hotel or did laundry and cooking in order to keep money coming in. Perhaps, like her friend Corinna Hinton Omohundro, she ran multiple businesses.

Robert Lumpkin had provided for her in death, but in the aftermath of the Civil War, when his bank was gone, his jail was closed, and the people he enslaved were set free, it would not be enough.

BEFORE EMANCIPATION, MOST of the Black men and women who had power were free multiracial people. Some of them were children of wealthy white fathers who recognized them, particularly in towns like Charleston and New Orleans. Black leaders came from this influential "mulatto elite" during the Civil War, and others would step up during Reconstruction.

When the South lost the war, some whites decided that "miscegenation"—a derogatory term for race mixing coined in 1864—was the sin that caused God to "forsake" the South and the reason for the North's victory. Multiracial people became a symbol of both defeat and the South's sin.

Black women were slightly less vulnerable to sexual abuse after the war, and the birth rate of multiracial children slowed. While they were still at the mercy of violent white men, Black women had been protected from them to some degree during the war because so many white men had gone off to fight for the Confederacy. After emancipation, fewer Black women lived in white men's households, and they were better able to resist abuse. The wartime deaths of some 289,000 Southern men, a great many of whom were white, resulted in a shift in sex ratios, with women outnumbering men. The ability of Black men to keep Black women safe had also improved. They could now encourage their wives to pursue work indoors rather than in the fields, where they were vulnerable to rape and abuse.

In the aftermath of the war, all Southern states except West Virginia legislated and restricted interracial relationships. The Alabama Constitution of 1865 directed the legislature to make interracial marriages between whites and people of African ancestry "null and void." Mississippi lawmakers legislated that "any person who shall so intermarry shall be deemed guilty of felony and, on conviction thereof, shall be confined in the state penitentiary for life."

In Virginia, laws that prohibited interracial marriage were fully developed after the war. In 1883, when the US Supreme Court decision *Pace v. Alabama* upheld the constitutionality of Alabama's laws banning interracial marriage, Virginia used the ruling to justify its own laws. Virginia would rely on the *Pace* decision until laws banning intermarriage were finally rejected by the Supreme Court.

Some states also created laws to punish whites who lived with a Black man or woman. Seven states, including Virginia, instituted a "one drop" policy, which defined a Black person as anyone with Black "blood." Under this policy, having a single Black ancestor meant one was considered Black. Virginia's "one drop" rule was part of the state's racial integrity laws passed between 1924 and 1930. A white person, as defined by the Racial Integrity Act of 1924, "has no trace whatsoever of any blood other than Caucasian."

The Ku Klux Klan was formed the year the Civil War ended when six veterans of the Confederacy met in Pulaski, Tennessee, to form a secret society that would punish whites who had relationships with Black people. The KKK's first grand wizard was Nathan Bedford Forrest, a former slave trader and high-ranking officer in the Confederacy whose cavalry had massacred approximately two hundred Black soldiers in April 1864 after they surrendered at Fort Pillow, Tennessee. In Louisiana, "crescendo" citizens created a vigilance committee to oppose white men dating Black women. Members of Mississippi's Anti Miscegenation

League, created in 1907, worked to secure evidence against those accused of committing the crime.

By the time Virginia passed its racial integrity laws, there had been centuries of rapes of enslaved people, and there were tens of thousands of multiracial people living in America. Many did not know their own racial background. Yet, in providing evidence that whites were not perfect—but instead were, as the historian Joel Williamson calls them, "fallen angels"—the very existence of multiracial people was a threat to white supremacy.

Legislation and KKK violence may have led mothers like Mary Lumpkin to suggest that their children and grandchildren try to pass for white when they were able. While she claimed her Blackness in Richmond after the war, worshiping in a Black church, some of her children may have made the decision on their own to never again speak of the conditions under which they were born and raised.

But other descendants lived as Black, and though her name was lost for a period, her brave actions to protect her children were never forgotten.

DURING THE WAR, the American Baptist Home Mission Society, established in New York in 1832 to found churches and minister to the poor, recognized the need for newly free Black people to get basic education.

After Abraham Lincoln issued the Emancipation Proclamation on January 1, 1863, the Mission Society's board decided to use its missionaries and teachers to help fill that void. In November 1863, a young white woman, Joanna P. Moore, became the first missionary appointed to the South when she was stationed at a Union Army encampment on the Mississippi River, north of Memphis, among "1,100 colored women and children in distress."

In the dead of winter, families slept in cabins and tents and children were dressed in nothing but "part of a soldier's old coat." Moore wrote to friends in the North asking for resources to help these women and children, who were technically free but had nowhere to go and no resources.

When the camp was moved to Helena, Arkansas, Moore went along and established a one-room school. She taught students in groups for ninety minutes each—"very little children, older children, adults who could read a very little, or rather those who wanted to learn, and the old people who could only listen as I read to them," she wrote later. At night, the families gathered around her cabin for family prayers.

In its early years, the Mission Society had achieved its goals using missionaries in foreign lands. Relying on that model, the society launched a National Theological Institute to prepare formerly enslaved men to enter the Baptist ministry as pastors. As the mission evolved, it offered courses to men and women at a variety of levels.

Days after Richmond collapsed, the Mission Society arrived in the former Confederate capital and began teaching classes for newly free Black men. By November 1865, the organization had established the Richmond Theological School for Freedmen. Harvey Morris, enslaved until the end of the war, walked one hundred miles and slept outdoors to get to the school. His wife had agreed to provide for the family's two children while he attended classes. He had no money or clothes when he arrived, and a friend had offered to pay his boarding costs. "I never went to school a day before I came here," Morris wrote in a letter thanking the friend.

Many of the schools for newly free Black people were established by aid agencies like the Mission Society in conjunction with the Freedmen's Bureau, which had been mandated to set up an educational system for the newly free Black men, women, and children as one of its first tasks. The American Baptist Home Mission Society and the Woman's American Baptist Home Mission Society, founded in 1877, would ultimately establish twenty-seven institutions of higher education for people freed after the Emancipation Proclamation was issued.

In Virginia, aid agencies found that they were unable to secure appropriate buildings for schools. Their teachers were denied homes to rent and were socially ostracized. The *Norfolk Virginian* described the teachers as Black "school-marms" who had taken "shelter, with their brood of black-birds, under the protecting wings of that all-gobbling, and foulest of all fowls, the well known buzzard . . . Freedmen's Bureau."

Schools were convened in "basement vestries, in audience rooms of churches—in rough barrack buildings, or hospital wards, without suitable furniture and appliances, often with two to six teachers and several hundred children in the same room." During the first school year, eight schoolhouses and churches were burned, and several teachers were assaulted or threatened. In spite of the roadblocks put up by whites, the schools were educating Black children—and many adults too. By March 1866, some 17,589 students were being instructed in 145 schools statewide.

Many white residents were displeased with their success. They accused the teachers who arrived in Virginia from New York and Connecticut of attempting to influence the newly free Black people through their teaching.

"Coming into conflict with the mores and attitudes of the white Virginians, and probably flaunting their Union victory in the faces of the defeated Confederates, they seem to have been the most important cause of white opposition to Negro schools," the historian William T. Alderson suggested in a 1952 paper. More likely, whites simply opposed Black education and empowerment, which threatened the white supremacy they hoped to maintain.

Finding a place to locate a school in Richmond had proved difficult for American Baptist Home Mission Society leaders for the same reason. The organization had been able to found a program quickly in Washington, DC, but it was stymied in the South by whites who had been deeply invested in slaveholding and remained opposed to empowering Black men. President Johnson's decision to overturn Field Order No. 15 also had a great impact on education. Without government funds to acquire land and buildings to create schools for Black children, classes were instead held at a variety of locations, and not on a set schedule. Richmond Theological School for Freedmen "hovered constantly on the edge of extinction," wrote Raymond Hylton, a white professor who compiled the school's early history.

Richmond Theological School's first leader was Joseph Getchell Binney, a former president of Columbian College, which later became George Washington University. He conducted classes at First African Baptist Church and in spare rooms in other buildings around town. Binney hoped to provide prospective pastors with biblical instruction as well as literary and scientific studies "sufficient enough to make them intelligent men and capable of leading colored churches," said his widow, Juliette Pattison Binney.

When Binney left Richmond in July 1866 for Myanmar, then known as Burma, where he had earlier founded a school, he was replaced by the determined white abolitionist Nathaniel Colver. A former minister at the Tremont Temple in Boston, Colver had for years preached against the system of slavery. When he learned of Black Americans' dire straits after the war, he compared the end of slavery to rescuing a drowning man in the winter.

"He had gotten his man out of the water onto the ice . . . but the poor fellow would freeze to death if not looked after," wrote Colver's successor, Charles Henry Corey, oozing paternalism in his *A History of the Richmond Theological Seminary.*

Colver could not find a building to house his school either. "How many white Christians were there in the South immediately after the war, when bad passions were still rampant, when hate prevailed and not love, who would have dared to sell a building or even lease a building in the face of their pro-slavery neighbors to be used as a school for negroes?" recalled James B. Simmons, the Mission Society administrator.

Simmons recounted that white property owners turned "pale with fear" when he asked to purchase their land for a Mission Society school. "No, no. Never, never. My neighbors would blame me," he recalled white landowners saying. One white man told Simmons, "Sir, the price of that land is one thousand dollars an acre, but as you want it for a Negro School, you cannot have it at *any* price!"

Colver had hoped to locate the Richmond Theological School in a Black church, but Black pastors were not receptive. He recalled that they "stood in doubt therefore as to the wisdom of my plans," incorrectly surmising that Black pastors were "afraid" of schools. "Slavery had taught them that schools and book learning were not for the black man, but only for the whites," he said.

More likely, Black preachers did not trust a white man to do right by them and their churches, which they finally controlled after so many years of ceding leadership to white preachers. Black Americans' desire to be educated was persistent, strong, and universal. Slave narratives are filled with stories of enslaved people's attempts to learn to read and write, and of the ways in which they were not only denied this opportunity by enslavers and lawmakers but beaten and punished if they tried.

Though Colver was perplexed by his inability to find a building to rent, he did not give up. In 1867, he spent a day fasting and praying as he considered how to proceed with a task that seemed impossible. In James B. Simmons's recounting, Colver recalled, "As the evening of that day approached, I went out of my place of prayer on to the streets of Richmond to see what answer the Lord might give me."

Colver was "close to despair" when he ran into a group of Black women on the street. Mary Lumpkin was among the women standing near First African Baptist Church, where she was a member. Perhaps their pastor, Reverend James H. Holmes, a formerly enslaved man, had paved the way for the conversation.

"I had not walked far when I met upon the sidewalk a group of colored people. I stopped them. I engaged them in conversation. I told them the story of my errand in Richmond and the obstacles I had encountered," Colver recalled.

He had finally found a receptive audience. "In the midst of that group was a large, fair-faced freed-woman, nearly white, who said she had a place which she thought I could have," Colver said later.

Described by Colver as "a pious and intelligent woman," Mary Lumpkin clearly valued education. She was literate herself and had made sure that her daughters had been educated too. Perhaps she viewed the act of renting the jail to him as a way to give back to her community, an investment in Black people after they had been denied so much. Maybe allowing the jail to be converted into a school felt like a religious act. Maybe she saw it as redemption for the many ways in which Robert Lumpkin had harmed enslaved people, or as her chance to act when for so long she had felt powerless to help the Black people imprisoned there. Or perhaps letting Colver use the jail was simply a way to pay her bills.

Meeting Mary Lumpkin was the answer to Colver's prayers. Two months later, he leased Lumpkin's Jail from Mary Lumpkin for three years at the cost of $1,000 a year. "The occupancy of those premises," Simmons wrote, "was wholly providential."

The building that had been an epicenter of pain and suffering for so many would take on a new life as a place of Black education.

COLVER WANTED TO transform Lumpkin's Jail into a place of healing where formerly enslaved men could build new lives.

As he opened the Richmond Theological School for Freedmen at the jail site, he sought the support of Black pastors such as Reverend James H. Holmes, who moved onto the campus with his family. Reverend Richard Wells of Manchester Baptist Church and, later, Ebenezer Baptist Church and Pastor George Jackson of Halifax County also backed Colver's efforts.

Within weeks, Black men like those once imprisoned at the jail knocked out the jail cells and pulled down the iron bars from the windows. A little over two years after the war ended, on September 1, 1867, classes began at the former Lumpkin's Jail with some thirty or forty pupils. "The old slave pen was no longer the 'devil's half acre' but God's half acre," Simmons noted.

On opening day, Colver preached from the porch of the boarding-house, acknowledging "the change that had taken place in the status of the colored people, and also to the different purpose to which the premises were about to be devoted." He also acknowledged changes to the "old jail, with the iron grating across the windows."

"No longer would there go up from within those walls from bro-kenhearted men, torn from their families forever, an agonizing wail to Heaven," Colver reportedly said.

Among the students were Holmes and Isaac P. Brockenton, a pastor from Darlington, South Carolina, whom Corey had assisted in found-ing a church after the war. Joseph Endom Jones, a formerly enslaved man who had been taught to read by another enslaved person and a Confederate soldier, entered the theological school to prepare for the ministry but would return as a teacher.

Peter Randolph also became a student, calling the school's location in Lumpkin's Jail "remarkable." "The groans and expressions of sorrow, that used to go up from this accursed spot, when husbands and wives, parents and children, were separated never more to meet, cannot be de-scribed by tongue or pen," he wrote. "How fitting it was that a school for the instruction of the freedmen, and especially the Christian ministry, should be erected, and occupy this place; verifying that scripture, that God makes even the wrath of men to praise him."

During a six-hour school day in the jail building, the institute's teach-ers taught grammar, math, geography, reading, and biblical knowledge. Some classrooms were in former jail cells, and former whipping posts were used as lecterns for the professors. Teachers and students boarded in other buildings on the jail grounds.

"So entirely absorbed were we in our arduous work of teaching these eager students, some of whom were already pastors, that our uninviting surroundings were unthought of by us," recalled H. Goodman-Smith, who taught at the institute for four years. Perhaps she was unbothered because she was white.

Though ill, Colver continued to lecture, teach, and serve as the school's administrator until 1868, when Charles Henry Corey was transferred to Richmond to replace him. Corey had spent the war ministering to soldiers in Texas, Louisiana, and South Carolina. Later, he helped organize Black churches, raise money for new buildings, and ordain ministers in Charleston. He had also taught at Georgia's

Augusta Institute, which would later become the HBCU Morehouse College.

When Corey arrived, he moved into Lumpkin's former home with his wife Fannie, failing to grasp the symbolism of a white authority figure making his home there. Corey acted as principal and taught biblical studies. In the afternoons, he and Fannie led an eighty-person class whose students included mothers and grandmothers.

In February 1869, the school was renamed the Colver Institute for its former principal, who continued to advise Corey. He suggested that in order to make the school viable over the long term, it needed to move out of the jail.

"The time will soon come," he wrote, "when that school must be put upon on a permanent basis."

IN THE AFTERMATH of the Civil War, Richmond was changing. In 1867, Black men voted for the first time, electing twenty-four Black men to Virginia's constitutional convention, which was called to write a new state constitution, as required by Congress before Virginia's representatives could be seated in Congress. Record numbers of Black students enrolled in school in 1868. The next year, Richmond residents petitioned the City Council for a citywide system of schools. A teacher for the Freedmen's Bureau was appointed superintendent.

In the fall of 1868, Mary Lumpkin, then in her midthirties, left Richmond, apparently for good. She returned to Philadelphia, reuniting with her children and her young grandchildren, Horace and Anna Kelsey. George E. Kelsey, to whom Mary Lumpkin had transferred ownership of the Philadelphia home when she went to Richmond after the war, transferred the house back to her control.

In Philadelphia, Mary Lumpkin did not have money to pay bills, a common problem for Black women of this era—apparently even for ones who had received an inheritance.

After Nathaniel Colver's retirement, he wrote to Charles Henry Corey inquiring about where things stood with Mary Lumpkin. Perhaps she was hoping that the Colver Institute would buy the jail from her. "Mrs. Lumpkin was ever so kind to us," Colver wrote, adding that he wished to give her "the kindest consideration in return."

Mary Lumpkin and Corey stayed in regular contact. He and his wife Fannie even visited her in Philadelphia. Corey also saw—or perhaps met for the first time—Martha Kelsey and Annie Lumpkin, whom he found "to be cultivated and refined, and contented and happy with families of their own." He was likely referring to Martha because Annie does not appear to have been married when he visited.

Mary Lumpkin wrote to Corey in March 1869, revealing she was having difficulty managing Robert Lumpkin's estate and asking for his assistance. "I would like for you to let me have one month's rent," she wrote, "as I have to raise $200 by next month, and if you could it will help me very much."

She probably had a tax bill coming due. She added, "I dislike to ask you but I am so worried about money affairs that I . . . hardly know what to do." After all she had endured, she was now also troubled about how to pay her bills.

As the Colver Institute sought to buy a building that could better suit its needs, she wrote Corey again to ask his assistance in settling up. "I asked for two thousand but would be satisfied with fifteen hundred," she wrote.

In her correspondence with school officials, she inquired about Reverend James H. Holmes, the caretaker and preacher of First African Baptist Church. "Remember me to Mr. Holmes and family," she wrote.

She continued to express support for the school that she had played a role in founding. She wrote, "I hope that the school is getting on very well."

WHILE THE COLVER Institute was operating out of the slave jail, Baptists had established schools for Black men in Southern cities such as

Raleigh, North Carolina; Columbia, South Carolina; New Orleans, Louisiana; and Nashville, Tennessee.

James B. Simmons, the American Baptist Home Mission Society administrator, regularly visited Richmond to look for a new, permanent location for the Colver Institute. He decided on the former United States Hotel at Nineteenth and Main streets. He bought the building for $10,000 with funds provided by the Freedmen's Bureau.

The L-shaped brick hotel had fifty rooms once frequented by state legislators. The building also had been used as a medical college and a Confederate hospital, and after the war it served as a school for Black children. Corey's students raised $1,000 toward improvements and spent hours after classes making repairs to the building. The Colver Institute opened in the hotel in the fall of 1870.

"It was a proud day when the students and teachers of Lumpkin's Jail marched up out of that slave-pen," Corey wrote, admitting that the symbolism of a slave jail as a school had weighed on him, and on the students too.

A few years later, in 1876, the Virginia General Assembly incorporated the school as the Richmond Institute. Corey, the school's longtime white leader, would serve as school administrator for thirty years. Corey's board of trustees included Black men, among them Reverend James H. Holmes and Reverend Richard Wells, but the school would not be run by a Black president until 1941.

In 1883, the Mission Society launched Hartshorn Memorial College, one of the first colleges for Black women in the country, after briefly admitting females to the Richmond Institute. At the college's founding, fifty-eight women were instructed in the basement of Richmond's Ebenezer Baptist Church, which had already hosted a Freedmen's Bureau school and one of Richmond's first public schools for Black students after the Civil War.

Hartshorn would graduate women like Bessye Banks Bearden of New Jersey, who became the first Black woman to serve on the New

York City Board of Education, and Tossie Permelia Frances Whiting, a Richmond native who became the first dean of women at the HBCU later known as Virginia State University. Ora Brown Stokes of Chester-field, Virginia, also graduated from Hartshorn. She became a civil rights activist and founded the Home for Working Girls, a safe place to live for Black women who moved to Richmond for work.

The Richmond Institute turned its focus to theology and in 1886 offered its first college degree—a bachelor of divinity. It reincorporated as the Richmond Theological Seminary, the central college for the ad-vanced theological training of Black Baptist ministers in the South. In 1899, after thirty-one years at the helm, Corey retired and the school merged with the historically Black Wayland Seminary, a Baptist insti-tution in Washington, DC. It was reincorporated as Virginia Union University, one of the oldest historically Black colleges and universities in America.

Mary Lumpkin, still alive then, had played an important role in the birth of Virginia Union University, whether she knew it or not. If she did, she must have been proud that she was able to take the old slave jail and turn it into something good—a place that would benefit Black men and women for generations.

After spending a year in Philadelphia with her children and grand-children, Mary Lumpkin left for New Orleans.

The journey of a formerly enslaved woman to this French and Spanish–influenced town, one thousand miles from Richmond, was a long time in the making. She had moved her children away from the riverbed jail to freedom. She had worked to protect them from a rela-tionship like hers with their father, a man twenty-five years her senior, a man who enslaved her. She had wanted them to be educated and to be provided for. She had seen to all that.

Now here she was in New Orleans, living in the same town as her longtime friend Lucy Ann Hagan. Clutching a letter tightly in her hand, she strode down the aisle of a Baptist church toward a group of

Black leaders meeting in the sanctuary. She handed the envelope to a pastor seated in the back of the church. The Reverend Armstead Mason Newman, who had also been enslaved in Richmond, took note of the "splendid looking" woman in front of him, but he didn't yet know that he had encountered her before.

He opened the letter and read it. "To whom it may concern: This is to certify that Sister Mary Jane Lumpkin is a member in good and regular standing in the First African Baptist church, city of Richmond, and is hereby dismissed by her own free will and consent to join with you," the letter read.

Newman looked up at Mary Lumpkin. He asked, "Is this Sister Lumpkin?" She nodded and replied, "This is Sister Lumpkin." In that moment, there must have been a flash of recognition. Years earlier, they had encountered each other behind the twelve-foot walls that surrounded Robert Lumpkin's slave jail. As an enslaved mother of enslaved children, Mary Lumpkin had noticed Newman, then a young enslaved boy not unlike her sons, who had been sent to the jail by his enslaver to be beaten for an infraction, perhaps a minor theft or talking back to a white person. The boy didn't know the punishment that awaited him.

"Have I not seen you before?" Mary Lumpkin asked Newman on that day in New Orleans.

"I expect you have," he replied.

A decade or more earlier, Newman had been the one carrying the letter. He had walked down Richmond's Broad Street, a note from his enslaver in his hand, "just as happy as a little fellow could be." He couldn't read and therefore didn't know the letter's contents. When he entered the slave jail and handed the letter to Robert Lumpkin or one of his caretakers, Mary Lumpkin had looked at him "rather piteously," he recalled. She likely knew the boy was about to be brutally beaten.

"I could not understand it," he recalled.

After Robert Lumpkin looked at the letter, he called out to one of his men. "Take this boy," he told the man. "Carry him back there and put him in."

Newman quickly surmised what was about to happen. "It seemed to me that my heart went right down," Newman recalled later.

The young Newman was escorted to the jail's whipping room. He was laid down on the floor, and his hands and feet were stretched out and fastened in metal rings that were attached to the floor. A man stood over him, flogging him, probably with a whip or lash. When he had been deemed sufficiently punished, he was unhooked and allowed to leave, and on his way out of the jail he encountered Mary Lumpkin again.

"When I came away, that same woman looked at me again, and it seemed to me that she was saying, 'poor child,'" he recalled.

Now Newman was face to face with the same woman, a woman who was well aware of Robert Lumpkin's brutality. Newman had learned to read and write. After attending seminary in Washington, DC, he had graduated with honors from what is now known as Colgate University. Selected to lead Common Street, or Tulane Avenue, Baptist Church in New Orleans, Newman would later serve as state missionary and president of the Louisiana Baptist State Convention.

Much had also changed for Mary Lumpkin since she had last seen Newman. She had lived as free in Philadelphia for years. She had transformed Robert Lumpkin's jail into a school for free Black men training as pastors—men just like Newman.

As she stood in a Black church in New Orleans, far away from that jail and the abuse she suffered there, recognition of Newman was surely settling into her bones. The past must have washed over them both that day, taking them back to the sounds of brutal beatings, to the fear of violence that coursed through their veins, to the stench of unwashed bodies, of death and dying.

"Are you not the little one that came one morning down to the jail with a note," Mary Lumpkin inquired of Newman, "and are you not the one that went into the back room?"

They both already knew the answer. They were free Black people building new lives, but they would never be completely free of their traumatic pasts.

ONCE MARY LUMPKIN could pick where to live without having to consider Robert Lumpkin, she chose to reunite with her longtime friend Lucy Ann Hagan.

It had been nearly twenty years since they were first separated as girls, but they had continued to see each other over the years. Hagan had made her last visit to Richmond in 1868, just before Mary Lumpkin left Virginia, apparently for good. Perhaps that is when they hatched a plan for Mary Lumpkin to head for New Orleans, where Hagan ran a boardinghouse.

Mary Lumpkin got to Louisiana in 1869 and stayed with Hagan for a while. In taking a "housekeeping" job, she was probably running a boardinghouse or working in one. Such work often entailed doing the cooking, cleaning, and washing for the people who boarded, as well as sewing for them or doing other chores they requested.

We don't know how Mary Lumpkin felt about moving away from her children and grandchildren, who had likely all stayed behind in Philadelphia. By 1870 they would be living in a different house than the one she owned there, in a different neighborhood. She may have wanted to give them freedom to pass as white, and her presence would have made that more difficult. She may have had complicated feelings about mothering since she was forced into the role by Robert Lumpkin. Or maybe she had met a man, wanted to be with him, and was taking that opportunity now that she could finally choose something for herself.

In New Orleans—or maybe earlier in Richmond, or Philadelphia—she met and partnered with an Army soldier. In 1872, Mary Lumpkin left New Orleans for New Richmond, Ohio, a prewar abolitionist stronghold named for the Virginia town where she had been enslaved for many years. It's unclear if she knew anyone else there, but she was likely following the US service member, who may have been from the small riverfront town or may have had friends there. Perhaps he belonged to Company K of the US Colored Infantry, a number of whose members lived in New Richmond. He and Mary Lumpkin may have married, but since Mary Lumpkin apparently never changed her name, it's possible

that they simply lived together. Regardless, she shows up in federal records years later as the widow of this unnamed soldier.

When she arrived in Ohio, it was not her first time. She may have
explored moving there or sending one or more of her children in 1847,
when she first traveled to Ohio. "I was in Cincinnati to see a lawyer," she
later recalled.

She would not have made the journey to Ohio alone as a young, enslaved woman, and Robert Lumpkin would probably have taken her himself or hired someone to make the journey with her. Perhaps she met with
Adam N. Riddle, the attorney and member of the Ohio Legislature appointed by Silas Omohundro to handle the legal issues of Louisa Tandy
Omohundro's relocation to Cincinnati, or maybe she had consulted with
an abolitionist attorney like Salmon P. Chase, who defended James G.
Birney, editor of *The Philanthropist*, an abolitionist newspaper, and who
later became governor of Ohio and chief justice of the US Supreme Court.
Regardless, Mary Lumpkin did not move to Ohio at that time.

For years, New Richmond had a large free Black population and was
Clermont County's largest and most prosperous Black community. The
town had been founded in 1814 at the base of a hill along the banks of
the Ohio River by the Revolutionary War hero Jacob Light. A cousin of
Light's from Richmond, Virginia, surveyed the land and named it, according to local lore. Land to the east was settled by Thomas Ashburn in
1816, and he named the town Susanna, for his wife. The villages merged
as New Richmond on January 11, 1828. The new town quickly became
a center of commerce because of its riverfront location, and local farmers brought produce to ship out on steamboats manufactured there. As
New Richmond grew, wool, saw, and grain mills opened. Furniture and
clothing factories were founded, along with distilleries and breweries.

During the slavery era, New Richmond had been a key stop on the
Underground Railroad, in part because of its location on the Ohio River
across from Kentucky, a slave state. When enslaved people escaped to
New Richmond, they could get assistance not only from white abolitionists but also from free Black families, who hid them in their homes.

The town's Presbyterian and Baptist churches passed resolutions denouncing slavery as early as 1834. Two years later Birney first published *The Philanthropist*, and a group of abolitionists attempted to protect him and the printing presses.

Black residents formed their own organizations, such as the Baptist Society of Colored Persons, which came together in 1850. The Union Association for the Advancement of the Colored Men of New Richmond formed in 1857, a half-century before the founding of the National Association for the Advancement of Colored People. In 1861, the Black Second Baptist Church was constructed.

The town became a destination for enslavers setting free the people they enslaved. In 1860, a Southern enslaver visited New Richmond to purchase a farm for his two multiracial sons. Like Robert Lumpkin, the man worried about his children being sold into slavery, and purchasing property for them went some way toward easing that anxiety.

Schools in the region had long educated Black children. Two miles south of New Richmond, in Clermontville, the integrated Clermont Academy, later known as the Parker Academy, had been founded in 1839 by the abolitionist preacher Daniel Parker and his wife Priscilla Parker. It is believed to have been one of the first in the United States with integrated and coed classrooms that included formerly enslaved children of white enslavers. Perhaps one of Mary Lumpkin's children attended.

One white Texas enslaver sent his four multiracial children to Parker Academy. Milton Taylor of Maysville, Kentucky, brought his three multiracial children there, and many of the county's abolitionists sent their children to the academy as well. Edwin Matthews, formerly enslaved by Birney, also attended. The academy was known locally as a station on the Underground Railroad.

Thirty miles south, the town of Ripley was settled by many former residents of Virginia and Kentucky. It was home to the minister John Rankin, who founded the Ohio Anti-Slavery Society and, according to local lore, used a lantern from his house on a hill above the Ohio River to signal to escaping enslaved people in Kentucky. He worked closely with the foundry owner John Parker, a formerly enslaved man who had purchased his own freedom in Virginia. Parker regularly went into Kentucky, a slave state, to help enslaved people cross the river and then delivered them to Rankin, who sheltered them and moved them north. Rankin penned his *Letters on Slavery* to his brother, Thomas Rankin, an enslaver in Virginia. John Rankin's call for the immediate emancipation of enslaved people moved his brother to bring the Black men and women he enslaved to Ohio and set them free.

New Richmond continued to attract Black residents after the war, including Black Union veterans. At least five New Richmond men served in Company K, which spent time in battle around Richmond, Virginia. Mary Lumpkin would become acquainted with Sarah Thomas, the Kentucky-born wife of Jacob Thomas, a Company K veteran born in Virginia. The two women eventually lived together when both were widowed.

Louisa Picquet had also moved to New Richmond. She had lived in New Orleans after being freed at her enslaver's death in 1847. She moved again in 1850, to Cincinnati, where she met her husband, Henry Picquet. Injured while serving in the Civil War, he became unable to work. The couple arrived in New Richmond in 1867 with Louisa Picquet's mother, Elizabeth Ramsay, whose freedom they had bought from Texas's first lieutenant governor, Albert Clinton Horton, in part with money they raised from abolitionists. Mary Lumpkin arrived in New Richmond five years after the Picquets, and they surely encountered each other. Perhaps they were friends, as they had much in common.

Mary Allen, a genealogist and New Richmond City Council member, said she was unsure what brought Mary Lumpkin to New Richmond, but thought perhaps she knew someone in the town, possibly one of Mary Allen's own ancestors. Allen's family has lived in New Richmond since the 1850s, when her great-grandfather, Howell Boone, was freed from slavery. The son of an enslaved woman and her enslaver's white brother, he opened Boone's Market, which served both white and

Black shoppers. He was also a founder of the Union Association for the Advancement of the Colored Men of New Richmond. Allen has for years researched the family trees of the town's longtime Black families, five of whom have lived in the town since the period from the 1850s to the 1880s, but she came across Mary Lumpkin only recently.

"She intrigues me," Allen said, "because I understand her significance to a lot of people, not just New Richmond."

AFTER MARY LUMPKIN moved to New Richmond, she transferred the Philadelphia house to Annie E. Lumpkin. That decision may indicate that Mary Lumpkin had married, or was preparing to, as Robert Lumpkin's will had stipulated that the property would go to their children if she wed.

The children were not able to hold onto the house. Annie Lumpkin sold the family's original home in Philadelphia a few months after Mary Lumpkin transferred it to her, probably splitting any proceeds with her siblings.

Not long after Mary Lumpkin moved to Ohio, tragedy struck Martha Kelsey's family. George Kelsey died, a devastating turn of events for Mary Lumpkin and her daughter. Their marriage had represented stability and potential for Martha and her siblings.

His death put Martha in a precarious financial position, and she decided to leave Philadelphia and relocate to New Orleans about 1873 or 1874. She likely did not want to be a burden on her brothers. Perhaps George Kelsey had family in New Orleans who offered to help his widow and children.

By 1876, Martha Kelsey had had a fourth child and was working in or running a boardinghouse in the French Quarter on the same street as the one run by Lucy Ann Hagan, who may have helped Mary Lumpkin's daughter land the job. Several years later, Martha Kelsey was working at two restaurants. In the span of a few years, she had gone from staying home with her children in Philadelphia to stringing together jobs in a new city to make ends meet.

Mary Lumpkin did not live in New Orleans but may have visited from Ohio. Before long, Annie Lumpkin would join her sister in New Orleans. In 1879, Annie Lumpkin petitioned the family's estate for money on behalf of William Edloe, Harriet Barber's son, who had taken the name of his late father. Robert Lumpkin had borrowed $600 from William Edloe just before he died, and he had given the young man a bond in exchange. Edloe was ready to cash it.

He and Annie Lumpkin, who had known each other for twenty years by then, may have been dating. On September 15, 1886, Annie Lumpkin and Edloe married in Manhattan. On the marriage certificate, Annie Lumpkin's maiden name is recorded as Lyttleton. Had she changed her last name to obliterate her past or was it a mistake in the government records? Martha Kelsey also used Lyttleton as her son George's middle name, and on Annie Lumpkin's death record, Lyttleton would be recorded as her father's last name instead of Lumpkin.

Like Annie, William Edloe was passing as white. When he moved west to Kansas for railroad work, the son of an enslaver and an enslaved woman created a narrative of being descended from an aristocratic family in Philadelphia. He and Annie Edloe had two children, both of whom died young.

In New Orleans, all four of Martha Kelsey's children apparently passed for white. They were surrounded by white neighbors and a few live-in Black servants. Martha's daughter, Anna E. Kelsey, would marry a white bookkeeper and live in the Bronx. Martha's son, Horace Kelsey, would move to Brooklyn, where he worked as a foreman in a railroad yard and married a white dressmaker. Their neighbors in Brooklyn were white, and in 1900 they had a live-in Irish servant.

By 1940, Horace's son had made the move to California that would firmly plant Mary Lumpkin's descendants on the West Coast. Martha's daughter Aileen married a white man from Virginia and moved with him to Montana, where he worked as a foreman in a mine. Martha's youngest, George Lyttleton Kelsey, was born in Louisiana, apparently after the death of her husband. He would later suggest on official documents that his father was a French man—in other words, not George Kelsey. He moved to Ohio and married a white woman, the daughter of an Englishman.

What happened to Mary Lumpkin's sons is not as clear. If Robert Lumpkin's namesake fought in the Civil War, he survived. All three men were alive in 1881. But by 1900, two of Mary Lumpkin's sons had passed away, and the third disappears from public records. He may have changed his name to George W. Lumpkins and moved to Bridgewater, Massachusetts, where he lived among the Wampanoag people and married a woman who had been born enslaved in Richmond. They may have stopped using their father's name.

"Whether they pass as colored or whites I do not know. But I presume no trace could be found of them under the name of Lumpkin; for in the very nature of things they would be more than willing that all records and recollections of their birthplace and pedigree should be blotted out forever," wrote James B. Simmons, the American Baptist Home Mission Society administrator, in an undated letter.

If Simmons was correct, all of Mary Lumpkin's children removed evidence of their relation to Robert Lumpkin and the violence he perpetrated. Some also moved away from their mother's Black roots.

On May 10, 1881, Mary Lumpkin said in a chancery case that she was "willing and desirous to turn over the said fund to her children," adding that she wanted to release her inheritance during her life rather than have it happen after her death. Also in 1881, Thurston Lumpkin's home in Alabama was sold in a sheriff's sale four years after his death, most likely because Mary Lumpkin could not pay taxes on it.

A few years later, in 1887, Frederika Hagan wrote to Mary Lumpkin to inform her that Lucy Ann Hagan had died, a loss that must have left a hole in her heart. In lives that were traumatic and difficult on many levels, lives that spanned from enslaved girlhood to free womanhood, their friendship had seen them through dark days. They had lost children and the fathers of their children. They had been enslaved and then become free. They had struggled to pay their bills, but their lives had been their own. Their friendship lasted through it all, a tool of survival and a form of resistance.

That year, Mary Lumpkin would prove her loyalty to Lucy Ann Hagan when she was asked to testify in a New Orleans court case about an inheritance. In her testimony, she was careful not to convey her dear friend's past as an enslaved woman. She also referred to Lucy Ann Hagan's relationship to John Hagan as a marriage, hiding the true nature of the connection. Mary Lumpkin must have considered it important to keep this information from a government body and anyone reading her testimony. She framed the story of their friendship in a way that left out altogether the women's enslavement and the years they had spent in slave jails. She omitted the sexual abuse that had resulted in them becoming mothers. She sanitized their history.

By 1900, if not well before, the man with whom Mary Lumpkin had partnered—perhaps her one true love—had died. Her grief at losing both her partner and her dearest friend must have been terrible; by then, two of her sons had died too. Her daughters had left or soon would leave New Orleans, and her children, grandchildren, and great-grandchildren were spread farther and farther apart, from New York to Montana.

In the final years of Mary Lumpkin's life, she lived in a Black neighborhood on New Richmond's Columbia Street, renting a room from Sarah Thomas. Her finances were surely in shambles. Her family did not live nearby. Yet in this tiny town of just 1,900 people, she could be seen and understood in all her complexity.

As she had done in Virginia, Pennsylvania, and Louisiana, she undoubtedly built community with other women in Ohio who had been enslaved and forced to have the children of their enslavers. She may have befriended women like Louisa Picquet and her mother, Elizabeth Ramsay, women who had survived, women who elevated and supported one another. Perhaps she viewed Sarah Thomas, who was much younger, as a daughter.

It must have brought her peace to think back on her life and know that she had removed her children from the slave jail where they had grown up. She had told Robert Lumpkin that "these children have to be free" and she had seen to it. Perhaps it made her proud knowing that she had not only given them an education but also ensured that generations of other free Black men and women had a chance to attend school too.

On November 11, 1905, Mary Lumpkin died at the age of seventy-two. She was buried in New Richmond's Samarian, or Good Samaritan, Cemetery. Located just outside of town on a steep embankment, it was the final resting place of twenty-three soldiers in the US Colored Infantry Troops. Jacob Thomas was buried there, along with Henry and Louisa Picquet and Elizabeth Ramsay. Perhaps her partner was buried there too.

Mary Lumpkin's grave was unmarked.

In June 2020, the image of George Floyd and the words "Black Lives Matter" are illuminated onto Richmond's Robert E. Lee statue, which became a headquarters for social justice. The statue was removed in September 2021 and surrounded with black chain link fencing. (Credit: Scott Elmquist)

10

"God's Half Acre"

By the start of the twenty-first century, the existence of Lumpkin's Jail and its role in the domestic trade of enslaved people had been all but forgotten.

The remnants of the slave business in Richmond, as in most Southern cities, were buried in the landscape, erasing the slaveholding history. There was little evidence of the horrific trade of humans that had gone on for decades in the city, of the slave auction sites and slave jails that had once been so visible.

"Black history in the U.S. has long been imperiled or rendered invisible," wrote *Richmond Times-Dispatch* columnist Michael Paul Williams, a Virginia Union University alumnus and Pulitzer Prize winner, of the destruction of an Underground Railroad house in nearby Petersburg in 2020.

From its early days, Richmond not only was complicit in its acceptance of slavery but benefited from it. The city was made by its exploitation of Black people. Yet Richmond has not adequately acknowledged that history or shared the stories of the wrongs that were committed. Slave trading cities like Charleston, New Orleans, and Natchez, Mississippi, have all buried their pasts too.

When the *New York Times* went looking in 2019 for slavery sites in cities and towns that played the most significant roles in the slave trade, it found that after the Civil War, "the auction blocks had largely been removed, and the auction houses that still stood had been repurposed."

"No one was eager to preserve these sites, or even remember them," the *Times* wrote. "And so they disappeared, year by year, generation by generation, until there was no living memory of what happened in these places."

Even fewer sites in America have explored the slave trade's impact on Black families who were brutalized, traumatized, exploited, and broken apart. Bryan Stevenson's Equal Justice Initiative opened a museum dedicated to the legacy of slavery in Montgomery, Alabama, on land where enslaved people were once warehoused. A museum with slavery at the center of its historical interpretation was founded at Whitney Plantation in Wallace, Louisiana, where enslaved people were forced to raise sugar cane. The International African American Museum was slated to open in 2022 on the waterfront where slave ships landed in Charleston, South Carolina.

In 2017, New Orleans mayor Mitch Landrieu addressed how little his city had done to memorialize slavery. At the time, New Orleans was having a public conversation about its Confederate monuments, which he said begged the question of "why there are no slave ship monuments, no prominent markers on public land to remember the lynchings or the slave blocks; nothing to remember this long chapter of our lives; the pain, the sacrifice, the shame . . . all of it happening on the soil of New Orleans." He called the absence of those memorials "a lie by omission."

Instead of publicly addressing that essential history in the aftermath of the Civil War, communities across the South put up heroic portrayals of Confederate figures in statue form. Erected during the Jim Crow era, these monuments are tools of white supremacy, designed to intimidate Black Americans.

"After the Civil War, these statues were a part of that terrorism as much as a burning cross on someone's lawn," Landrieu said. "They were erected purposefully to send a strong message to all who walked in their shadows about who was still in charge."

They were also intended to change the story told about the Civil War. The "Lost Cause" narrative, which presents the war from the point of view of the Confederacy, romanticized the South as a chivalrous society and made the case that slavery was not the primary cause of the war.

One of the largest Confederate monuments in the country was located a few blocks from my home in Richmond. Cast in bronze and sitting on a forty-foot granite and marble base, the statue of Robert E. Lee atop his horse, Traveller, loomed over my neighborhood and the city, casting a decidedly ominous shadow.

While Virginia is the birthplace of many of the country's founding fathers, the commonwealth and the city of Richmond chose to honor Confederates instead. In 1886, Governor Fitzhugh Lee, a nephew of Robert E. Lee, consolidated two groups that had been fundraising for fifteen years to build the statue. The new association ordered a statue of him cast in Paris at a cost of $77,500—roughly $2.2 million today.

John Mitchell Jr., editor of the Black newspaper *Richmond Planet*, criticized its placement. "The South may revere the memory of its chieftains. It takes the wrong steps in so doing, and proceeds to go too far in every similar celebration. It serves to retard its progress in the country and forges heavier chains with which to be bound," he wrote. Mitchell, a former City Council member, had voted against allocating funds. A later City Council, however, approved funding for an event to celebrate the statue's placement.

When the twelve-ton, twenty-one-foot-tall statue of Lee arrived in Richmond by boat, some 10,000 people helped move it with ropes to a tobacco field that was to become a subdivision for Richmond's white elite. When the statue was unveiled in 1890, approximately 150,000 attended, among them thousands of former Confederate soldiers in uniform who marched with their units.

After the Lee statue was placed in Richmond, more Confederate statues followed, rising up on a tree-lined Monument Avenue, with a generous green median running down the middle. The statues made it appear as if the Confederacy had won the war—the revisionism of the Lost Cause on full display. Lavish brick homes began to be constructed in the area in 1901, and in 1907 an equestrian statue of James Ewell Brown "Jeb" Stuart, one of the most prominent officers of the Confederacy, went up nearby.

The same year, a likeness of Jefferson Davis, who led the Confederacy, was erected with an inscription reading "Exponent of Constitutional Principles" and "Defender of the Rights of States," along with Davis's ridiculous assertion that he acted "not in hostility to others." In fact, he had approved the execution of Black prisoners-of-war and the white Union officers who commanded them, and he suggested that all free Black men and women should be enslaved. Even two decades after the war's end, he did not repent, saying, "If it were all to do over again, I would again do just as I did in 1861."

Statues depicting Thomas "Stonewall" Jackson, a high-ranking Confederate officer who had served in the US military, arrived on Monument Avenue in 1919, and a decade later, Matthew Fontaine Maury, who had served as a Confederate Navy official. Confederate sympathizers had successfully created what the historian Charles Reagan Wilson termed a "sacred road" of "Southern civil religion." The late Raymond H. Boone, the trailblazing founder and publisher of the *Richmond Free Press*, a Black newspaper, called it "Losers' Lane." From the time he and his wife, Jean Patterson Boone, established the paper in 1992, he called for the monuments to be removed.

For the 131 years that Confederate statues stood in Richmond, the monuments would do exactly what they were intended to do— rewrite history. For generations, Black residents of Richmond—and anyone else who happened to be driving through the city—could not avoid those idols of white supremacy, which were designed to keep them subservient.

BLACK RESIDENTS OF Richmond have worked for decades to bring the story of the city's role in the slave trade to the forefront, to ensure that this dark chapter of history is not forgotten and that it is taught to generations of Americans. It is a story Black Virginians, Black scholars, and the Black press know well and have been telling for years.

After taking a trip to Senegal, Virginia governor L. Douglas Wilder, the grandson of enslaved people and the nation's first elected Black governor, dreamed up the United States National Slavery Museum in 1993 and spent a decade trying to bring it to fruition.

The museum was slated to be built on a thirty-eight-acre parcel on the Rappahannock River in Fredericksburg, Virginia. The presidents of historically Black Hampton and Howard Universities joined his museum board, along with the actor Bill Cosby, the late historian John Hope Franklin, and various business leaders. Wilder planned for the museum to open in 2004, but after a series of delays and false starts, supporters of Wilder's vision believed that his project was dead. In 2012, his organization declared bankruptcy and donors asked for the return of artifacts, including leg shackles and a bill of sale for enslaved people. Wilder later raised the idea of placing the museum in Richmond and suggested that it could be located at the original location of First African Baptist Church.

By then, momentum for memorializing slavery in Virginia had shifted to Richmond's Slave Trail Commission, formally established in 1998. The commission worked to help preserve and share the history of slavery in Richmond by creating a walking trail that chronicles the history of the slave trade in Virginia. Unveiled in 2011, the trail begins at Manchester Docks, which served as a port in both the transatlantic trade and the domestic trade, and weaves through the sites of some of the former slave markets of Richmond, passes the Lumpkin's Jail site and the African burial ground, and ends at the former home of First African Baptist Church.

The route also includes the Reconciliation Statue, unveiled in 2007 to memorialize the transatlantic British, African, and American trade route. The statue was installed on Fifteenth Street after the Virginia General Assembly voted to express profound regret for the state's role in the slave trade and for the exploitation of Indigenous people. The measure passed 97–0 on a roll call vote in the Virginia House and a voice vote in the Senate the same day. At the time, the expression of collective regret was said to be the first of its kind in the country.

When Virginia delegate Delores McQuinn joined the commission, members talked about finding a way to tell the story of Richmond slavery through firsthand accounts. Ben Campbell, a founding member, recalls first hearing about Lumpkin's Jail from the late Nancy Jo Taylor, a Black Richmond public school educator, as she led a tour of sites in Richmond's hidden Black history. After commission members became aware of the jail's existence, they began investigating its history and trying to determine where it might have been located. McQuinn remembers visiting the potential site in 2003 and feeling "a presence" and "a bond."

"I started weeping and couldn't stop," she told *Smithsonian Magazine*. "It's a heaviness that I've felt over and over again."

The commission decided to search for archaeological remnants of the jail and requested bids for the work in 2005, but with one caveat: members were not sure of the exact location of the Lumpkin property. The Virginia archaeologist Matthew R. Laird attempted to pinpoint the site so that his employer, James River Institute of Archaeology, could bid on the project. He spent months researching the history of the property and looking at deeds for the parcels acquired by Robert Lumpkin in 1844. He pulled out 1830s-era city maps, located the land on those maps, and then overlaid the old maps on newer photographs of Shockoe Bottom. Though development had dramatically changed the neighborhood, the street grid was the same.

One morning in 2006, Laird stood in an asphalt parking lot in Shockoe Bottom near Main Street Station. As cars and tractor trailers zoomed past on Interstate 95, he unfolded the map, looked at it, and knew he was standing on the spot where the jail had been located in antebellum days. A few months later, he returned with a city contract and a backhoe driver to look for remnants of antebellum Richmond, but he didn't know if any would remain.

"I was honestly thinking we would get in there . . . and we would find a jumbled mess and everyone would turn around and walk away," he confessed.

The backhoe driver lifted one thin layer of fill at a time, and eventually, to Laird's delight and astonishment, the backhoe hit the jail's brick foundation. The preliminary dig was a jackpot—a once-in-a-lifetime archaeological experience.

Not only had Laird pinpointed the parcel where Lumpkin's Jail was located, but he had determined that its foundation had been preserved.

WHEN MARY LUMPKIN rented out the jail building to a school for free Black men, she could not have predicted how long it would be in existence.

When the Richmond Theological Seminary was reincorporated as Virginia Union University just before the turn of the century, the school moved onto a new campus built on a former sheep pasture. Once known as Sheep Hill, the area had been settled in the 1840s by Jewish and German immigrants. In 1899, Virginia Union University held its first founders' day on the new campus, which consisted of nine "noble buildings" built from Virginia granite and Georgia pine.

Sheep Hill had been renamed for the Black inventor George Washington Carver, and the vibrant Black community served as an extension of Jackson Ward, the adjacent Black business district known as "the Harlem of the South," which was home to Maggie Lena Walker, the first Black female bank founder and president. These Black neighborhoods, a mile from wealthy Monument Avenue, tended to be underdeveloped and did not have sewer lines, water mains, regular garbage collection, or paved streets. City leaders had passed restrictive covenants ensuring that only white families could live near Monument Avenue, and in 1911 they limited Black residents to city blocks where Black people were a majority.

Virginia Union's permanent home was near Hartshorn Memorial College, which in 1884 had acquired part of a nearby former plantation. The schools merged in 1932, making the new Virginia Union University coeducational. In 1964, Virginia Union also absorbed the assets and alumni of Storer College, which closed in 1955. Founded in 1867 in Harper's Ferry, West Virginia, by Freewill Baptists of New England, with assistance from the wealthy Maine merchant John Storer, the college had acquired land in Harper's Ferry and over the years sold it to Black residents and alumnae, ensuring that some 75 percent of Black residents owned property. Frederick Douglass had served as a trustee of the school.

Before the groundwork for Virginia Union was laid, the Institute for Colored Youth and Lincoln University had been founded in Pennsylvania, in 1837 and 1854, respectively. In 1856, Wilberforce University was established by the white Methodist Episcopal Church at Tawawa Springs in Xenia, Ohio. Named for the British abolitionist William Wilberforce, the school closed temporarily in 1862 as students withdrew to fight in the Civil War. The African Methodist Episcopal Church bought the school in 1863 and named Bishop Daniel A. Payne the first Black American college president.

In the aftermath of the Civil War, dozens of historically Black colleges and universities were founded to educate newly free Black people, and they became the primary way in which Black Americans could earn an education after high school. More than ninety institutions had been founded by 1900 to train teachers and preachers, but by the twentieth century many HBCUs began promoting Black scholarship instead. Many would seek autonomy from the white leaders and white churches that had been at the helm of the schools since they were founded.

Historically, Black men and women were routinely denied admission to predominantly white institutions, or PWIs. Before America's colleges and universities were desegregated in the 1950s and 1960s, nearly every Black student who went to college in America attended an HBCU. By providing Black men and women with access to higher education in a protective setting, HBCUs have helped them achieve individual success and progress as a group. The institutions have given Black students the kind of support that they can't always find at predominantly white institutions, many of which have a legacy of slavery, including Harvard, Yale, Georgetown, and the University of Virginia.

"Going to an HBCU gave me a real sense of my promise," said W. Franklyn Richardson, president of the board of trustees for Virginia Union and a graduate of the university.

Barbara Grey, a 1947 graduate, recalled that her parents moved her and her three sisters to Richmond from rural Virginia to attend Virginia Union because it was a college where they could afford to send all four girls. John Malcus Ellison, the college's first Black president, told her mother to let him know if she ever had difficulty making tuition payments. "To us, it meant everything," Grey said.

In 2021, Virginia Union was one of 101 HBCUs still in existence in America—99 of which are accredited. They are spread across nineteen states, Washington, DC, and the US Virgin Islands. University officials claim that Virginia Union is one of only two HBCUs where a Black woman is involved in the founding story. The other, Bethune-Cookman University, was established in Daytona Beach, Florida, by Mary McLeod Bethune, whose parents were born enslaved. Bethune founded the school in 1904 as Daytona Literary and Industrial Training School for Negro Girls. In 1935, she would establish the National Council of Negro Women.

Many HBCUs were born in church basements, homes, or old schoolhouses by white philanthropists or Black ministers with help from the American Missionary Association and the Freedmen's Bureau. The all-female Spelman College was founded as Atlanta Baptist Female Seminary in 1881 by a pair of white women and later named for donor John D. Rockefeller's wife and mother- and father-in-law, who were abolitionists.

The story of Mary Lumpkin as the mother of Virginia Union is one that the school has long recognized but only recently reclaimed. Students are now taught the role she played in the school's founding in first-year seminars and history courses. In 2020, a road that runs through campus was named Mary Lumpkin Drive, and the university installed a marker recognizing her as "the Mother of VUU" and expressing gratitude to her for providing space at the jail to give newly emancipated people an opportunity for education and advancement.

Across America, HBCUs annually enroll approximately 300,000 students, 70 percent of whom are from low-income families. Centered on Black liberation, they have served as training grounds for generations of activists and Black leaders, including Ida B. Wells, Booker T. Washington, Martin Luther King Jr., and W.E.B. Du Bois. Thurgood Marshall, who argued *Brown v. Board of Education* in front of the US Supreme Court, was trained at Lincoln University. Vice President Kamala Harris is a graduate of Howard University.

Virginia Union's activist roots have been central to its identity. One of the school's first graduates, Reverend Richard Wells, served on the five-person delegation that met with President Andrew Johnson at the White House soon after the Civil War ended to report that Black men and women in Richmond were being mistreated by city officials and soldiers.

During the civil rights era, students and faculty marched to downtown Richmond department stores to join the efforts that had begun in Greensboro, North Carolina, to desegregate whites-only lunch counters. On February 22, 1960, thirty-four Virginia Union students staged a sit-in at the lunch counter of the elegant fourth-floor Richmond Room in Thalhimer's department store, where Black men and women were allowed to shop but not to eat.

The students, referred to as the "Richmond 34," were arrested on charges of "trespassing" and were bailed out with funds raised by the NAACP and others. A Virginia Union sorority canceled its cotillion and instead used the funds to help students who had been arrested, and the university's vice president and his wife put up their home as collateral. College president Samuel Proctor had supported students behind the scenes, engaging in their plans to force arrests and garner attention for the cause of desegregation.

Following a boycott of its store, Thalhimer's integrated its lunch counters in January 1961. Yet the charges against the students were not dropped until lawsuits filed on their behalf made their way to the US Supreme Court, which in 1963 overturned the trespassing charges against the students. The protest became a defining story in Virginia Union's history and, like its origin story, central to its identity.

HBCUs have also historically served as safe spaces for their students. Beyond the reach of white students and faculty—who can be unsupportive at best and menacing at worst—HBCU campuses shelter young Black students from a world that can be dangerous for them, particularly during times of political strife like the presidency of Donald J. Trump. Instead of meeting Black students with low expectations or hostility, HBCUs create a nurturing environment and instill a sense of belonging.

"HBCUs are critical to the future of the African American people," said Richardson, senior pastor at Grace Baptist Church in Mount Vernon, New York.

Virginia Union was attended by Henry Allen Bullock, who won the Bancroft Prize for his book *A History of Negro Education in the South: From 1619 to the Present*, and by Lyman Tefft Johnson, whose legal challenge at the University of Kentucky opened the school to Black students in 1949. Wyatt Tee Walker, a key strategist behind civil rights protests who served as chief of staff to the Reverend Dr. Martin Luther King Jr., completed his graduate studies at Virginia Union. Dr. Lucille Brown, who served as a Richmond City Schools superintendent, and Jean Louise Harris, Virginia's first Black cabinet member, are graduates.

GIVEN THE NATURE of the founding of HBCUs, their history of activism, and their role in protecting and promoting Black men and women, they have been historically underfunded and neglected by the US government.

Private funders also have not stepped up for Black institutions, which white leaders in America historically have deemed unimportant. Therefore, HBCUs have never had the enormous endowments that support the many financial needs of majority-white institutions. "They were viewed as educating the people who weren't going to become much anyway," W. Franklyn Richardson said.

A number of HBCUs have struggled, some for years. The 125-year-old Saint Paul's College shut down its Lawrenceville, Virginia, campus in 2013 after accreditation and financial problems resulted in declining enrollment. Atlanta's Morris Brown College, named for the Charleston preacher, was stripped of accreditation for twenty years because of its debt. Wilberforce University has struggled with financial challenges and in 2019 joined with Central State University, an adjacent public HBCU, in order to keep its accreditation.

Virginia Union University has struggled too. In recent years, the university saw enrollment figures for incoming freshmen and transfers drop by a half. The school reported that its undergraduate enrollment dipped to a twenty-five-year low of 1,153 students for the 2019–2020 school year, down from a student body of between 1,300 and 1,500. In response, the board lowered tuition by nearly one-third in order to attract more students. Enrollment climbed to 1,276 in 2020–2021, during the pandemic, and school officials hoped it might inch above 1,300 for 2021–2022. The school reported it retained 70 percent of its freshman class, its highest retention rate in history.

While enrollment is a persistent worry for school leaders, Richardson is circumspect about the challenges facing Virginia Union. "Historically Black Colleges have had to struggle to exist," Richardson said. "Their story is the story of struggle."

University officials are developing new graduate programs, acquiring land to expand the school's campus, and setting fundraising goals at $30 million in the short term and $100 million over the long term. In 2021, the institution announced that it would award more than $6.35 million to 1,344 students to eliminate education loan debt, with the help of the federal Coronavirus Aid, Relief, and Economic Security Act. The school has also partnered with Richmond public schools to give scholarships to fifth- and eighth-graders. The university, Richardson said, is "in a place of promise and possibility."

The endowments of all 101 HBCUs total $3.4 billion, which is less than the endowment of predominantly white Brown University, the least well-endowed of the Ivy League schools. In recent years, wealthy Americans have taken note. The novelist and philanthropist MacKenzie Scott donated $560 million to HBCUs in 2020. In the commonwealth, Virginia Union was bypassed, but Scott gave $40 million to Norfolk State University and $30 million to Virginia State University, both public institutions.

In 2020, Netflix cofounder Reed Hastings and the film producer Patricia Quillin gave $40 million each to the United Negro College Fund, Morehouse College, and Spelman College. LeMoyne-Owen College in Memphis received $40 million from the Community Foundation of Greater Memphis. In 2021, Calvin Tyler, a retired United Parcel Service senior executive and board member, pledged $20 million to Baltimore's Morgan State University.

Hastings and Quillin said that they hoped their gifts would help reverse "generations of inequity in our country" and inspire others to donate to historically Black colleges and universities. "HBCUs have a tremendous record, yet are disadvantaged when it comes to giving," the couple said in a statement. "Generally, white capital flows to predominantly white institutions, perpetuating capital isolation."

Black Americans have long known the value of HBCUs, but wider recognition of their importance, particularly on the part of white Americans, is essential for them to be funded equitably. Michael L. Lomas, president and chief executive of the United Negro College Fund, predicted in 2021 that donor support would soon pick up at HBCUs across the country. When Howard University signed Black journalists and MacArthur genius grant recipients Nikole Hannah-Jones and Ta-Nehisi Coates as professors, Lomas said that it signaled that the school can be "a nationally recognized platform for creativity, for insight, for voice to the Black community," and he expected it to a have a ripple effect.

"This is a renaissance for Black colleges," he said.

After Matthew R. Laird determined the location of Lumpkin's Jail in Shockoe Bottom, the city of Richmond awarded his team a contract in 2008 to conduct a full archaeological dig.

Laird knew that the site would be difficult to excavate, for two reasons. First, the location posed access challenges, as the foundations for Robert Lumpkin's home and boardinghouse were most likely buried under Interstate 95 and the rest of the slave jail property was adjacent to the highway. Second, the back part of the property, where the jail sat, sloped down to Shockoe Creek, requiring the removal of many layers of fill dirt. He didn't expect the third challenge: the creek would fill the dig site with water.

Workers started by digging an 80-by-160-foot plot. Slowly and methodically, they removed layers of soil, which were then hauled away by a waiting dump truck. Within days, and working in view of thousands of people who passed the site on Interstate 95, the team reached pieces of china and doll parts, remnants of the jail property buried under the modern landscape. They also found a carved bone ring and a wooden toothbrush. Over the course of four months, the site—and its intense history—was uncovered bit by bit.

Laird's team revealed the footprint of a separate kitchen building, located a little farther back on the property. Then the workers found the remains of a brick retaining wall where the property dropped seven or eight feet to the jail and sloped down a terraced hillside to Shockoe Creek.

Standing next to the dig site, they peered down at a cobblestone courtyard, a brick gutter, the footprint of a kitchen, and the top of the brick retaining wall that divided Lumpkin's land into upper and lower levels. "It was like a sealed cityscape—like Pompeii, peeling back the layers," Laird told me.

"It was so compelling," he recalled more than a decade later. "It was like you climbed down into a time capsule. You were standing on the ground surface of what had been an antebellum slave trading complex."

In the final weeks of the dig, the footprint of the jail was also exposed, some fifteen feet below the surface soil. The property Mary Lumpkin walked countless times a day was revealed. Peering down into it, Delores McQuinn knew that Richmond had what it needed to tell slavery's story in a special way that would attract slave heritage tourism. Ghana, for example, has brought visitors to its castles and forts where captured African people were kept before they were forced onto slave ships and sent across the Atlantic.

"What people are looking for across the country are authentic sites," McQuinn said. "We don't have to make it up. . . . In doing the excavation and researching, we have found the actual site."

When the archaeologists reached the jail footprint, the dig site started filling with water. "We could not keep the water out of it," Laird recalled. "It was flowing in from the sides and underneath. We were constantly pumping it."

While the water posed complications for the archaeologists, they also knew that it was exactly what had preserved the site, sealing it in a mud bubble that oxygen could not penetrate. More than a dozen feet of fill dirt had also kept it exactly as it had been.

In 1873, the hotel proprietors Andrew Jackson Ford and his wife, Mary Lucy Ford, had bought the jail property and used some of the buildings to house their employees. When the dilapidated jail was demolished on March 10, 1888, newspaper reports noted that the building was "more widely known through the south in slave days than any similar edifice here." One paper reported that Libby Prison, which housed Union prisoners during the Civil War, also would soon be taken down. "The new South is about to forget both structures and the occasion for their use," read one report—a fairly accurate prediction.

In 1892, the Fords sold the lots to the founders of Richmond Iron Works, and truckloads of fill dirt were brought in to level off the sloping parcel. Huge piles were constructed on top to support a brick building where architectural ironworks, stationary engines, and supplies for electric railroads would be manufactured. Had it not been for the fill dirt, the slave jail remnants would have been entirely destroyed.

"They would have blasted through the Lumpkin-era features, and there wouldn't have been anything left at all," Laird said.

By 1909, the ironworks site had been demolished, and Seaboard Air Line Railway had constructed a large freight depot. Then, in the 1950s, a section of the jail site was covered by the construction of the Richmond and Petersburg Turnpike, which later became Interstate 95. Lumpkin's Jail had been buried in plain sight for more than a century, enabling Richmond and the rest of the white South to forget its role in the slave trade.

Now that it finally had been uncovered, the power of the site was revealed. Yet the money allocated for the project had been spent, and with winter approaching, the bricks and stones uncovered in the archaeological dig were exposed and at risk of freezing, which would jeopardize their integrity. Loads of fill dirt were brought back in to protect the site.

Once again, the history of Lumpkin's Jail was being buried. Would it be permanent this time?

IN 2013, THEN Richmond mayor Dwight C. Jones, a Black preacher and Virginia Union alumnus, proposed an $80 million minor league baseball stadium for the Richmond Flying Squirrels to be constructed in Shockoe Bottom.

Once the location of slave jails, an African burial ground, and the execution of Gabriel, the enslaved leader of the 1800 uprising, Shockoe Bottom was in danger of becoming a mixed-use project. The proposal placed the stadium in a neighborhood already covered in asphalt, its important American history paved over. The stadium would bring a hotel, a grocery store, residential units, and commercial office space.

In the negotiations, Jones vowed to set aside $5 million for the creation of a slavery museum in the neighborhood and to make improvements to the Richmond Slave Trail and the African burial ground. But activists worried that slave trading sites would be destroyed in the process. Many believed that the proposed project endangered important archaeological remains—including ones that have not yet been uncovered. The proposal ignored the neighborhood's slave history, they said as they launched into action. "No stadium on sacred ground!" opponents chanted as Jones unveiled his plans.

Richmond residents were joined in their protests by descendants of Solomon Northup, including one who read from his ancestor's account of the time he spent at a Shockoe Bottom slave jail in 1841 before being shipped to New Orleans. No descendants of Mary Lumpkin or Robert Lumpkin emerged to participate in the discussion.

"This history remains dormant, buried under asphalt and covered by weeds, but it is one that pulses in veins of the millions of living ancestors of the men and women and children whose lives were forfeited on the auction blocks, in the slave pens and on the gallows pole," wrote Linsey Williams, Northup's great-great-great-great-granddaughter, in a petition to protest the stadium. "It is a history that is very much alive."

Lupita Nyong'o, an actor in *Twelve Years a Slave*, the movie depicting Northup's kidnapping and life as an enslaved man, called for the site's history to be preserved. "The tactic of the enslaver was to systematically erase all memory of the African's past," she wrote. "Let us not repeat this ill by contributing to the erasure of this past in America, too."

The Black *Richmond Free Press* opposed the project, while the *Richmond Times-Dispatch* initially supported it. "A stadium appears to be a strong way to draw attention to slavery and to commemorate the lives of human beings held in bondage," the newspaper argued in February 2014.

Often criticized for its support of school segregation and other racist policies, the paper's editorial page later changed its stance, announcing its opposition to the baseball stadium's "sketchy financing." Jones's argument that a slavery museum would not happen without the baseball stadium did not hold water, an editorial read, noting that the Virginia

Holocaust Museum had been constructed in Richmond without partnering with a sports entity.

The outcry over the possible destruction of slave history was too loud for city officials to ignore. In meetings around the city, Jones could not drum up the needed support for the project, and he withdrew his proposal in May 2014 rather than see it defeated in a City Council meeting.

That year, the National Trust for Historic Preservation declared Lumpkin's Jail one of the nation's eleven most endangered sites and added the archaeological dig site to its "National Treasures" program because of the threat that the baseball stadium project had generated. The trust suggested that eight blocks around the jail site be preserved as a "site of conscience" to memorialize "this dark chapter of American history."

When the archaeological dig was re-covered with layers of dirt, Laird expected that the site would soon be reopened and preserved. He envisioned visitors arriving to view the outline of a slave jail property in its original location. He knew that revealing the dig site would create a unique opportunity for Americans to get a glimpse of a cobblestone courtyard where enslaved people once walked, to show visitors up close a place where the devastation of slavery had occurred, and to make them feel as if they were there. Perhaps no place in America was better equipped to tell the story of the domestic slave trade.

"Every time I drive by on the interstate," Laird said, "I look down and imagine what it could be."

BEFORE SHE KNEW Mary Lumpkin's name, Carolivia Herron had long heard of her great-great-grandmother's efforts to protect her children. When Herron was nine and pretending to sleep on the rug in her grandmother's parlor in Washington, DC, an aunt came in with friends and shared details about their enslaved ancestor.

Herron remembered her aunt recounting that the ancestor had demanded money of her enslaver for the enslaved children she had been forced to bear. "My unnamed female ancestor had managed to get power over him," Herron said.

She recalled her aunt's descriptions of the enslaver's cruelty and that his job assisted enslavers. Herron also knew that her ancestor had freed her children to three states—Louisiana, Ohio, and Massachusetts. Later, an uncle made another revelation: "We changed our name," he once said to her. He told Herron that her great-great-grandmother's name was Mary, which he learned from his grandfather, George W. Lumpkins—presumably Mary's son who had changed his first name and added an "s" to his last name.

Herron's mother, Georgia Johnson Herron, a longtime Washington, DC, public school teacher, said it makes sense for her to be descended from a woman like Mary Lumpkin. "Our family has been known for strong women and that falls right into place," she said.

When I tracked down other descendants—great-great-grandchildren and great-great-great-grandchildren—they did not know any of Mary Lumpkin's story. She had been completely forgotten. Her name, her race, her background as an enslaved woman—all gone. Her role as the mother of her enslaver's children—lost. For generations, this branch of the family tree has lived as white, oblivious to her past and its important place in American history. They did not know Robert Lumpkin's legacy as a slave trader either.

Martha Kelsey's children had passed as white and married spouses identified as white by government officials. They had lived in white neighborhoods, setting the stage for subsequent generations to continue passing. In so doing, Martha Kelsey's children were attempting to use whiteness to fit into a world that valued white lives above others. In the aftermath of the Civil War, when white people were angry about Black men and women's freedom, there were lots of reasons a Black person would want to pass as white, the most important of which was not having to worry about being harassed or killed.

The Lumpkin children apparently were divided in how they wanted, or were able, to racially identify. Herron has a photo of George W.

Lumpkins, who was dark-skinned with light eyes, and she noted he could not have passed. He married a light-skinned woman, Rowena Nelson. Also born enslaved in Richmond, she was likely the child or grandchild of a white enslaver who was sent to Massachusetts to be freed and protected by the Wampanoag people. The couple married around 1875 and lived in Bridgewater, Massachusetts, with the Wampanoags, and Rowena didn't know until later in life that she was Black. She was so disgusted by white people's treatment of Black Americans she vowed to "make her descendants Black," Herron said.

When the family moved to Washington, DC, Rowena Nelson Lumpkins "rejected the inclination to pass as white vigorously," Herron said. When her daughter Lucy had three suitors, her mother forced her to marry the darkest one. Herron has a saying about how her great-grandmother's decision to live as Black impacted the family line: "White to Black in three generations."

But other descendants who lived as white probably stopped talking about Mary Lumpkin so long ago that none of her descendants alive today ever had a chance to know her story. Countless families who passed as white after slavery are not aware of their Black ancestors. Yet as DNA testing has become more popular through genealogy websites, a number of Americans who believed they were white have learned otherwise. Some 4 percent of white US residents have at least 1 percent or more African ancestry, which indicates they had a Black ancestor within the last six generations, 23andMe scientist Kasia Bryc found. Based on those numbers, as of the 2010 census, some 7.8 million Americans who identified as white would have been classified as Black according to "one drop" rules.

When I reached out to some of Mary Lumpkin's descendants who live as white, they seemed truly surprised to learn of their connection and were pained to hear of the trauma she had endured as an enslaved woman. Several told me they wished her legacy had not been kept from them. For generations, the history of trauma and enslavement has been hidden in their DNA.

That Martha Kelsey's family's telling of its history made no mention of Mary Lumpkin or her children being Black or enslaved speaks to the structural racism at the heart of America. One descendant said that she was told that the family was descended from a white indentured servant. Another descendant noticed that a space next to George Kelsey's name was blank where Martha Kelsey's should have been. "We're not supposed to talk about this," she was told by her mother. "Your great-great-grandfather married an Indian woman. He was ostracized from the family."

Martha Kelsey's name and race were kept secret from subsequent generations even after her racial identity became more palatable to most Americans. By making her an indentured servant, she became white. By turning her into an Indigenous person, the family had acknowledged this country's aversion to Blackness and engaged in the historical practice of using an Indigenous background to erase Blackness.

Perhaps Mary Lumpkin was indeed part Indigenous. After all, hundreds of thousands of Indigenous people were enslaved in America. George W. Lumpkin connected with, and was accepted by, Indigenous people in Massachusetts who may have protected him when he escaped slavery, Herron said. But claiming that Martha Kelsey was Indigenous, and presumably descended from an Indigenous mother, may have been a story her descendants told in order to hide that they were Black.

Over time, through marriage to white spouses, some or all of Martha Kelsey's descendants easily passed for white and accepted its inherent privileges. A potent mix of shame and racism may have kept descendants from acknowledging her and her mother at that time—and from acknowledging their slave trader ancestor too. Instead, false narratives were concocted and passed down to generations of unsuspecting offspring, many of whom might never have known their true roots if I had not called. And yet they may have carried the unexplained pain of not knowing exactly who they are.

Deciding to hide or ignore our pasts—and not share them with our offspring—is one of many ways in which Americans have refused to acknowledge this country's violent history of enslavement. Many of us are descended from enslaved people, from enslavers, or both. This history still lives with us and reverberates today.

Whether Mary Lumpkin's descendants know it or not, the violence perpetrated by their ancestor Robert Lumpkin is woven into their lives, as is the trauma that Mary Lumpkin endured. The resilience she demonstrated and the joy she surely experienced, despite the terrible conditions of her enslavement, are also part of their constitution.

As a scholar of Black history, Carolivia Herron learned about Lumpkin's Jail years ago but for a long time was not aware of its role in her life. When she gave a talk in Richmond in 2014, she visited the site for the first time and connected the dots. This Mary Lumpkin was the "Mary" she had been told about—the one who demanded money from her husband and freed her children. After realizing what her kin had endured at the slave jail, Herron walked into the middle of the adjacent African burial ground and fell to the ground, overwhelmed by grief.

"I've come. I've returned," she whispered into the grass, speaking to her ancestors. "I was able to survive, and you won't be forgotten. I will hold you up. I hope you can have peace."

Though she did not grow up with all the facts about her ancestors, visiting the site cemented her connection to the history. "This was my family," she said. "I belong here."

The archaeological dig had convinced some community leaders that Lumpkin's Jail should not only be preserved but also showcased.

Six years after the dig was completed, in 2014, the state and city set aside a combined $20 million for a pavilion and slavery museum. A foundation would be created to raise the additional funds needed.

In 2015, the city held a series of public forums about creating a slavery memorial, and participants requested that the scope be widened beyond Lumpkin's Jail. They asked for both a memorial and a museum that would acknowledge the history of Shockoe Bottom through interpretation of artifacts and explore the wider impacts of enslavement.

Residents wanted a site that would provide context for Richmond's role in the domestic slave trade and a place for reflection.

Sharing the history of slavery is essential in Richmond, where it informs life for so many people. As a hub of the domestic trade, the city has the potential to tell a big piece of the slave trade story and to confront a dark past that many Americans find too painful to consider.

"The opportunity to create a destination for Black tourists and people interested in the broadening narrative of the American story—we've got that," said Ana Edwards, a longtime Richmond activist. "We've got the goods here in Richmond."

Since slavery ended, white Americans have not wanted to acknowledge the role of their ancestors as enslavers or the damage they inflicted. Some Black Americans find enslavement just too painful to discuss. The gulf between competing understandings of slavery can seem too wide to cross. Many white people exist in a state of denial, unwilling to learn about slavery, downplaying its significance, and claiming that their ancestors were kind and benevolent enslavers. Meanwhile, some Black Americans don't want to process how devastating slavery and its aftermath were for their ancestors.

Really digging into a discussion about enslavement would require that Americans look at the ways in which the country's policies since the Civil War have echoed enslavement. A reckoning would require that white Americans acknowledge not just white privilege and systemic racism but the violence against Black bodies perpetrated by their white ancestors in the form of enslavement, lynchings, and rapes—violence still being perpetrated today through mass incarceration, the forced labor of prisoners, the drug wars, and the killing of Black citizens by police. Such a reckoning would require the dismantling of these racist systems.

In Richmond, the city and the Virginia Department of Transportation have spent years working to reimagine Shockoe Bottom as a transportation hub, investing millions of dollars to have multiple train lines and bus systems converge at Main Street Station next to the Lumpkin's Jail site. A forty-year, $86 million renovation of the train station, a national historic landmark, was completed in 2017 and includes a breathtakingly beautiful, five-hundred-foot-long glass event space.

Could Shockoe Bottom, this transportation hub, also be a hub of truth-telling? Could it be a place where people go to explore the rarely acknowledged history of the land?

In recent years, the Lumpkin's Jail site, surrounded by tall metal fences and construction projects, was nearly impossible for visitors to locate. When Virginia's legislative Black caucus hosted a memorial of the four-hundredth anniversary of slavery at the site in 2019, Delegate Delores McQuinn had her staff make handwritten signs to mark the entrances. Even after the fences came down, there was no indication of how important this site is to America's story. More than a decade after the extraordinary archaeological dig, the site, though a stop on the Richmond Slave Trail, remains a patch of grass on the edge of a highway, unseen and unknown.

But Lumpkin's Jail is too important to keep hidden. It's time to bring Richmond's history in the domestic slave trade into the light.

Michael Twitty, a culinary historian, knows what a gem Richmond has in the "Devil's Half Acre" site. His research into his enslaved ancestors has revealed that some were sold through the Richmond slave market—perhaps at Lumpkin's Jail. He frequently travels by train and when he passes through Main Street Station, he often initiates conversations about the area's history.

"You know what's down here?" he asks fellow passengers. "That's the second-largest slave market in America."

Sitting in a railcar above the former slave jail, he experiences the pain of the region's history and takes a moment to sit with it. "I feel it every single time," he says.

Looking down on Shockoe Bottom from the train, Twitty says a prayer for the people who came before him. "I let my ancestors know, 'I haven't forgotten about you.'"

AFTER THE BLACK American artist Kehinde Wiley visited Richmond in 2016 and saw the collection of Confederate statues that lined Monument Avenue, he decided to create a statue of his own to mock them.

"They're designed to terrorize and menace," he told National Public Radio. "They're designed to remind the Black citizenry of Richmond that they have a place in society and that they need to stay within those confined spaces."

His twenty-seven-foot-tall *Rumors of War*, cast in bronze, features a modern-day Black man dressed in a hoodie and high-top Nikes, his hair in dreadlocks and tied back in a ponytail. He is seated atop a horse, reminiscent of the Black cavalry who first liberated Richmond. The Virginia Museum of Fine Arts bought the piece, the most expensive single artwork the museum had acquired at a price tag of $3 million. Wiley, who painted Barack Obama's presidential portrait, unveiled the statue in Times Square first before bringing it to Richmond, where three thousand people cheered its December 2019 installation in front of the museum.

The museum sits on Arthur Ashe Boulevard, renamed for the Black tennis icon raised in Richmond, and adjacent to the headquarters for the United Daughters of the Confederacy, which raised money to put up many of the Confederate statues around the South. The organization was also provided taxpayer money for the upkeep of Confederate cemeteries.

Wiley's creation made a statement about Confederate statues, and when it was installed, only a select few American cities had removed the statues from their glorified positions of power and idolatry. Before the coronavirus shut down much of the United States in March 2020, statues in New Orleans and Chapel Hill, North Carolina, were removed in the dead of night, to avoid confrontation. Richmond leaders, reluctant to claim the city's history of enslavement, had not publicly debated taking down the city's Confederate statutes.

When Levar Stoney, an ambitious young Black politician, was elected mayor in 2016, he did not publicly support removing Confederate statues, probably because he knew the issue was a political hot potato. In

2017, he appointed historians and academics to study Richmond's collection, among the largest in the South, and to recommend what to do with them. The Monument Avenue Commission rather timidly proposed in 2018 that signage be added to "contextualize" the statues and suggested the removal of Jefferson Davis. But it did not happen.

"I wish these monuments had never been built," Stoney said at the time, "but like it or not they are part of our history in this city, and removal will never wash away that stain."

That year, white supremacists gathered in Charlottesville for a "Unite the Right" rally when its City Council was debating whether to remove its Robert E. Lee statue, and one of them drove his car into a crowd, killing thirty-two-year-old Heather Heyer. After the tragedy, Stoney did not change his public stance about Richmond's Confederate statues. As a politician with wider ambitions, he must have calculated that calling for their removal would be tantamount to political suicide at that time.

Stoney's focus in 2018 seemed to be on finding revenue for the city via a $1.5 billion proposal to redevelop downtown Richmond by building a concert venue. Stoney trumpeted Navy Hill as "the largest economic development project in the city's history." Richmond residents complained that it had not been properly vetted and would take money from the city's desperately underfunded public schools. The Richmond City Council voted down the project in February 2020, perhaps hoping to avoid bleeding public resources.

A few months later, Stoney was dealing with a whole new set of challenges. The coronavirus pandemic had shut down America, and when George Floyd was killed by a police officer in Minneapolis in May 2020, protests broke out across the country, including Richmond. In the early summer, activists gathered around the Confederate statues on an almost daily basis. Protestors burned a municipal bus, broke glass windows on businesses throughout the city's gentrifying downtown, and used Molotov cocktails to set fire to the United Daughters of the Confederacy headquarters, causing $1.2 million in damage. Stoney told reporters that a small group of people was responsible.

The activists—a multiracial coalition of Richmond residents—demanded an end to systemic inequities and racially motivated violence against Black people. They called for cutting the Richmond Police Department's budget and putting those funds into social service programs. They asked for the formation of an independent civilian review board to study accusations of police misconduct. They also wanted the Confederate statues to come down.

When protesters attempted to pull down the J.E.B. Stuart statue one night after weeks of protests, police responded—under Stoney's direction and supplemented by state troopers and officers from other localities—with force and chemical agents. The next day, the Richmond police force, in broad daylight, confronted protesters at the Robert E. Lee statue and fired tear gas into a crowd that included young children. It felt to many people that police were protecting the Confederate statues.

On June 2, hundreds of angry residents shouted at Stoney on the steps of City Hall as he attempted to apologize via megaphone for the use of force. "It was wrong and it was inexcusable," he said. But nothing seemed to change.

As protests continued for weeks, state and local police continued to use the same tactics. They dressed in riot gear and forced protesters away from the statues by blocking paths with their bodies, releasing "flash bangs," and making arrests. Police planes and helicopters hovered over the neighborhood, shining spotlights on protesters in order to facilitate arrests by officers on the ground. Neither then nor anytime thereafter did Stoney adequately address the violent tactics that police used in his city against protesters who were marching in opposition to police brutality against Black Americans.

During this time, the Lee statue, isolated on a platform in the middle of a traffic circle on Monument Avenue, was transformed, seemingly overnight, from a foreboding space into a park for the people and an outpost for a racial justice movement. Protesters renamed the circle for Marcus-David Peters, a Virginia man killed by Richmond police in 2018.

A constantly evolving work of public art, the statue was repainted daily in graffiti, enabling residents to celebrate the statue's reclamation through public protest. At night, a pair of video artists splashed the statue with photographs of Floyd, historic images of civil rights leaders, and iconic videos of Martin Luther King Jr. giving his "I have a dream" speech. In its new form, the statue was embraced by a diverse array of Richmond residents, but particularly by its Black population.

Visitors parked nearby to walk the circle and admire the statue in its evolving state. High school graduates posed for photos in their graduation gowns, while Black dancers in tutus went en pointe and families took portraits of themselves, dressed in matching shirts, in front of the statue. Community members picnicked on the lawn surrounding the statue, firing up a grill to cook burgers and playing music, while others played pickup basketball on a net that had been wheeled in. A garden was planted, and activists posted laminated photos of Americans killed by police, transforming the site into a sacred space where people could consider, and mourn, the death of Black citizens at the hands of police. Some referred to it as a "healing circle."

People drove from around the region to witness and participate in the history unfolding. *National Geographic* featured a photograph of the graffiti-covered statue on its cover. The *New York Times* deemed the statue in that moment the most influential work of protest art since World War II.

As police attacked protesters in Richmond and elsewhere, Confederate statues around the country began to come down, in part to protect residents from accidents when protesters attempted to topple them. In some cases, their removal was meant to protect the statues themselves from destruction. The Confederate Soldiers and Sailors Monument, an obelisk, was removed in Birmingham, Alabama, after protesters attempted to topple it, and a bronze likeness of Admiral Raphael Semmes, an officer in the Confederate Navy, was removed from downtown Mobile, Alabama. In Alexandria, Virginia, the United Daughters of the Confederacy took down its statue commemorating Confederate soldiers.

In some places, protesters did not wait for authority figures to take down the statues. In Bristol, England, an eighteen-foot bronze statue of Edward Colston, a seventeenth-century slave trader, was dragged to a harbor and dumped in the River Avon. Statues in Richmond started to get pulled down too—three in a week's time. In June 2020, a statue of Williams Carter Wickham, a Confederate officer, was pushed off its pedestal in a city park. A few days later, a crowd gathered at Byrd Park to consider the struggles of Indigenous and Black people in America. That evening, using ropes, protesters tore down a likeness of Christopher Columbus—the explorer who initiated the Atlantic slave trade and the genocide of Indigenous people—set it on fire, and tossed it into a lake. The next day, protesters splashed pink paint across the bronze Jefferson Davis statue on Monument Avenue and later pulled it down after dark, using a car and ropes. After police responded, the felled statue was hauled away by a tow truck.

A few days earlier, on June 4, 2020, Virginia governor Ralph Northam had announced that he planned to remove the likeness of Lee, the only Confederate statue on Monument Avenue that sits on state land. A year earlier, Northam had come under national scrutiny after discovery of a photo on his medical school yearbook page of a person wearing blackface and another dressed in a KKK robe. He said that he didn't think either person was him, though he admitted to wearing blackface under another circumstance. Under pressure to resign, Northam declined, vowing instead to devote the remainder of his term to addressing racial inequality.

When the removal of Lee's statue was announced, Virginia delegate Jay Jones, a Black lawmaker from Norfolk, was elated. "That is a symbol for so many people, Black and otherwise, of a time gone by of hate and oppression and being made to feel less than," he said.

The Lee statue removal was delayed by a lawsuit originally filed by a descendant of the deed signatories, who contended that when the land was granted, the state had promised to "faithfully guard" the statue. A group of residents took the case to the Virginia supreme court in June 2021, arguing that neither the governor nor the legislature could revoke an agreement for how the land would be used. The state argued that it should have the authority to do so.

After Northam's June 2020 announcement that the state would remove the Lee statue, Stoney ordered the removal of the city's other Confederate statues, defying the acting city attorney. On July 1, 2020, hundreds of people gathered to witness Stonewall Jackson's likeness come down. They stood for hours in the rain to watch as the statue was lifted from its pedestal by a crane operator, amid claps of thunder. The crowd broke into cheers when it was finally removed, and the bell pealed from the adjacent First Baptist Church—a bell that was nearly melted down to make Confederate weapons when the congregation voted to donate it during the Civil War.

"Times have changed, and removing these statues will allow the healing process to begin," Stoney said then. "Richmond is no longer the capital of the Confederacy. It is filled with diversity and love for all."

By September 2020, Richmond had removed eighteen Confederate statutes or symbols—more than any other locality in the country. Stoney cited public safety as the reason for the decision to remove the statues.

A few months later, in January 2021, the state closed off the reclaimed public space around the Lee monument, erecting an enormous black chain-link fence that cut off access to the statue as well as its memorials and garden. Officials claimed to be preparing for the statue's removal, but the fence was likely put up in response to complaints from wealthy residents about the steady stream of visitors. In September 2021, the state supreme court ruled against the neighbors' lawsuit, allowing for the statue's removal. It was the last Confederate statue on Monument Avenue to go.

This was a celebrated moment of reckoning, forced in large part by Black activists. But what comes next?

When it came down, observers stressed that while taking down the statues is symbolically important, it is not the real work of dismantling structural racism—work the city has hardly begun. City schools are starved for resources, and gentrification threatens Black neighborhoods that were created by redlining and have long been neglected. Discussions about police reform have been met with bureaucratic roadblocks.

"The statues coming down is the tip of the iceberg," said Zyahna Bryant, who called for the removal of Charlottesville's Robert E. Lee statue. "There are larger systems that need to be dismantled."

ANA EDWARDS, AN activist and descendant of enslaved people sold out of Richmond in the 1840s, has worked to persuade city leaders to acknowledge its slave trading history and to extend it beyond Lumpkin's Jail.

Edwards publishes Richmond's *Defender*, a community newspaper, with her husband, Phil Wilayto, and she chairs the Sacred Ground Historical Reclamation Project of the Virginia Defenders for Freedom, Justice and Equality, which has advocated making the Shockoe Bottom history a more inclusive story. The Defenders wrote and promoted a plan for creating a Shockoe Bottom Memorial Park, a sixty-acre space that would combine "preservation, commemoration, education, and equitable revitalization at a scale proportionate to Shockoe Bottom's nationally significant heritage." The Defenders' proposal called for the city to procure nearly nine acres in order to tell a fuller story, a stance similar to that of the National Trust for Historic Preservation, which recommended a more comprehensive archaeological study of the neighborhood.

Mayor Stoney shared the challenges of developing and preserving Shockoe Bottom in National League of Cities meetings, and he was subsequently selected for a land use fellowship sponsored by the league and the Urban Land Institute. Experts from around the country came to Richmond to advise the city on how to protect the neighborhood's history and resources while transforming it into a destination. A stakeholder group of archaeology experts, historians, residents, business owners, housing advocates, and developers was formed to create a shared vision for the neighborhood that would memorialize the slave trading history and guide private investment.

The Shockoe Alliance agreed to utilize a wider area for its master plan, as Edwards's group had asked. The new area included the African burial ground and the site of Lumpkin's Jail, and it extended two blocks east to encompass the location of many slave traders' businesses. Stoney's acknowledgment that those blocks "contain significant, historical sites with future archaeological potential," together with the steps he took to acquire additional parcels, now make it possible for a bigger slavery memorial park to be built.

In 2020, Stoney announced that, over a five-year period, the city would spend between $25 million and $50 million to commemorate slavery in Shockoe Bottom. He said that $3.5 million would immediately be put toward building a memorial park. Governor Northam also announced that he would allocate an additional $9 million for improvements to the Slave Trail and for the development of a slavery museum and memorial—essentially converting to cash the money already committed to the project—and said that the city would be in charge. In 2021, construction of a national slavery museum was projected to cost up to $220 million.

"At a time when this Commonwealth and country are grappling with how to present a complete and more honest picture of our complex history," Northam said, "we must work to enhance public spaces that have long been neglected and shine light on previously untold stories."

By the fall of 2021, the plans for Shockoe Bottom were beginning to reflect Edwards's vision, as the city claimed it was acquiring the land she wanted preserved. The Shockoe Alliance had approved a plan that mapped the area and set priorities for development. In January 2022, city council members voted to establish a foundation to fundraise to build a National Slavery Museum. The city also provided $1.3 million in seed funding to enable the foundation to hire an executive director and pay for more design work. Its members will include some from the city's defunct Slave Trail Commission, who have asked the new governor, Republican Glenn Youngkin, to fund $45 million in additional excavation work at the Lumpkin's Jail site.

All city council members expressed support for the slavery museum and several spoke about the importance of it being built. "Richmond is not where it is today without the labor of enslaved Africans," Councilman Michael Jones said. "Something is owed."

The city hired SmithGroup—the architectural firm that designed the iconic $540 million National Museum of African American History and Culture on the Mall in Washington, DC—to create conceptual designs for a museum that would utilize the Lumpkin's Jail footprint as the ground floor while also taking into consideration new floodplain maps. Early drawings featured an airy, triangular-shaped museum building that appeared to float above Interstate 95 with a garden on the hypotenuse and a reflective pool connecting the Lumpkin's Jail site with the African burial ground, the Slave Trail, and Shockoe Creek. Will there ever be enough momentum for a museum to be built?

After his reelection in 2020, Levar Stoney stated that he would focus on closing the divide between Black and white Richmonders, pointing to policies around public education, generational wealth, economic empowerment, and housing that needed to be addressed. He did not cite finding a way to tell the history of the slave trade in the city as a priority.

But it should be. Erecting a truthful interpretation of the city's history is an important step toward healing. It's a way to make amends for the harm caused by Confederate iconography. It's a way to teach the city's—and America's—true history. If Stoney does not make this project a priority for his administration and take the lead, how will a museum memorializing the enslaved ever move forward?

I wonder: Will Richmond shine a light on its own participation in the downriver slave trade and the role that slave jails played? Will it address the ways in which enslaved people—and women in particular—were harmed? Will it tell the story of Mary Lumpkin's power and her pain? Or will it continue to keep this history hidden, maintaining white supremacy at all costs?

Will Richmond's leaders be bold enough, courageous enough, to share a story that showcases the city at its worst but is also critical to America's reckoning with its past?

LITTLE IS KNOWN about how Mary Lumpkin felt about her life in Richmond.

We don't know what her days were like in the jail where she was forced to live. We can't know how she viewed Robert Lumpkin. And yet her life, even in its erasure, is meaningful.

It's meaningful to Virginia Union students and alumni. It's meaningful to her descendants, even the ones who are only now learning her story. It is meaningful to Richmond residents, and it is meaningful to women, particularly Black women across the country and the world.

Faithe Norrell, a Richmond resident who is descended on both sides of her family from enslaved women who were forced to have the children of their enslavers, said that she sees similarities between her ancestors' histories and Mary Lumpkin's.

"I would be very passionate about telling her story," said Norrell, who works for the Black History Museum and Cultural Center of Virginia.

In the shadow cast by Mary Lumpkin, we can imagine a life forged out of limited opportunities. We can picture the family she built, the school she played a role in founding, the young nation she helped shape.

"We have tried to find her all the time," said Hakim J. Lucas, the Virginia Union president. As in the passing down of African history, he acknowledged, "we have created her stories. We have created our fables."

We see Mary Lumpkin using her agency throughout her life. We glimpse her efforts to educate her children, to move them to safety, to seize freedom for them—and for herself. We witness her resilience. We see her actively creating a better life for herself and her descendants.

If we follow her family line through the years, we can glimpse her children living as free people in Philadelphia and New Orleans. We witness them marrying and having children. We see them moving west for opportunity, for a life free of the chains of slavery and its memories.

We see tens of thousands of Black students who have been educated and empowered over a century and a half as a result of Mary Lumpkin's decision to allow the "Devil's Half Acre" to be transformed into a school for free Black men. We see the value of this safe, nurturing university for Black men and women in a world where white supremacy still makes daily life treacherous for so many.

We acknowledge that Mary Lumpkin struggled as an enslaved woman, even with the opportunities afforded her as the mother of her enslaver's children. And we notice that her challenges continued after she was free and had secured an inheritance. We see that her life as a Black woman was not an easy one. And yet she lived.

In all that she was and all that she became, she represented multitudes. A woman with both white and Black heritage. The oppressed and the oppressor. A mother to her own children, and a mother to thousands of students.

Perhaps in hearing the story of her journey, Americans will strive to better understand the complicated space that Mary Lumpkin occupied. A woman caught between two worlds. A woman who, even in freedom, was never truly free.

Bury Me in a Free Land

Make me a grave where'er you will,
In a lowly plain, or a lofty hill,
Make it among earth's humblest graves,
But not in a land where men are slaves.

—Frances Ellen Watkins Harper

*This book is written
in memory and in honor of
enslaved women
who were taken from their parents
and separated from their children*

Acknowledgments

This book has been a long time in the making, and I appreciate the people who supported my goal to tell Mary Lumpkin's story.

I am grateful to Virginia Humanities for a fellowship that funded my research on this project, and to Matthew Gibson and Jeanne Siler for their assistance. I am appreciative of the Library of Virginia for hosting me for my fellowship research, and I am incredibly grateful to Sandra Treadway, Librarian of Virginia, for allowing me to stay an extra year. Her library staff was amazing, and I especially appreciate the coaching of John Deal and his team. The edits provided by Mari Julienne and Brent Tarter improved this book tremendously, and I am so thankful for the many ways in which they have assisted me. I am appreciative of Greg Crawford and Gregg Kimball for their research ideas and advice. Dave Grabarek saved the day by fetching records from across the country. I enjoyed sharing ideas with Catherine Fitzgerald Wyatt, Barbara Batson, Matt Gottlieb, Cindy Marks, Ann Henderson, Emma Ito, and Ashley Ramey. The institution's librarians, particularly Ginny Dunn and Kevin Shupe, were enormously helpful. I am grateful to have crossed Virginia Humanities' fellowship paths with Nicole Mauritano and Kim O'Connell, who immediately became good friends. Gregory Smithers always provided great advice. Tom Kapsidelis gets the gold medal for encouraging me to apply for the fellowship.

In Richmond, I'm grateful to Ana Edwards for answering questions for years and for her tours of important sites in Shockoe Bottom. I appreciate Delores McQuinn's willingness to share her passionate pursuit of sharing the history of slavery in Richmond. I am grateful to Faithe Norrell for sharing the story of her ancestors with me. I loved talking with Barbara Grey about her fascinating life. I am grateful to Niya Bates for sharing her expertise. Ben Campbell was always just a phone call away, and I am grateful. Matthew Laird has my heart for his beautiful archaeological dig report. My thanks to Joseph Rogers for telling me some of his family's stories. I am grateful for Michael Twitty's willingness to talk with me about his connections to Richmond. I am indebted to the Virginia Union University Archives and Special Collections and to the school's historian, Raymond Hylton. My thanks also go out to the archivists at the Virginia Museum of History and Culture and The Valentine.

In New Richmond, Ohio, Greg Roberts was a wonderful tour guide and a font of knowledge. Mary Allen shared her family's amazing history in the village. Kelly Mezurek briefed me on her research on the US Colored Troops and gave me advice during an epic four-hour Zoom call. The employees of the Clermont County Records Management Division were incredibly helpful too.

In Massachusetts, Meghan Petersen, archivist at the Ipswich Public Library, and the fine people at the Ipswich Museum, including Berni Angelo and Katherine Chaison, were incredibly helpful. Thanks also to the staff of Archives and Special Collections at Mount Holyoke College. I am appreciative of the American Antiquarian Society for hosting me and assisting in my research. In Philadelphia, I am grateful to the Library Company of Philadelphia for providing housing and research help, and to the employees at the Philadelphia Archives who worked tirelessly to help me find property records. I am also deeply indebted to the University of North Carolina's "Documenting the American South" project, which put many of the books I needed online.

I am appreciative of other scholars who are doing work in this area. I am forever grateful to William Julius Wilson for his support. I owe

Alexis Broderick thanks for being a sounding board. Kari J. Winter was incredibly encouraging. Troy Valos kindly shared his knowledge on George Apperson. Amrita Chakrabarti Myers was generous enough to share her paper on Julia Chinn. Joshua D. Rothman kindly answered my questions. I am also appreciative of the scholars who did work on Mary Lumpkin long before I arrived on the scene, including Hannah Craddock and the late Philip J. Schwarz. Although we have never met, Alexandra J. Finley was a wealth of information on Corinna Hinton Omohundro and Lucy Ann Hagan, and I am grateful for her research and writing.

I was so happy to make my first Ancestry friend, Tom Baxter, who enabled me to make incredible connections between Harriet Barber and Mary Lumpkin's family. I am also grateful to historian Katherine Clay Bassard for her generosity in sharing with me her work on Peter Randolph. I am so grateful to the descendants of Mary Lumpkin for their ßopenness and am particularly appreciative of Carolivia Herron for sharing her stories. Thank you also to Georgia Johnson Herron for talking with me. I am also appreciative of the contributions to this project of Rene Tyree and Mark Young.

I am grateful to Rachel Beanland for encouraging me on this long road, listening to every new discovery, and making the manuscript much better with her smart edits. I'd be lost without her. I am thankful for Rosa Castellano's insightful reading of the text. Her deep knowledge of the subject matter enabled me to make this book more nuanced than it otherwise would have been. I appreciate Regina Boone for pushing me to think more deeply and sharing Richmond knowledge. I am indebted to Michael Paul Williams, Richmond's Pulitzer Prize–winning columnist, for providing early feedback. I am grateful to Ellen Brown for keeping me on task with our daily check-ins and always saying the right thing to propel me forward. Thank you to Anisha Walker for reading an early version and for her loving support. I appreciate Taikein Cooper for always weighing in when asked. I appreciate Mia Zuckerkandel's insights and steady encouragement. Thanks also to Rebecca Ruark for being an early reader. I am grateful to Trudy Hale for providing a truly beautiful work retreat.

Thank you to my friends who have supported me on this path, especially Crissy Pascual, Jane Archer, Sarah Roe, Rachel Machacek, Nicole Velez, Tamsen Kingry, Melissa Sinclair, Flavia Jimenez, Martia Rachman, Cheryl Carlyon, Katherine Smothers, and Emily Dalton.

My heartfelt thanks to my agent Chad Liubl for seeing the power of this story and potential in me. I have loved having him on my side. I also appreciate the support of the Janklow & Nesbit team. My editor, Emi Ikkanda, has been a wonderful partner in this book. She shared my vision and made the book immeasurably better by pushing me while at the same time being incredibly encouraging. I am appreciative of her editorial assistant, Madeline Lee. I am grateful for Cindy Buck's work to make my copy sing and to Melissa Veronesi for pulling the whole package together. Thank you to Ivan Lott for spreading the word about the book. I owe Ann Kirchner a debt of gratitude for the gorgeous cover. Thank you to the rest of the team at Seal Press, including Lara Heimert, Liz Wetzel, and Jessica Breen.

I am so grateful for my mom and dad, to whom this book is dedicated, for the beautiful life they have given me. I'm lucky to have an amazing family: brothers Chaz, Ben, and Aaron; sisters-in-law Jill and Erinn; and my awesome nephews Myles, Jack, Conner, and Tanner. I'm appreciative of my in-laws JB, Ginny and Noel, and John and Terrie.

Without my husband Jason and his steadfast belief in me, this book would not have been possible. I appreciate all he did to lovingly support me in this effort and in everything I do. I am so grateful for the encouragement of my daughters, Amaya and Selma. They both regularly reminded me, "You can do this, Mommy!" I did it, and I hope I make them proud.

Recommended Reading

Baptist, Edward E. *The Half Has Never Been Told: Slavery and the Making of American Capitalism*. New York: Basic Books, 2014.

Berry, Daina Ramey, and Kali Nicole Gross. *A Black Women's History of the United States*. Boston: Beacon Press, 2020.

Blay, Yaba. *One Drop: Shifting the Lens on Race*. Boston: Beacon Press, 2021.

Cooper, Brittney. *Eloquent Rage: A Black Feminist Discovers Her Superpower*. New York: Picador, 2018.

Deyle, Steven. *Carry Me Back: The Domestic Slave Trade in American Life*. New York: Oxford University Press, 2005.

Finley, Alexandra J. *An Intimate Economy: Enslaved Women, Work, and America's Domestic Slave Trade*. Chapel Hill: The University of North Carolina Press, 2020.

Gudmestad, Robert H. *A Troublesome Commerce: The Transformation of the Interstate Slave Trade*. Baton Rouge: Louisiana State University Press, 2004.

Jacobs, Harriet. *Incidents in the Life of a Slave Girl*. Boston: Published for the author, 1861.

Johnson, Walter. *Soul by Soul: Life Inside the Antebellum Slave Market*. Cambridge, MA: Harvard University Press, 1999.

Jones-Rogers, Stephanie E. *They Were Her Property: White Women as Slave Owners in the American South*. New Haven, CT: Yale University Press, 2019.

Kendi, Ibram X., and Keisha N. Blain. *Four Hundred Souls: A Community History of African America, 1619–2019*. New York: Random House/One World, 2021.

Miles, Tiya. *All That She Carried: The Journey of Ashley's Sack, a Black Family Keepsake*. New York: Random House, 2021.

Perdue, Charles L. Jr., and Thomas E. Barden. *Weevils in the Wheat: Interviews with Virginia Ex-Slaves*. Bloomington: Indiana University Press, 1980.

Piquet, Louisa, and Hiram Mattison. *Louisa Picquet, the Octoroon: or Inside Views of Southern Domestic Life*. New York: Published for the author, 1861.

Rothman, Joshua D. *The Ledger and the Chain: How Domestic Slave Traders Shaped America*. New York: Basic Books, 2021.

Schermerhorn, Calvin. *The Business of Slavery and the Rise of American Capitalism, 1815–1860*. New Haven, CT: Yale University Press, 2015.

Smith, Clint. *How the Word Is Passed: A Reckoning with the History of Slavery Across America*. New York: Little, Brown, 2021.

Sterling, Dorothy, ed. *We Are Your Sisters: Black Women in the Nineteenth Century*. New York: W. W. Norton, 1984.

Tadman, Michael. *Speculators and Slaves: Masters, Traders, and Slaves in the Old South*. Madison: University of Wisconsin Press, 1989.

Takagi, Midori. *Rearing Wolves to Our Own Destruction: Slavery in Richmond Virginia, 1782–1865*. Charlottesville: University of Virginia Press, 1999.

Wilkerson, Isabel. *Caste: The Origins of Our Discontents*. New York: Random House, 2020.

Notes

To piece together the life of Mary Lumpkin and track her descendants, I used documents on Family Search and Ancestry.com. Among the documents were US census reports, city directories, marriage certificates, death certificates, burial records, wills, court cases, and deeds. I also searched newspapers through newspapers.com, the Library of Congress's Chronicling America, and the Library of Virginia's Virginia Chronicle.

To do reporting, I spent time on the ground in Richmond and also traveled to Ipswich, Massachusetts, Philadelphia, and New Richmond, Ohio, where I interviewed stakeholders and visited local repositories of records. To write about the experience of the enslaved, I read deeply, delving into firsthand accounts by formerly enslaved people and interviews conducted by the Works Progress Administration with formerly enslaved people from multiple Southern states.

The work of others on the slave trade in Richmond was incredibly helpful, including Elizabeth Kambourian's work mapping jails and auction houses, "Slave Traders in Richmond," *Richmond Times-Dispatch*, February 24, 2014, https://richmond.com/slave-traders-in-richmond /table_52a32a98-9d56-11e3-806a-0017a43b2370.html.

What follows is a chapter-by-chapter sampling of books, papers, and articles that I think will be most useful to readers.

PROLOGUE

One of the best sources for the book is Matthew R. Laird's "Archaeological Investigation of the Lumpkin's Jail Site, Richmond, Virginia" (Williamsburg, VA: James River Institute for Archaeology, May 2006). I also interviewed Laird about the project.

To get a handle on the number of girls and women who were enslaved, I used Dorothy Sterling's *We Are Your Sisters: Black Women in the Nineteenth Century* (New York: W. W. Norton, 1984).

One of the best sources of information on Mary Lumpkin is Charles Henry Corey's *A History of the Richmond Theological Seminary, with Reminiscences of Thirty Years' Work Among the Colored People of the South* (Richmond: J. W. Randolph Co., 1895). Mary Lumpkin's great-great-granddaughter Carolivia Herron was also a source.

For a discussion of how enslaved people preserved their history through retelling, see Henry Clay Bruce, *The New Man: Twenty-Nine Years a Slave, Twenty-Nine Years a Free Man* (York, PA: P. Anstadt & Sons, 1895).

I was thrilled to learn of Julia Chinn, whose story is told by Amrita Chakrabarti Myers in "Disorderly Communion: Julia Chinn, Richard Mentor Johnson, and Life in an Interracial, Antebellum, Southern Church," *Journal of African American History* (Spring 2020).

To understand why enslaved women's stories weren't told, I read about "triple constraints." Particularly fascinating is Bernice McNair Barnett's "Invisible Southern Black Women Leaders in the Civil Rights Movement: The Triple Constraints of Gender, Race, and Class," *Gender and Society* 7, no. 2 (June 1993).

One of the most helpful books for framing the erasure at the heart of this story was Daina Ramey Berry and Kali Nicole Gross's *A Black Women's History of the United States* (Boston: Beacon Press, 2020).

I enjoyed reading Anna Malaika Tubbs's book about the mothers of three civil rights leaders whose stories have been overlooked; see *The Three Mothers: How the Mothers of Martin Luther King Jr., Malcolm X, and James Baldwin Shaped a Nation* (New York: Flatiron Books, 2021).

For first-person accounts by enslaved women who were in situations that in some ways mirrored Mary Lumpkin's, I turned to Harriet Jacobs's *Incidents in the Life of a Slave Girl*, edited by L. Maria Child (Boston: Published for the author, 1861), and Louisa Picquet and Hiram Mattison's *Louisa Picquet, the Octoroon: or Inside Views of Southern Domestic Life* (New York: Published for the author, 1861).

For an explanation of why enslaved women typically didn't run away permanently, I used the late Stephanie M. H. Camp's *Closer to Freedom: Enslaved Women and Everyday Resistance in the Plantation South* (Chapel Hill: University of North Carolina Press, 2004).

CHAPTER 1

Henry Box Brown's story of a mother's fear of losing her child was imprinted on my mind throughout the writing of this book. I used his first-person account, *Narrative of the Life of Henry Box Brown, Written by Himself* (Manchester, UK: Lee and Glynn, 1851).

I also found Peter Randolph's story of his mother mourning her lost children particularly moving: *From Slave Cabin to the Pulpit: The Autobiography of Rev. Peter Randolph: The Southern Question Illustrated and Sketches of Slave Life* (Boston: James H. Earle, 1893). I used his book extensively in discussing his move to Boston and sharing insight about Harriet Barber.

For the story of an enslaved man named Pete, as told by a British visitor, I used Stephen V. Ash's *Rebel Richmond: Life and Death in the Confederate Capital* (Chapel Hill: University of North Carolina Press, 2019).

To understand Kasia Bryc's work, I read Henry Louis Gates Jr.'s "How Many 'White' People Are Passing?" *The Root*, March 17, 2014.

Michael Tadman writes searingly of children being separated from their families in *Speculators and Slaves: Masters, Traders, and Slaves in the Old South* (Madison: University of Wisconsin Press, 1989). For the story of a sleeping baby being sold, I relied on Daina Ramey Berry's *The Price for Their Pound of Flesh: The Value of the Enslaved, from Womb to Grave, in the Building of a Nation* (New York: Random House, 2018).

Frederic Bancroft does a great job of explaining how common it was for children to be taken from their parents in *Slave Trading in the Old South* (New York: Frederick Ungar Publishing, 1959).

For the section on Richmond becoming the center of the domestic slave trade in Virginia, I used Robert H. Gudmestad's master's thesis, "The Richmond Slave Market, 1840–1860," University of Richmond (May 1993). A report on the archaeology of the Bruin Slave Jail in Alexandria, Virginia, explains why the trade shifted away from Alexandria.

A classic book for learning about the city's early development is Samuel Mordecai's *Richmond in By-Gone Days; Being Reminiscences of an Old Citizen* (Richmond: George M. West, 1856). For what Richmond looked like as the slave trade developed, I also used Jack Trammell's *The Richmond Slave Trade: The Economic Backbone of the Old Dominion* (Charleston, SC: History Press, 2012), and Jay Worrall Jr.'s *The Friendly Virginians: America's First Quakers* (Athens, GA: Iberian Publishing Co., 1994).

To write about leasing out enslaved people, I used Midori Takagi's *Rearing Wolves to Our Own Destruction: Slavery in Richmond Virginia, 1782–1865* (Charlottesville: University of Virginia Press, 1999).

To discuss how slavery became Virginia's most profitable industry, I turned to David W. Blight's *A Slave No More* (Orlando, FL: Harcourt, 2007). I also used a presentation by Scott Nesbit, Robert K. Nelson, and Maurie McInnis, "Visualizing the Richmond Slave Trade," American Studies Association, San Antonio (November 2010). It was a project of the Digital Scholarship Lab at the University of Richmond.

For descriptions of the slave trading district, I talked with the historian Kari J. Winter and used her book, *The American Dreams of John B. Prentis, Slave Trader* (Athens: University of Georgia Press, 2011).

Descriptions of the Lumpkin's Jail property came from a few places. Corey provides some of the best descriptions. But perhaps the most helpful was Charles Emery Stevens's *Anthony Burns: A History* (Boston:

John P. Jewett and Co., 1856). The Swedish traveler Fredrika Bremer does a great job of providing more general descriptions of multiple Richmond jails in her book *The Homes of the New World: Impressions of America* (New York: Harper & Brothers, 1853).

For more about slave traders, I used Stephanie Jones-Rogers's *They Were Her Property: White Women as Slave Owners in the American South* (New Haven, CT: Yale University Press, 2019), and Anna North's "How White Women's 'Investment' in Slavery Has Shaped America Today," *Vox*, August 19, 2019.

To learn about the day-to-day lives of traders, I gained some insight from George William Weatherstonhaugh's *Excursion Through the Slave States, from Washington on the Potomac, to the Frontier of Mexico; with Sketches of Popular Manners and Geological Notices* (New York: Harper & Brothers, 1844). I was excited to discover an account of a Louisiana trader buying enslaved people in Virginia in David O. Whitten's *Andrew Durnford: A Black Sugar Planter in the Antebellum South* (New Brunswick, NJ: Transaction Publishers, 1995).

The best assurance I have that Robert Lumpkin was not married came from Robert Lucid's *The Journal of Richard Henry Dana Jr.*, vol. II (Cambridge, MA: Belknap Press of Harvard University Press, 1968). Dana talked at length with Bill Robinson, a formerly enslaved man who had served as an overseer for Robert Lumpkin.

The Library of Virginia has some great records in which I found hints of how Robert Lumpkin got his start. One was the record of condemned enslaved people and free Black people executed or transported, 1781–1865, Accession APA 756, box 10, folder 10.

I also got a glimpse of Robert Lumpkin's family life in a Library of Virginia document in which he requests that four enslaved people who had been owned by his father be sold so that he can get his share; see Petition 21682703, Henrico Chancery, filed December 23, 1827.

Jeff Forret explores the system of enslaved convicts sold by slave traders in his book *Williams' Gang: A Notorious Slave Trader and His Cargo of Black Convicts* (Cambridge: Cambridge University Press, 2020).

The very first article I read about Robert Lumpkin, which mentions Mary Lumpkin, was Abigail Tucker's "Digging up the Past at a Richmond Jail," *Smithsonian Magazine*, March 2009.

In attempting to understand the extent of the rape of enslaved women by enslavers, I read Joel Williamson's *New People: Miscegenation and Mulattoes in the United States* (Baton Rouge: Louisiana State University Press, 1995). John W. Blassingame writes that enslavers were known to use gifts to get women to comply in his book *The Slave Community: Plantation Life in the Antebellum South* (New York: Oxford University Press, 1972).

I learned that for many years Black women could not claim to have been raped by white men in Sharon Block's *Rape and Sexual Power in Early America* (Chapel Hill: University of North Carolina Press, 2006).

I read Joshua D. Rothman's book about Franklin and Armfield, *The Ledger and the Chain: How Domestic Slave Traders Shaped America* (New York: Basic Books, 2021).

One of the first books I read while conducting research was Walter Johnson's *Soul by Soul: Life Inside the Antebellum Slave Market* (Cambridge, MA: Harvard University Press, 1999), and I was fascinated by his explanation that enslavers were selling other men a fantasy.

The Half Has Never Been Told: Slavery and the Making of American Capitalism by Edward E. Baptist (New York: Basic Books, 2014) was life-changing. I had to stop numerous times to put down the book because the subjects he explores are so painful. His discussion of traders sharing enslaved women was useful for this book.

Thomas S. Berry explains why tobacco production slowed and what it meant for the slave trade; see "The Rise of Flour Milling in Richmond," *Virginia Magazine of History and Biography* 78, no. 4 (October 1970): 387–408.

Steven Deyle's analysis of how enslaved children became Virginia's most important export was an important source for this book; see "An Abominable New Trade: The Closing of the African Slave Trade and the Changing Patterns of US Political Power, 1808–1860," *William and Mary Quarterly* (Third Series) 66, no. 4 (October 2009): 833–850.

I was incredibly moved by Edward Ball's exploration of the size of the forced resettlement of enslaved people in "Retracing Slavery's Trail of Tears," *Smithsonian Magazine*, November 2015. This article was a pivotal read for me.

One of the most revolting realizations of my research was that enslavers sometimes bought enslaved girls with their sexual future in mind. Solomon Northup discusses this in *Twelve Years a Slave: Narrative of Solomon Northup, a Citizen of New-York, Kidnapped in Washington City in 1841, and Rescued in 1853, from a Cotton Plantation Near the Red River in Louisiana* (New York: Miller, Orton & Mulligan, 1856).

CHAPTER 2

Records of Bacon Tait's first jail in Richmond are important for understanding the jail that Robert Lumpkin would buy. I particularly enjoyed William Lloyd Garrison mocking Bacon Tait's advertisement for his jail in "Private Jails," *The Liberator*, December 27, 1834.

Bethany Veney describes the fences that surrounded a jail in which she was imprisoned in Richmond before she went on the auction block the next morning in *The Narrative of Bethany Veney, A Slave Woman* (Worcester, MA: Press of Geo. H. Ellis, 1889). For another description of Richmond slave jails, see Seldon Richardson, *Built by Blacks: African American Architecture and Neighborhoods in Richmond* (Mt. Pleasant, SC: History Press, 2008).

For an incredible explanation of how slavery became racialized, see Peter Wallenstein, "Race, Marriage, and the Law of Freedom: Alabama and Virginia 1860s–1960—Freedom: Personal Liberty and Private Law," *Chicago-Kent Law Review* 70, no. 2 (December 1994).

A good explanation of how the future of slavery rested on Black women once the transatlantic trade was outlawed can be found in Deirdre Cooper Owens and Sharla M. Fett's "Black Maternal and Infant

Health: Historical Legacies of Slavery," *Home American Journal of Public Health* (June 14, 2019).

Jennifer L. Morgan explains how the legal principle *partus sequitur ventrem* was used to determine the fate of Black people in America; see *"Partus sequitur ventrem*: Law, Race, and Reproduction in Colonial Slavery," *Small Axe* 22, no. 1 (55) (March 2018): 1–17.

James Hugo Johnston points out the paradox of white women being punished for having sex with Black men in his *Race Relations in Virginia and Miscegenation in the South, 1776–1860* (Amherst: University of Massachusetts Press, 1970).

For a description of how Solomon Northup had hoped to pull off a mutiny, I read David Fiske, Clifford W. Brown, and Rachel Seligman's *Solomon Northup: The Complete Story of the Author of "Twelve Years a Slave"* (Santa Barbara, CA: Praeger, 2013).

My sources for the slave mutiny on the *Creole* were Calvin Schermerhorn, *The Business of Slavery and the Rise of American Capitalism, 1815–1860* (New Haven, CT: Yale University Press, 2015); Edward D. Jervey and C. Harold Huber, "The Creole Affair," *Journal of Negro History* 65, no. 3 (1980): 196–211; and George Hendrick and Willene Hendrick, *The Creole Mutiny: A Tale of Revolt Aboard a Slave Ship* (Chicago: Ivan R. Dee, 2003). For background on insuring enslaved people, Rachel L. Swarns's article in the *New York Times* of December 18, 2016, "Insurance Policies on Slaves: New York Life's Complicated Past," was helpful.

For information on the development of slave jails, Winter's book was useful, as was Robert H. Gudmestad's *A Troublesome Commerce: The Transformation of the Interstate Slave Trade* (Baton Rouge: Louisiana State University Press, 2003). For exploring the slave trade in Washington, DC, I used Candyce Carter's "What Happened When Anna Jumped from the Window: The Domestic Slave Trade in Antebellum Washington, DC," Stanford University (2017).

To describe how enslaved people were cleaned up for sale, I used William Wells Brown's incredible book *Narrative of William W. Brown, A Fugitive Slave* (Boston: The Anti-Slavery Office, 1847). Josiah Quincy points out an example of women objecting to being sold in his *Figures of the Past: From the Leaves of Old Journals* (Boston: Roberts Brothers, 1884).

Edward Baptist writes more about the abuse of enslaved women in his paper "'Cuffy,' 'Fancy Maids,' and 'One-Eyed Men': Rape, Commodification, and the Domestic Slave Trade in the United States," *American Historical Review* 106, no. 5 (December 2001): 1619–1650.

The late Judith Kelleher Schafer wrote about Theophilus Freeman in *Slavery, the Civil War, and the Supreme Court of Louisiana: The Business of Slavery* (Baton Rouge: Louisiana State University, 1994).

CHAPTER 3

Writing this account, I had to imagine that Mary Lumpkin may not have wanted to have children with her enslaver, a scenario confirmed by Elizabeth Keckley in *Behind the Scenes, or, Thirty Years a Slave and Four Years in the White House* (New York: G. W. Carleton & Co., 1868). Cooper Owens explores the networks that women created to help each other with childbirth on plantations in *Medical Bondage: Race, Gender, and the Origins of American Gynecology* (Athens: University of Georgia Press, 2018).

Stephen E. Ambrose discusses the American presidents who owned slaves in his "Founding Fathers and Slaveholders: To What Degree Do the Attitudes of Washington and Jefferson Toward Slavery Diminish Their Achievements?" *Smithsonian Magazine*, November 2002. Betty Kearse adds to the list of presidents and vice presidents who fathered children with enslaved people in her beautiful book *The Other Madisons: The Lost History of a President's Black Family* (Boston: Houghton Mifflin Harcourt/Mariner Books, 2020).

To learn about Sally Hemings, I used Annette Gordon-Reed's amazing *Hemingses of Monticello* (New York: W. W. Norton & Co., 2008). I enjoyed reading more about Madison Hemings in a piece by Steven H. Hochman, "A Note on Evidence: The Personal History of Madison Hemings," *Journal of Southern History* 41, no. 4 (1975): 523–528.

Philip Kennicott wrote one of my favorite newspaper accounts about Monticello finally deciding to recognize Sally Hemings in "Jefferson's Monticello Finally Gives Sally Hemings Her Place in Presidential History," *Washington Post*, May 13, 2018.

I enjoyed the journalist Sydney Trent's exploration of Mary Lumpkin's relationship to Robert Lumpkin: "She Was Raped by the Owner of a Notorious Slave Jail. Later, She Inherited It," *Washington Post*, February 1, 2020.

I was completely absorbed by Jermain Loguen's compelling story, *The Rev. J. W. Loguen, as a Slave and as a Freeman: A Narrative of Real Life* (Syracuse, NY: J.G.K. Truair & Co, 1859). He describes his free Black mother being kidnapped into slavery.

The often-quoted Mary Boykin Chesnut vividly explores denial among white women about the children fathered by their husbands with enslaved women in *A Diary from Dixie* (Cambridge, MA: Harvard University Press, 1980).

I enjoyed the account of Virginia-born John Mercer Langston's family by Lorraine Boissoneault, "The Unheralded Pioneers of 19th-Century America Were Free African-American Families," *Smithsonian Magazine*, June 19, 2018.

Though Richmond had a large population of free Black people, their status was carefully regulated, as explained by Carey H. Latimore in "Surviving War and the Underground: Richmond Free Blacks and Criminal Networks During the Civil War," *Virginia Magazine of History and Biography* 117, no. 1 (2009): 2–31.

CHAPTER 4

Some of Lucy Ann Cheatham Hagan's life story can be found in government records. Her probate file (New Orleans, Civil District Court Papers, nos. 21664–21741, 1887) was a great source on her life and on Mary Lumpkin's. I was able to watch her being shipped from Richmond to New Orleans through my Ancestry.com account, where I found her in a New Orleans slave manifest of December 1848 for the barque *Cyane*.

Alexandra Finley has written extensively about Corinna Hinton Omohundro. I enjoyed reading "'Cash to Corinna': Domestic Labor and Sexual Economy in the 'Fancy Trade,'" *Journal of American History* (September 2017): 410–429. Her book *An Intimate Economy: Enslaved Women, Work, and America's Domestic Slave Trade* (Chapel Hill: University of North Carolina Press, 2020) came out while I was writing this book, and it was incredibly helpful to me.

A fascinating book by Maurie D. McInnis tells the story of the slave trade through art, and Richmond plays a prime role; see *Slaves Waiting for Sale: Abolitionist Art and the American Slave Trade* (Chicago: University of Chicago Press, 2011).

There were many rewards for free Black people and enslaved people seeking freedom in Ohio, but there were also risks. A good primer is Jill E. Rowe's "Mixing It Up: Early African American Settlements in Northwestern Ohio," *Journal of Black Studies* 39, no. 6 (July 2009): 924–936. Greg Hand's "Ohio Was Not Home-Free for Runaway Slaves," *Cincinnati Magazine*, February 18, 2016, was also useful.

The story of the Omohundro family as told by family member Malvern Hill Omohundro is fascinating, especially for what is left out. See *The Omohundro Genealogical Record; The Omohundros and Allied Families in America; Blood Lines Traced from the First Omohundro in Westmoreland County, Virginia, 1670, Through His Descendants in Three Great Branches and Allied Families Down to 1950* (Staunton, VA: McClure Printing Co., 1950–1951).

Chapter 5

Phillip Troutman explores the ways in which Mary Lumpkin may have been allowed to move around in Lumpkin's Jail in "'Black' Concubines, 'Yellow' Wives, 'White' Children: Race and Domestic Space in the Slave Trading Households of Robert and Mary Lumpkin and Silas and

Corinna Omohundro," Sixth Conference on Women's History of the Southern Association of Women Historians, Athens, GA, 2003.

Anthony Burns's story is well told by Albert J. Von Frank, *The Trials of Anthony Burns: Freedom and Slavery in Emerson's Boston* (Cambridge, MA: Harvard University Press, 1998).

Katherine Clay Bassard edited Peter Randolph's accounting of his life, with wonderful results. Her book, *From Slave Cabin to the Pulpit* (Morgantown: West Virginia University Press, 2016), was incredibly useful for learning about Randolph as well as about Harriet Barber and her children. To learn more about the people enslaved by Carter Edloe, I used his will and chancery case in the Index, 1855-020, Library of Virginia.

Samuel May described greeting Peter Randolph in Boston in his letter to John Bishop Estlin of October 31, 1847, held by the Boston Public Library's Rare Books Department.

Also useful was Kathryn Grover and Janine V. da Silva, "Historic Resource Study: Boston African American National Historic Site," December 31, 2002, www.nps.gov/parkhistory/online_books/bost/hrs.pdf.

For background on the Fugitive Slave Act, Northup's *Twelve Years a Slave* is essential. I also used Thomas D. Morris's *Free Men All: The Personal Liberty Laws of the North 1780–1861* (Baltimore: Johns Hopkins University Press, 1974), and Gordon S. Barker's "Secession and Slavery as a Positive Good: The Impact of the Anthony Burns Drama in Boston on Virginia," *Virginia Magazine of History and Biography* 118, no. 2 (2010): 136–173. Also useful was C. Evan Stewart's "The Trial of Anthony Burns and the Coming of the Civil War," *Federal Bar Council Quarterly* (August 21, 2014).

For understanding how Massachusetts was changed by the Burns trial, I utilized Thomas Wentworth Higginson's sermon *Massachusetts in Mourning* (Boston: James Munroe and Co., 1854).

CHAPTER 6

To understand how enslaved people could be offered as collateral, I read Bonnie Martin, "Slavery's Invisible Engine: Mortgaging Human

Property," *Journal of Southern History* 76, no. 4 (November 2010): 817–866. Matthew Desmond paints a picture of how routine this was in his depiction of Thomas Jefferson mortgaging enslaved people to build Monticello in "In Order to Understand the Brutality of American Capitalism, You Have to Start on the Plantation," *New York Times*, August 14, 2019.

When I wanted to learn about banks' involvement in financing slavery and using slavery as payment, I read David Teather's "Bank Admits It Owned Slaves," *Guardian*, January 21, 2005; and Richard Slawsky's "Bank One Seeks to Make Amends for Past Ties to Slavery," *Louisiana Weekly*, February 14, 2005. Two other good pieces were Cheryl Corley's "Lehman Brothers Admits Past Ties to Slavery," National Public Radio, December 11, 2003; and Ken Magill's "From JP Morgan Chase, an Apology and $5 Million in Slavery Reparations," *New York Sun*, February 1, 2005. I also read Daryl Fears, "Seeking More than Apologies for Slavery," *Washington Post*, June 20, 2005.

Robert Lumpkin may have feared that creditors would take his children, as described by Stanley Feldstein in *Once a Slave: The Slaves' View of Slavery* (New York: William Morrow & Co., 1971). Jermain Loguen spells out in his book exactly how his father sold him, his siblings, and his enslaved mother when creditors came calling.

I was thrilled to learn of John Hemphill, who escorted his daughters with an enslaved woman to school, as described by David Furlow in "Theodora Hemphill's Guide to the Texas Constitution," *Journal of the Texas Supreme Court Historical Society* 5, no. 1 (Fall 2015).

To understand the British government's decision to reimburse Robert Lumpkin and other slave traders for enslaved people lost in the *Creole*, I used Walter Johnson's "White Lies: Human Property and Domestic Slavery Aboard the Slave Ship *Creole*," *Atlantic Studies* 5, no. 2 (2008): 237–263.

One of Robert Lumpkin's relatives suffered from mental illness, and it was blamed on the *Creole* mutiny. For information, I consulted "Wilson Lumpkin, Richmond City Husting Court Minutes 1846–48," reel

91, p. 389, Library of Virginia; records of Eastern State Hospital, 1770–2009, accession no. 23459; and admissions records, vols. 2 and 3, state government records collection, Library of Virginia.

To learn about the panics of 1856 and 1857, I read Harvey Wish, "Slave Insurrection Panic of 1856," *Journal of Southern History* 5, no. 2 (May 1939): 206–222; and James Huston, "The Panic of 1857, Southern Economic Thought, and the Patriarchal Defense of Slavery," *The Historian* 46, no. 2 (February 1984): 163–186. Austin E. Hutcheson also explores the panic of 1857 in "Philadelphia and the Panic of 1857," *Pennsylvania History: A Journal of Mid-Atlantic Studies* 3, no. 3 (July 1936): 182–194.

I am so sad that I never got the chance to meet or talk with the late Hank Trent, who did amazing research into Bacon Tait. I treasure his book, *The Secret Life of Bacon Tait, a White Slave Trader Married to a Free Woman of Color* (Baton Rouge: Louisiana State University Press, 2017).

I gleaned some information from the petition for freedom of Lucy Ann Hagan, Louisiana, Orleans Parish, Fifth District Court of New Orleans, May 10, 1856, petition 20885631b. Even more information comes from the will of John Hagan, found at Louisiana Wills and Probate Records, 1756–1984 (for John Hagan), Orleans (Parish), Will Book, vol. 10, 1855–1857 (Ancestry.com). His gravestone was also helpful.

To understand Lucy Ann Hagan's role in running a boardinghouse, I read Loren Scheweinger's "Property Owning Free African American Women in the South, 1800–1870," *Journal of Women's History* (Winter 1990): 13–44.

Gladys J. Gray explores the decision by a free Black mother living in Richmond to move her children to Massachusetts, where they could attend school, in "George Lewis Ruffin," *Negro History Bulletin* 5, no. 1 (October 1941): 18–19. I read Morris to learn more about legislators' attempts to make Massachusetts safer for Black residents. For details on Judge Loring's removal, I read Kevin L. Gilbert's PhD dissertation,

"The Ordeal of Edward Greeley Loring: Fugitive Slavery, Judicial Reform, and the Politics of Law in 1850s Massachusetts," University of Massachusetts–Amherst (1997).

I loved reading about Mary Lyon, the founder of the Ipswich Female Seminary. I used Eleanor M. Gaunt, "Pioneer for Equality," *Boston Globe*, March 9, 1987; Kelley Bouchard, "Ipswich Teacher's Career Advanced Women's Education," *Peabody Times*, March 19, 1991; and "Mary Lyon, Pioneer," *Boston Globe*, March 1, 1897, p. 6.

To get a primer on the quaint seaside town of Ipswich, I read Joseph B. Felt's "History of Ipswich, Essex, and Hamilton" (Cambridge, MA: Printed by Charles Folsom, 1834), held in Ipswich Female Seminary Collection, box 2 of 2. I also used "An Observer: Seminary for Female Teachers, at Ipswich Mass.," *American Annals of Education (Boston, 1830–1839)* 3, no. 2 (February 1833).

To explore the concept of passing for escaped slaves, I read Martha J. Cutter's "'As White as Most White Women': Racial Passing in Advertisements for Runaway Slaves and the Origins of a Multivalent Term," *American Studies* 54, no. 4 (2016): 73–97. Rachel L. Swarns explores the discussion by white people after the *Dred Scott* decision about whether Black people should be re-enslaved in *American Tapestry: The Story of the Black, White, and Multiracial Ancestors of Michelle Obama* (New York: Amistad, 2012).

I discovered the story of Ann Matthews and her connection to Robert Lumpkin through two articles: "Adjudged a Slave," *Richmond Enquirer*, November 25, 1853; and "To Be Heard," *Daily Dispatch*, November 22, 1853.

I learned about the role of Lancaster County, Pennsylvania, in helping enslaved people from Virginia get free in Nilgun Anadolu Okur's "Underground Railroad in Philadelphia, 1830–1860," *Journal of Black Studies* 25, no. 5 (May 1995): 537–557. Joe Napsha's "Effort Under Way to Resurvey Mason-Dixon Line Will Be First Complete Survey in Decades," *York Daily Record*, March 10, 2020, helped me better understand the significance of the location. In exploring the lives of Silas

Omohundro's children with Corinna Hinton in Pennsylvania, I read Calvin Schermerhorn's *Unrequited Toil: A History of United States Slavery* (Cambridge: Cambridge University Press, 2018).

Erica Armstrong Dunbar was an incredible source for learning about life in Philadelphia for newly emancipated women. I quoted extensively from her *A Fragile Freedom: African American Women and Emancipation in the Antebellum City* (New Haven, CT: Yale University Press, 2008).

CHAPTER 7

I found it fascinating that Mary Lumpkin and her children ended up in Philadelphia's Seventh Ward. I enjoyed reading W.E.B. Du Bois's book about his study of the neighborhood, *The Philadelphia Negro: A Social Study* (Philadelphia: University of Pennsylvania Press, 1899).

I explored the growing multiracial population in the city using Karsonya Wise Whitehead's *Notes from a Colored Girl: The Civil War Pocket Diaries of Emilie Frances Davis* (Columbia: University of South Carolina Press, 2014), and Alison Duncan Hirsch's "Uncovering 'the Hidden History of Mestizo America' in Elizabeth Drinker's Diary: Interracial Relationships in Late Eighteenth-Century Philadelphia," *Pennsylvania History: A Journal of Mid-Atlantic Studies* 68, no. 4 (Autumn 2001): 483–506.

A good primer on the abolition movement as it related to women is Jean R. Soderlund's "Black Women in Colonial Pennsylvania," *Pennsylvania Magazine of History and Biography* 107, no. 1 (January 1983): 49–68. For the history of the Pennsylvania Abolition Society, I used Richard S. Newman's "The PAS and American Abolitionism: A Century of Activism from the American Revolutionary Era to the Civil War," Historical Society of Pennsylvania (n.d.), https://hsp.org/sites /default/files/legacy_files/migrated/newmanpasessay.pdf.

I thoroughly enjoyed Dunbar's incredible book recounting Ona Judge's escape from slavery while George Washington was packing to return to Virginia. See *Never Caught: The Washingtons' Relentless Pursuit of Their Runaway Slave, Ona Judge* (New York: 37 Ink/Atria Books, 2017).

To learn about schools for Black children in Philadelphia, I read John C. Van Horne, "The Education of African Americans in Benjamin Franklin's Philadelphia," in *"The Good Education of Youth": Worlds of Learning in the Age of Franklin* (Newcastle, DE, and Philadelphia: Oak Knoll Press and University of Pennsylvania Libraries, 2009); and Elise Kammerer, "Uplift in Schools and the Church: Abolitionist Approaches to Free Black Education in Early National Philadelphia," *Historical Social Research* 42, no. 1 (159) (2017): 299–319. I also enjoyed Michael Coard's piece on the Philadelphia Female Anti-Slavery Society, "Black, White Philly Sistahs Help Abolish Slavery," *Philadelphia Tribune*, December 7, 2018. Juliet E. K. Walker's exploration of Robert Purvis in "Racism, Slavery, and Free Enterprise: Black Entrepreneurship in the United States Before the Civil War," *Business History Review* 60, no. 3 (Autumn 1986): 343–382, was helpful to my understanding of the family.

To tell the story of John Brown, I used Hannah N. Geffert's "John Brown and His Black Allies: An Ignored Alliance," *Pennsylvania Magazine of History and Biography* 126, no. 4 (October 2002): 591–610. For background on what led to his revolt, I read the full text of Senator Charles Sumner's speech "Crime Against Kansas," May 19–20, 1856 (Boston, Cleveland, and New York: John P. Jewett & Co., 1856), www.senate.gov/artandhistory/history/resources/pdf/CrimeAgainst KSSpeech.pdf. For information on the caning of Senator Sumner, I consulted United States Senate, "The Caning of Senator Charles Sumner, May 22, 1856," www.senate.gov/artandhistory/history/minute/The _Caning_of_Senator_Charles_Sumner.htm.

To tell the beautiful love story of Harriet and Dangerfield Newby, I used an account by Geffert. I also relied on Eugene L. Meyer's "Five Black Men Raided Harpers Ferry with John Brown. They've Been Forgotten," *Washington Post*, October 13, 2019; and "The Heartbreaking Love Letters That Spurred an Ohio Blacksmith to Join John Brown's Raid," *Zacalo Public Square*, October 12, 2019.

I was fascinated by Frederick Douglass's decision not to support the raid on the armory. David W. Blight offers insight in *Admiration and*

Ambivalence: Frederick Douglass and John Brown: A Manuscript from the Gilder Lehrman Collection (New York: Gilder Lehrman Institute of American History, n.d.) and in his book *Frederick Douglass: Prophet of Freedom* (New York: Simon & Schuster, 2018). I was also interested in how Douglass reflected on John Brown later in life in his address "John Brown: An Address by Frederick Douglass at the Fourteen Anniversary of Storer College," Harper's Ferry, WV, May 30, 1881.

DeNeen L. Brown offers details of John Brown's execution in "'Unflinching': The Day John Brown Was Hanged for His Raid on Harpers Ferry," *Washington Post*, December 2, 2017.

CHAPTER 8

Deyle explains that by the time of John Brown's raid, Virginia had lost its position of power. I also relied on Nelson Lankford's take in "Virginia Convention of 1861," in *Encyclopedia Virginia* (Charlottesville: Virginia Humanities, February 1, 2021).

Latimore and Takagi explain how Richmond was selected as the capital of the Confederacy. I also read Mary DeCredico and Jaime Martinez's "Richmond During the Civil War," in *Encyclopedia Virginia* (Charlottesville: Virginia Humanities, July 20, 2021). I found John B. Jones's description of the city's quick transformation in *A Rebel War Clerk's Diary* (New York: Sagamore Press, 1958) very helpful.

To learn about the moment when the United States took New Orleans, I read "The Capture of New Orleans," *St. Albans Weekly Messenger*, May 1, 1862, p. 2; and Adam Rothman's "'Nothing to Stay Here For': How Enslaved People Helped to Put Slavery to Death in New Orleans," *Slate*, September 22, 2015. The decision to enlist Black troops there is outlined in Howard C. Westwood's "Benjamin Butler's Enlistment of Black Troops in New Orleans in 1862," *Louisiana History: The Journal of the Louisiana Historical Association* 26, no. 1 (Winter 1985): 5–22.

To understand the results of the Emancipation Proclamation, I read Alexander Manevitz's "The Failures of Reconstruction Have Never Been More Evident—or Relevant—than Today. Americans' Failure to Secure

Genuine Racial Equality After the Civil War Continues to Haunt Us," *Washington Post*, June 11, 2020.

Thomas Morris Chester provides a wonderful accounting of Black Union troops in *Black Civil War Correspondent: His Dispatches from the Virginia Front*, edited by R.J.M. Blackett (Baton Rouge: Louisiana University Press, 1989). To learn about John Wayles Jefferson, Jefferson's grandson by Sally Hemings who served in the Civil War as a white soldier, the Monticello website has a wonderful accounting (www .monticello.org/getting-word/people/john-wayles-jefferson).

To get details on the death of Silas Omohundro's son, I read several local newspaper accounts: "A Case of Sympathy," *The Star of the North* (Bloomsburg, PA), January 1, 1862; "Sad Case of Sympathy: Death of a Son of a Richmond Merchant," *Richmond Dispatch*, December 21, 1861; and *The Local News* (Alexandria, VA), December 11, 1861.

One source of information on Thomas Knox was the chapter on the Home for Aged Colored Women in Grover and Silva's "Historic Resource Study: Boston African American National Historic Site." Latimore provides a good accounting of food shortages during the Civil War. Also helpful were Mary Elizabeth Massey, "The Food and Drink Shortage on the Confederate Homefront," *North Carolina Historical Review* 26, no. 3 (July 1949): 306–334; and Michael B. Chesson, "Harlots or Heroines? A New Look at the Richmond Bread Riot," *Virginia Magazine of History and Biography* 92 (April 1984). I also read accounts in "The Rebel Bread Riots," *New York Times*, April 10, 1863; and "Spirit of the Morning Press," *Evening Star* (Washington, DC), April 9, 1863.

Calvin Schermerhorn writes about Silas Omohundro's death in *Money over Mastery, Family over Freedom: Slavery in the Antebellum Upper South* (Baltimore: Johns Hopkins University Press, 2011).

Nelson Lankford offers a detailed accounting of the final days of the Civil War and addresses slave traders' experiences during the war in *Richmond Burning: The Last Days of the Confederate Capital* (New York: Viking, 2002). Ernest B. Furgurson's *Ashes of Glory: Richmond at War* (New York: Alfred A. Knopf, 1996) is another amazing account. I also enjoyed Michael E. Ruane's "War's End," *Washington Post*, March 27, 2015; and Edwin Slipek Jr.'s "After the Fire: The South Fell, and Richmond Went Up in Flames. But the Civil War Is Still Here—if You Know Where to Look," *Style Weekly*, May 10, 2011. I also enjoyed reading details of the evacuation from the *Richmond Whig*, April 8, 1865.

Ellen Chapman explores the Liberation Day holiday in "Richmond's Archaeology of the African Diaspora: Unseen Knowledge, Untapped Potential," *African Diaspora Archaeology Newsletter* 15, no. 1 (Spring 2015).

The absolutely thrilling story of Garland White is recounted in detail in "Striking Meeting in Richmond," *Caledonian Mercury* (Edinburgh, Scotland), July 31, 1865; and also in Edward A. Miller Jr., "Garland H. White, Black Army Chaplain," *Civil War History* 43, no. 3 (September 1997). For an account of soldiers opening the jails to free enslaved people, see Leon F. Litwack's *Been in the Storm So Long: The Aftermath of Slavery* (New York: Alfred A. Knopf, 1979).

For a description of Abraham Lincoln's visit to Richmond two days after the city fell, I read "From Richmond: Visit of President Lincoln to Richmond," *New York Times*, April 8, 1865. Bob Deans recounts "Lincoln's March Through Richmond" in the *Richmond Times-Dispatch*, March 28, 2015. In a letter to Thurlow Weed dated March 15, 1865, Lincoln declined to place blame for the war (holograph letter [215] Digital ID al0215, Library of Congress).

William T. Alderson provides a wonderful resource in "The Freedmen's Bureau and Negro Education in Virginia," *North Carolina Historical Review* 29, no. 1 (January 1952): 64–90. I enjoyed reading Harriet Jacobs and Louisa Jacobs's "Letter from Teachers of the Freedmen," *National Anti-Slavery Standard*, April 16, 1864. The historian Elvatrice Belsches takes a modern look at bureau records in "When Freedom Came, Part 3," *Richmond Free Press*, April 9, 2015. I enjoyed reading about freed Black men taking control of their churches in John T. O'Brien's "Factory, Church, and Community: Blacks in Antebellum

Richmond," *Journal of Southern History* 44, no. 4 (November 1978): 509–536.

Jonathan W. White writes about slave jails and slave markets being used for other purposes after the war in "When Emancipation Finally Came, Slave Markets Took on a Redemptive Purpose," *Smithsonian Magazine*, February 26, 2018.

Winnifred K. MacKay's "Philadelphia During the Civil War, 1861–1865," *Pennsylvania Magazine of History and Biography* 70, no. 1 (January 1946): 3–51, was helpful for considering what the Lumpkin children's lives might have looked like in Pennsylvania.

CHAPTER 9

I found Robert Lumpkin's pardon on Ancestry.com; "US Pardons Under Amnesty Proclamations, 1865–1869," vol. 10, June–August 1865, sent me down a fascinating rabbit hole. Barton Myers's explanation of "Sherman's Field Order No. 15" (*New Georgia Encyclopedia*, July 9, 2021) is wonderful. Alexander Manevitz offers a damning assessment of its revocation in "The Failures of Reconstruction Have Never Been More Evident—or Relevant—than Today," *Washington Post*, June 11, 2020.

The death of Robert Lumpkin was covered in the *Richmond Enquirer*, October 27, 1866, and the *Daily Dispatch*, October 27, 1866. I found information about his burial at Richmond City, Bureau of Cemeteries, Shockoe Cemetery 1822–1982, mis. reel 929 (Library of Virginia); Shockoe Hill Cemetery, plot range 17, section 11, memorial ID 151097932. I also used his will, dated February 14, 1866, and the court response, Richmond City, hustings wills, no. 24, 1866–1867, reel 852, pp. 419–422, Library of Virginia.

I found information about the sale of Thurston Lumpkin's property in "Sheriff's Sale," *Huntsville Weekly Democrat*, September 7, 1881. I learned that Mary Lumpkin owed a little over $200 in back taxes through the "List of Delinquent Taxes," *Richmond Dispatch*, February 20, 1871.

On the regulation of race mixing after the war, Williamson and Wallenstein were very useful resources. A good history is *Ku Klux Klan: A History of Racism and Violence*, 6th ed., compiled by the staff of the Klanwatch Project (Montgomery, AL: Southern Poverty Law Center, 2011).

The history of the Baptist Home Mission Societies is on its website (https://abhms.org). I also used an accounting by Joanna P. Moore, the first missionary appointed to the South, *In Christ's Stead* (Chicago: Women's Baptist Home Mission Society, 1902).

Virginia Union History, from the Campus History Series (Mt. Pleasant, SC: Arcadia Publishing, 2014), is a history of VUU penned by the college historian, Raymond Pierre Hylton. Harry Kollatz did a nice job with "'God's Half Acre': How Richmond's Most Notorious Slave Jail Became an Institution That Unleashed the Shackles of Oppression," *Richmond Magazine*, April 2, 2015. Karin Kapsidelis wrote "VUU Celebrates Its Miraculous Rise," *Richmond Times-Dispatch*, April 4, 2015.

I loved Samantha Willis's story about the Mission Society's opening of a college for Black women in Richmond: "'Ahead of Its Time': Richmond's Hartshorn Memorial College Pioneered an Atmosphere of Higher Learning That Nurtured and Prepared Black Women for a Lifetime of Leadership," *Richmond Magazine*, September 19, 2018.

The incredible story of Newman and Mary Lumpkin meeting in New Orleans is recounted in Corey's book. To learn more about Newman's background, I read William Hicks's *History of Louisiana Negro Baptists from 1804 to 1914* (Nashville, TN: National Baptist Publishing Board, 1915).

To learn some of the history of New Richmond, Ohio, I went on a great tour with the town manager, Greg Roberts, in 2020. I interviewed City Council member Mary Allen, whose family has lived in the town for generations. I read Gary L. Knepp's *Freedom's Struggle: A Response to Slavery from the Ohio Borderlands* (Milford, OH: Little Miami Publishing Co., 2008). I also used *History of Clermont County, Ohio, with Illustrations and Biographical Sketches of Its Prominent Men and Pioneers*

(Utica, KY: McDowell Publications, 1880). Jeff Suess's "River Towns Celebrate Milestones: New Richmond 200, Ludlow 150," *Cincinnati Enquirer*, September 15, 2014, was also helpful.

To learn about John Rankin, I read Larry G. Willey's "John Rankin, Antislavery Prophet, and the Free Presbyterian Church," *American Presbyterians* 72, no. 3 (Fall 1994): 157–171.

CHAPTER 10

To understand the failure of American cities to acknowledge their history, I read Heather Greenwood Davis's "Plantations Are a Dark Chapter in American History—Here's Why to Visit," *National Geographic*, February 8, 2019; and New Orleans mayor "Mitch Landrieu's Speech on the Removal of Confederate Monuments in New Orleans," *New York Times*, May 23, 2017.

To understand the history of Richmond's Monument Avenue, I read Andrew Lawler's "The Origin Story of Monument Avenue, America's Most Controversial Street," *National Geographic*, July 27, 2020. For details on the Robert E. Lee statue, I read Steve Hendrix and Lynda Robinson's "When Confederate Gen. Robert E. Lee's Statue Arrived in Richmond in 1890, It Was Greeted by 10,000 Admirers," *Washington Post*, June 3, 2020. The historian Kevin M. Levin wrote a fantastic piece, "Richmond's Confederate Monuments Were Used to Sell a Segregated Neighborhood," *Atlantic*, June 11, 2020.

Other articles that were useful for providing context were Ian Millhiser, "The Night They'll Tear Old Dixie Down," *Vox*, June 24, 2020; and Michael Kranish, "Richmond Split over Confederate History," *Boston Globe*, July 4, 2015, which features Ana Edwards. Also useful were Laura Vozzella, "Virginia Confederate Monuments: 'We're Going to Hold Hands on This Journey as Brothers and Sisters,'" *Washington Post*, March 5, 2020; and Thad Williamson, "The Almost Inevitable Failure of Justice," *Boston Review*, April 4, 2018.

For the "Devil's Half Acre" project, a good primer was Ned Oliver's "Richmond Slavery Memorial to Explore Enduring Impact of Slavery,

'How Persistence Overcomes Horror,'" *Richmond Times-Dispatch*, September 24, 2017.

Susan Svrluga's "Two Decades Later, Donors Wonder What Happened to Plans for Slavery Museum," *Washington Post*, February 11, 2012, outlines why Governor Wilder's project went amiss.

For background on Wilberforce, I consulted Joan Baxter, "The History of Wilberforce University," *Xenia Gazette*, February 19, 2018. Also useful was the US Department of Education, Office for Civil Rights, "Historically Black Colleges and Universities and Higher Education Desegregation," March 1991, www2.ed.gov/about/offices/list/ocr/docs /hq9511.html.

For understanding the place of HBCUs in America, useful sources are Samara Freemark, "The History of HBCUs in America," *APM Reports*, August 20, 2015; and "Why Historically Black Colleges and Universities Matter in Today's America," *The Conversation*, August 12, 2015.

Two articles have explicated the financial difficulties of HBCUs: Denise B. Hawkins, "After 125 Years of Service, St. Paul's College Shutting Down June 30," *Diverse Issues in Higher Education*, May 31, 2013; and Ernie Suggs, "18 HBCUs That Didn't Make It," *Atlanta Journal-Constitution*, August 21, 2019.

Also useful were Ronald E. Carrington, "VUU Surprised by $1M Announcement on Founders Day," *Richmond Free Press*, February 14, 2020; and Jeremy M. Lazarus, "VUU Announces $5,000 Tuition Cut," *Richmond Free Press*, January 2, 2020.

Stories about donations to HBCUs include Nick Anderson and Lauren Lumpkin, "'Transformational': MacKenzie Scott's Gifts to HBCUs, Other Colleges Surpass $800 Million," *Washington Post*, December 18, 2020; and Elizabeth Redden, "A Fairy Godmother for Once-Overlooked Colleges," *Inside Higher Ed*, January 4, 2021.

To learn the date on which Lumpkin's Jail was torn down, I used a "Ford's Hotel" advertisement that appeared in the *Wilmington Morning Star* on October 4, 1870, and "Lumpkins Jail: Tearing Down a

Celebrated Slave Pen at Richmond, Va.," *Cincinnati Enquirer*, March 11, 1988.

Background on the Richmond Iron Works is available at "RVA Legends—Richmond Iron Works," RvaHub, May 14, 2019, https://rvahub .com/2019/05/14/rva-legends-richmond-iron-works.

To learn about the ballpark proposal, I read Michael Martz and Graham Moomaw's "Update: Shockoe Bottom Plan Draws Protesters," *Richmond Times-Dispatch*, November 11, 2013; and "'12 Years a Slave' Figure's Descendants Join Rally," Associated Press, April 4, 2014. I read the editorial "Say Yes: Stadium et al.," *Richmond Times-Dispatch*, February 25, 2014, and then the subsequent change of heart, "Ballpark in the Bottom? Definitely Not," *Richmond Times-Dispatch*, June 20, 2015. For a story covering the rejection of the stadium, see Graham Moomaw, "Mayor Withdraws Shockoe Ballpark Proposal," *Richmond Times-Dispatch*, May 27, 2014.

For information about Kehinde Wiley, I read Bilal Qureshi, "Artist Kehinde Wiley's 'Rumors of War' Now Stands in Former Capital of the Confederacy," National Public Radio, December 11, 2019; and Susan Stamberg, "'Rumors of War' in Richmond Marks a Monumentally Unequal America," National Public Radio, June 25, 2020.

To understand the hesitancy to remove the Confederate monuments, see Ned Oliver, "Mayor Stoney: Richmond's Confederate Monuments Can Stay, but 'Whole Story' Must Be Told," *Richmond Times-Dispatch*, June 22, 2017; and "Neo-Nazi Who Killed Charlottesville Protester Is Sentenced to Life in Prison," National Public Radio, June 28, 2019.

For useful coverage of the Black Lives Matter protests, see Andrew Ringle, "Police Use Chemical Agents to Disperse 'Unlawful' Gathering at J.E.B. Stuart Statue in Richmond," *Commonwealth Times*, June 22, 2020; and "A Timeline of a Month of Protests in Richmond" WVTF, July 1, 2020. The police use of chemical weapons against protesters is described by Schneider in "Hundreds of Angry Residents Shouted at Him on the Steps of City Hall, and He Seemed to Have Lost Control of the City in a Poorly Managed Press Conference," *Washington Post*, November 7, 2020.

For the governor's plan to remove the Lee statue, I used Ben Pavior's "Descendants of People Enslaved by Virginia's Governors Are Reframing History," National Public Radio, October 1, 2020; and Schneider's "Northam's Case for Removing Lee Statue Was Devised by a Lawyer Descended from Slaves," *Washington Post*, June 22, 2020. Alan Suderman and Sarah Rankin's "Virginia Governor to Announce Removal of Lee Statue," Associated Press, June 3, 2020, was also useful.

In writing about the removal of statues, I used "In Bristol, Toppling of Slave Trader's Statue a Major Moment," Associated Press, June 8, 2020. I also relied on "Columbus Statue Torn Down and Thrown in Byrd Park Lake," *Richmond Times-Dispatch*, June 9, 2020; and Mark Katkov, "Protesters Topple Jefferson Davis Statue in Richmond, Va.," National Public Radio, June 11, 2020. Bill Lohmann documents the removal of the Davis statue in "Confederate Soldiers Almost Used This Richmond Bell for Munitions; Wednesday It Rang in a New Era on Monument," *Richmond Times-Dispatch*, July 2, 2020.

Sabrina Moreno tracks the city's progress in "Richmond Has Removed the Most Confederate Symbols in the Country since the Killing of George Floyd," *Richmond Times-Dispatch*, September 4, 2020. Dionne Searcey writes about Kehinde Wiley's response in "Kehinde Wiley on Protests' Results: 'I'm Not Impressed Yet,'" *New York Times*, August 28, 2020.

To read about the plan for Shockoe Bottom of the Virginia Defenders for Freedom, Justice and Equality, see the group's website (sacredground project.net). Ideas for the new museum and memorial are on the website of Lumpkin's Slave Jail Site/"Devil's Half Acre" Project (lumpkinsjail .org). Gary Robertson makes a case for telling the slavery history in "It's Time We Tell the Whole Story," *Richmond Magazine*, January 26, 2016.

The mayor's efforts in Shockoe are described in Mark Robinson, "At First Meeting of Shockoe Alliance, Stoney Kicks Off Planning Effort to Memorialize Area's History of Slavery," *Richmond Times-Dispatch*, April

15, 2019; and Kenya Hunter, "Stoney Announces Multimillion-Dollar Proposal to Commemorate Shockoe Bottom Slave Trade," *Richmond Times-Dispatch*, July 28, 2020.

Michael Paul Williams weighs in with his thoughts in "By Any Name, Half-Acre of Slave Trade History Not Enough," *Richmond Times-Dispatch*, May 8, 2017; and "Navy Hill Happened, Then the Coronavirus. But Let's Not Forget the Commemoration of the Slave Trade in Shockoe Bottom," *Richmond Times-Dispatch*, May 26, 2020.

Index

Credit: Julia Righetti

Kristen Green is the author of the *New York Times* best-seller *Something Must Be Done About Prince Edward County*, which received the Library of Virginia Literary Award for Nonfiction and the People's Choice Award. A newspaper reporter for two decades, she worked for the *Boston Globe*, the *San Diego Union-Tribune*, and the *Richmond Times-Dispatch*. She holds a master's in public administration from the Harvard Kennedy School. Green lives with her husband and two daughters in Richmond, Virginia.